W. T. Greene

Birds of the British Empire

W. T. Greene

Birds of the British Empire

ISBN/EAN: 9783743309265

Manufactured in Europe, USA, Canada, Australia, Japa

Cover: Foto ©Andreas Hilbeck / pixelio.de

Manufactured and distributed by brebook publishing software
(www.brebook.com)

W. T. Greene

Birds of the British Empire

BIRDS OF THE BRITISH EMPIRE

THE IMPERIAL LIBRARY,

CONDUCTED BY FRANCIS GEORGE HEATH,

will be issued in a series of Volumes which, elegantly bound, will be published at 5/- each, net.

"The Imperial Library" is to consist of works of far-reaching interest, giving information upon every subject concerning our great Empire—all designed to aid the noble movement, now progressing, for strengthening the ties which unite the Mother Country to the splendid Colonies which are the power and the pride of "Greater Britain."

The great and far-reaching object for which "The Imperial Library" has been founded is to bring home to the minds of the millions of our splendid Empire a knowledge of what they, as citizens in their huge commonwealth, are so proud to possess; and thus, it is hoped, may be built up, by gradual means, and at a cost that may come (by easy instalments) within the pecuniary resources of the humblest of intelligent readers, a storehouse of information collected with one object and under one system; and ultimately, it may reasonably be hoped, there will be produced an Encyclopædia Britannica such as no private person at present possesses.

LONDON:

THE IMPERIAL PRESS, LIMITED,

21 SURREY STREET, VICTORIA EMBANKMENT, W.C.

BIRDS

OF THE

BRITISH EMPIRE

BY

DR. W. T. GREENE, F.Z.S.

AUTHOR OF

"The Song Birds of Great Britain,"
"Favourite Foreign Birds,"
"The Amateur's Aviary of Foreign Birds,"
"Feathered Friends, Old and New,"
Etc., Etc.

LONDON
THE IMPERIAL PRESS, LIMITED
21 Surrey Street, Victoria Embankment, W.C.
1898

PREFACE

As something like 5,000 species of birds—about half the number known to exist in the habitable globe—are to be found in the dominions of our Queen, it must be obvious that the briefest description of them could not be included within the compass of a small volume like the present one, as its size is necessarily restricted by the limits imposed upon each book in the series of "THE IMPERIAL LIBRARY." Nevertheless, it is hoped that the present "glance" at a big subject will prove interesting and valuable to many people. The number of persons interested in birds is unquestionably enormous; but the proportion is probably much smaller of those who require an exhaustive treatise carried out with cosmopolitan comprehensiveness; and, in any case, the expense of such a work would be a bar to a wide sale.

Later on, if this epitome should secure popular favour, it will be easy to supply the demand for more.

With regard to the illustrations in this volume, it should be noted that no attempt, for obvious reasons, has been made to furnish them to exact scale—the great object being to give the best available drawings; but in the letterpress descriptions the size of each bird has been carefully given, and the INDEX at the end of the volume will enable the reader to immediately find what he may be looking for, and probably all familiar, and many unfamiliar, names will be found, modest though the proportions of the book are.

BELVEDERE, KENT,
January, 1898.

CONTENTS

		PAGE
Part	I. British Birds	1
"	II. The Birds of India	168
"	III. The Birds of Africa	231
"	IV. The Birds of America	273
"	V. The Birds of Australia	287

BIRDS OF THE BRITISH EMPIRE.

PART I.

BRITISH BIRDS.

THE British Empire! What a world of thought that apparently simple expression is capable of evoking from the "vasty deep" of the human imagination. An Empire well-nigh co-extensive with the globe on which it is situated, and on which, if the use of a hackneyed expression may be permitted in such a connection, the sun never sets; an Empire immensely vaster than either Alexander or Cæsar dreamt of in the wildest flights of their insatiable ambition; an Empire containing every variety of the human race, every species of animal, almost, that is known to exist, every reptile, fish, and bird to be met with in the universe.

Yes, every bird, or feathered fowl, from the gorgeous inhabitants of the tropical forests of remote New Guinea, so resplendent in the exuberant glories of many-tinted and strangely developed plumes as to have been styled the birds of paradise, down to the humble sparrow of our own house-tops; from the stately ostrich of Southern Africa to the tiny golden-crested wren of our verdant English woods, or the minute humming-bird of the north-western slopes of British Columbia, as well as almost every conceivable intermediate form and kind.

To review minutely, within the limits at the writer's disposal, all these marvels of creation is manifestly impossible; to make a selection from them for the same purpose would be invidious; but we can include them in a passing glance, in groups, as a migratory bird takes in a glimpse of the varied scenes through which it passes in its instinct-guided flight over vast tracts of land and sea. But where begin?

In the dear old mother country, of course, that small body so pregnant with life that its arms can stretch out with irresistible power to the furthest extremities of the earth's surface, for we include in our avi-fauna some of the most delightful warblers in the world, and at their head, according to the system of classification in vogue at the London Zoological Gardens, stand

THE THRUSHES.

Family—*Turdidæ.*

Genus—1. *Turdus.*	*T. musicus.*	Song Thrush.
	T. pilaris.	Fieldfare.
	T. iliacus.	Redwing.
	T. viscivorus.	Missel Thrush.
	T. merula.	Blackbird.
	T. torquatus.	Ring-Ouzel.
2. *Daulias.*	*D. luscinia.*	Nightingale.
3. *Sylvia.*	*S. cinerea.*	Whitethroat.
	S. curruca.	Lesser Whitethroat.
	S. atricapilla.	Blackcap.

4. *Phylloscopus.*	*P. sibilatrix.*	Wood-Warbler.
	P. trochilus.	Willow-Warbler.
	P. loquax.	Chiffchaff.
	P. rufa.	Rufous Chiff-chaff or Dartford Warbler.
5. *Acrocephalus.*	*A. streperus.*	Reed-Warbler.
6. *Accentor.*	*A. modularis.*	Hedge-Sparrow.
7. *Saxicola.*	*S. œnanthe.*	Wheatear.
8. *Pratincola.*	*P. rubetra.*	Whinchat.
9. *Ruticella.*	*R. phœnicurus.*	Redstart.
10. *Erithacus.*	*E. rubecula.*	Redbreast.

Song Thrush.—Upper parts olive brown, greyer in the female; throat white, with a yellowish tinge, and a black line on each side; sides of neck and breast pale reddish white, with dark brown spots in shape like a heart reversed; belly white, with oval spots. Length, 8½ inches; wings open, 13; tail, 3½. Resident.

Fieldfare.—Migratory, arriving in winter from the north. Upper parts ashen grey, with some blackish spots on top of head; eyebrows white; throat and upper breast rusty yellow, with black, heart-shaped spots; remaining under parts white, with black, heart-shaped spots on sides, more elongated towards vent and under tail coverts. Length, 10¾ inches; wings open, 17; tail, 4.

Redwing.—Migratory, winter visitor from the north. Upper parts brown; eyebrows white; throat, neck, and breast white, with dart-shaped blackish spots; sides and under wing coverts reddish fawn; belly, vent, and under surface of tail, pale grey. Length, 8 inches; wings open, from tip to tip, 13½; tail, 3¼.

Missel Thrush.—Upper parts brownish grey, lighter on rump; throat and breast white, with dart-shaped spots pointing upwards; legs and feet yellow; bill dusky yellow. Length, 11½ inches; tail, 4; open wings, 19. Female a little less, and lighter in colour. Resident.

BLACKBIRD.—General colour of male jet black; bill and circle round eyes orange. Female brownish black, spotted more or less indistinctly on breast; her bill is greyish horn-colour. Length, 9½ inches; wings, from tip to tip, 15; tail, 4. Resident.

RING-OUZEL.—A summer visitor from the south. General colour black, each feather bearing an edging of a lighter shade; a broad shield-like "ring" marks the meeting of the neck and breast; bill pale yellow; legs and feet lead grey. Length, 11 inches; wings, 19; tail, 4. Female more of a brown shade, and narrower ring.

FIG. 1.—*The Missel Thrush.*

NIGHTINGALE.—A summer visitor from the south. Upper surface brown, deepening to red on the rump and tail; under surface greyish white; eye full and black. When hopping about, flaps wings and raises and depresses tail. Female much resembles male. Length, 6 inches; wings open, from tip to tip, 10½; tail, 3. The young are mottled with yellow on the back, and with reddish brown on the lower surface.

WHITETHROAT.—Upper surface greyish brown, with a shade of slate on head and rump; under surface white,

Fig. 2.—*The Blackbird.*

shading to grey on vent and under tail coverts; wings brown, edged with yellowish brown. Female lighter in colour. Length, $5\frac{1}{2}$ inches: tail, $2\frac{3}{4}$; open wings, from tip to tip, $8\frac{1}{2}$.

Lesser Whitethroat.—General colour grey, darker on upper surface than on lower: throat pale grey; belly nearly white: not much brown on wings. Length, 5 inches: tail, $2\frac{1}{4}$; open wings, 8.

Blackcap.—Head of male jet black; of female brown. Upper surface dark ash, with a tinge of olive; under surface grey, fading to white at hinder parts. Length, $5\frac{5}{8}$ inches; tail, $2\frac{1}{2}$: open wings, $9\frac{1}{4}$.

Fig. 3.—*The Nightingale.*

Wood-Warbler.—Upper surface light olive green, tending to yellow on upper tail coverts; wing and tail feathers edged with yellowish green: under parts almost white. Female closely resembles male. Length, $5\frac{1}{4}$ inches: tail, 2: open wings, $8\frac{3}{4}$.

Willow-Warbler.—Upper parts greenish yellowish brown; under parts white tinged with yellow. Sexes alike. Length, 5 inches: tail, 2; wings, 8.

Chiffchaff.—Upper parts greyish olive; under, white with a tinge of yellow; white line above, and dark line behind eye; wing feathers edged with light brown. Length, $4\frac{1}{2}$ inches: tail, $1\frac{3}{4}$; wings, 6.

Rufous Chiffchaff.—Unlike the eight preceding species, which are migratory, the Dartford Warbler remains in this country all the year round. Upper parts ashen grey, laced with dark edging on head; tail very dark grey; chin white, each feather edged with black;

throat and breast rusty brown; belly and vent greyish white. The female has the top of the head of a

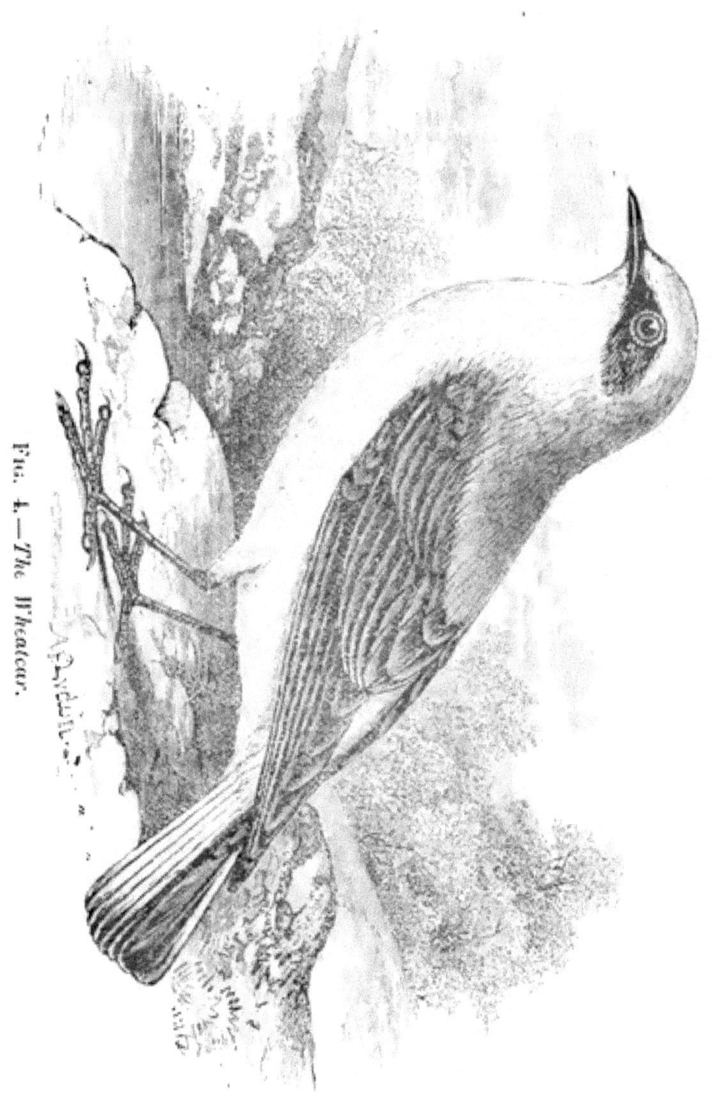

FIG. 4.—*The Wheatear.*

greenish grey shade. Length, 5½ inches; tail, 2¼; open wings, 6¾.

REED-WARBLER.—Upper parts greenish grey, tinged with olive; eyebrows long and yellow; under parts yellowish white. Length, 5 inches; tail, 2; wings, 6. Migratory.

FIG. 5.—*The Redstart.*

HEDGE-SPARROW, also called DUNNOCK.—A resident species. Upper parts greyish brown, spotted with greyish black marks; under parts slate grey, with some reddish spots on side; inside of bill pink. Female greyer. Length, 5½ inches; tail, 2¼; open wings, 8¾.

WHEATEAR. — Migratory. Forehead light grey; neck and back brownish grey; rump and tail coverts white; tail grey black, with white bush to all but middle pair; chin white; neck and breast rusty red; wings dark greyish brown; large wing coverts edged with yellow; belly and vent white. Female duller in appearance. Length, 6½ inches; tail, 1¾; open wings, from tip to tip, 12½.

WHINCHAT.—Summer visitor like the last. Upper surface brownish grey, with large black spots; white patch on wing coverts, and long white line over eyes; chin, throat, and breast ruddy buff, fading into yellowish grey on hinder parts; tail white, with black lower third; bill dark slate; legs and feet same, but darker shade. Length, 5 inches; tail, 1¾; wings open, 9¼. Female like male, but paler. Young much speckled with grey and white.

REDSTART.—Summer visitor. One of our handsomest

birds. Forehead, throat, and upper breast jetty black; crown white; nape and back slate blue; rump, lower breast, and half of belly bright red; central tail feathers reddish brown, the rest bright red; wings brown; vent and under tail coverts reddish grey; bill black; legs and feet dark slate grey. Female, upper parts yellowish brown; throat and under parts pale yellowish grey; tail brownish red, much resembling that of the nightingale. The young are mottled with orange on the breast. Length, $5\frac{3}{4}$ inches; tail, $2\frac{1}{4}$; open wings, $8\frac{3}{4}$.

Redbreast.—Upper surface olive-brown, except the forehead, which, with the cheeks, chin, and breast, are orange red; remaining under parts pale brownish grey. Female less red, and greyer on back. The young have no red, and are mottled all over with yellowish grey spots. Length, $5\frac{3}{4}$ inches; tail, $2\frac{1}{4}$; wings, $9\frac{1}{4}$. Resident.

Fig. 6.—*The Robin.*

The Thrushes proper and the Blackbirds feed on worms, snails, and insects of all kinds, also berries and small fruit.

Accentor. — Small seeds and insects.

Warblers.—Insects, especially small caterpillars, and aphides and berries, especially in the autumn.

Robin.—Insects of all kinds, and garden worms, also a few berries.

Wheatear, Whinchat, and Redstart.—Insects.

All the foregoing birds are more or less gifted with the power of song, though the nightingale, by general consent, comes first, the blackcap makes a good second, and the song thrush is not much behind as third, though the blackbird runs him close for fourth place, and the remainder are more or less gifted, the whitethroat taking perhaps the first place in the second rank, closely followed by the robin redbreast, in comparison with which the rest are nowhere.

All these birds do infinitely more good than harm to the agriculturist and gardener, in spite of the fact that the first six eat fruit when they can find it, but the depredations of the remainder are so insignificant that they do not admit of comparison with the good effected in the destruction of myriads of insect pests.

The nests of the thrushes are marvels of construction, being all made more or less with mud, the song thrush taking the lead in this respect, and the blackbird coming next.

As the object of this work is not to assist oologists in forming "collections," not much will be said about the eggs, except to mention that those of the dunnock are of the most lovely turquoise blue; that those of the whinchat somewhat resemble them in colour, but are smaller; and that those of the nightingale are of a uniform olive tint.

The blackcap makes a compact nest of grass stems, lined with hair, in an open bush; but the nest of the whitethroat is so flimsily put together that in those cases where it is placed at a few feet elevation from the ground the spectator standing below can see the eggs through it.

The nest of the nightingale is clumsily built of leaves and grass, and is placed among brambles near the ground, and never far from the stem of a tree.

The willow, wood, and Dartford warblers make domed nests among leaves on, or close to, the ground, and the redstart nests in holes of trees or walls; her six eggs are dull blue. The robin nests in all manner of places, and makes a loose nest somewhat like that of the nightingale; the eggs are white, spotted and streaked with brick-red.

None of the birds in the foregoing list are eaten by cats, although these animals will kill them fast enough if they get the chance, for which reason, surely, they are also unfit for human food. A very young and inexperienced pussy, or one that is on the verge of starvation, will sometimes venture on one of them, but if she does swallow it, she is immediately afterwards violently sick, and seldom repeats the experiment. Yet most of them are greedily devoured by our continental neighbours, with whom everything is game that falls to their gun.

Seeing that all these birds consume such a large quantity of destructive molluscs, worms, and insects, they should be given every possible protection, instead of being relentlessly persecuted as they are in many parts by the members of sparrow clubs, one of whom recently advertised, with apparent pride, the shameful fact that in less than two years he had shot about nine hundred blackbirds and thrushes.

Had he ever calculated how much money he expended in ammunition? or given a moment's consideration to the number of his worst enemies, insects, that would have been eaten by these poor slaughtered birds?

It is no wonder that insects of all kinds increase when the police appointed by Nature for their repression are so ignorantly destroyed every year.

It is curious that so shy a bird as the blackbird should elect to sing in a conspicuous situation, as he often does, perched in a bush or tree of no great height, and well in view of all passers-by; but it is stranger still that his courtship should be performed in the face of the world, generally in an open field under trees, but often on a lawn in a garden, and the way he capers about his mate, and generally "shows himself off" is very entertaining.

The song thrush and the missel thrush both sing perched on high trees, often the highest in the neighbourhood, whereas at other times they are rather chary of letting themselves be seen.

Hunger often drives these birds, as well as the migratory thrushes, close to a house, and they will even feed upon a window-sill; but it is sad to think that so many of the latter perish from the combined effects of hunger and thirst, not to speak of the murderous gun.

Among the warblers it is surprising how the chiffchaff can find its way across vast expanses of water when it is noticed that its flight from bush to bush is so wavering and apparently feeble; but there is no doubt it does, though probably many of them perish by the way, and a curious feature of their migration is that the young of the year always set out on their journey first, and not, as many suppose, in the company of their parents and elders.

While bearing a general resemblance, the eggs of all birds vary a good deal, often a great deal, in appearance, those in one nest differing conspicuously in detail from those in another, a fact that should always be borne in mind when describing them, and which also accounts for the fact, otherwise puzzling, that scarce two writers give the same description of the eggs of birds.

There are exceptions, of course. For instance, those of the dunnock differ little, if at all, from each other, and the same observation applies to those of the redstart, the nightingale, and a few others; but these form the exception, not the rule.

It can never be too often repeated that all the birds included in the thrush family, many of which, but not all, have been mentioned in the preceding paragraphs, feed, for at least nine months in the year, entirely on insects and other pests of the gardener, arboriculturist, and farmer, and during the remaining three months (unless abnormally numerous in a given locality) do far less mischief than is commonly supposed, their destruction having always been followed by far greater evil than any they might have caused, namely, the multiplication of noxious insects of all kinds, which the birds had kept in check, as the latter would have been by the hawks and owls if these had not been destroyed off the face of the earth by game-preservers and their satellites, to say nothing of farmers who kill a sparrow-hawk for swooping at one chick, but forget the benefit the bird has conferred by destroying shoals of mice.

THE DIPPER AND THE BEARDED TIT.

These birds are now separated, the one from the thrushes and the other from the tits, a differentiation which we think to be superfluous, but accept for the sake of uniformity, as well as for facility of reference. The first of the two is familiarly known as the Dipper.

Family—*Cinclidæ.*
Genus—*Cinclus. C. aquaticus.*

Head and upper part of the back of the neck dark rusty brown; the remaining upper parts of the body greyish black, except the flights, which are blackish brown; chin, throat, and upper half of the breast white; lower half of the breast ruddy brown; belly and under tail coverts greyish-black: bill, legs, and feet, slate grey. Length, $7\frac{3}{4}$ inches; tail, 2; wings, from tip to tip, $12\frac{3}{5}$.

This bird is tolerably widely distributed throughout the British Isles, from the Hebrides in the north, to Devon and Cornwall in the south. It also occurs in the neighbourhood of streams throughout Ireland.

FIG. 7.—*The Dipper.*

It feeds on aquatic insects, worms, molluscs, and spawn and fry of fish, though to a much less extent in the case of the latter than is supposed, as it prefers the former.

In shape the dipper resembles the starling rather than the thrush, but its head is rounder and thicker than that of the former.

The female is a trifle smaller, lighter in colour than the male, and the white of her neck and breast has a grey tinge.

The nest is very compactly built of moss and leaves and stems of aquatic plants, is large, and varies a good deal in shape according to circumstances. Thus, if placed in the open, it is domed; but if a convenient site can be found under a projecting ledge of rock, the upper portion is dispensed with, and the interval only between the two stones is filled up. The eggs are four or six in number, of an oval shape, and white; and the young leave the nest before they are able to fly.

Not only does the dipper walk into the water, and along the bottom of the stream or pond in search of its food, but it uses its wings, when submerged, like the penguins, and actually flies through the water. The argument against its being able to do so being that, to the reasoning powers of the objector, it does not seem possible, is not of sufficient force to call for further attention. Its feet are constructed so as to afford a very firm hold of the surface over which it walks, so that no effort on its part is required to enable it to keep its place below the surface; and, as might be expected, it walks badly on dry land, seldom availing itself of that mode of progression.

In the north of Scotland the dipper is known as the kingfisher, and a price is put upon its head, which has led to its almost complete extinction there, which is a pity, for it is by no means proved that it eats the fry of trout and salmon, while the spawn is generally about when more favourite food is abundant. Unless more protection is afforded to it, the dipper will soon be extinct in Britain. The song is agreeable and flute-like, and the bird can be readily domesticated and preserved for a number of years in an out-door aviary, where the conditions that obtain in its native haunts are imitated for its benefit. The young are easily reared on ants' eggs, meal worms, and other insects, eked out with a little bread and milk.

The second bird referred to at the commencement of this section is known by the name of Bearded Tit.

Family—*Panuridæ.*
Genus—*Panurus biarmicus.*

This handsome bird was at one time fairly common in England, but of late years is but rarely seen, even in the eastern counties, which used to be its favourite haunt. The upper parts are ruddy fawn, but the forehead and cheeks have a tinge of grey; the wing coverts are brown with yellow margins, and the flights are slate grey; the chin and sides are white, changing to pale fawn on the breast and belly; the vent is black, and the lores, as well as a broad line extending from them down the sides of the face, are of the same colour, and from their shape and position give the bird its trivial name. The outer tail feathers are white, the bill yellow, and the long legs and feet dark slate.

Small insects of all kinds, but chiefly flies, gnats, and midges, are its diet. In the house, ants' eggs, young meal worms, black beetles, and silk-worms will keep it in health and beauty for a long time; but on artificial food, no matter how cunningly devised and cleverly compounded, it will not long survive. Some observers credit the bearded tit with eating the seeds of grass, sedge, etc.

Beauty of plumage, elegance of shape, sprightly deportment, and pleasing song, are its attractive qualities. It is perfectly harmless and entirely useful, and needs all the protection that can be afforded to it, if it is to remain in the list of our native birds.

Most examples of this species that are to be met with in

the bird shops and at the dealers are imported from the Continent, and chiefly from Holland. The nest is built among reeds, and the eggs, four or five in number, are white, faintly marked with reddish brown.

THE TITS.

This important family, from which the last species has been somewhat arbitrarily separated, consists of one English genus and several species, which are mostly familiar to even the most ordinary observers.

Family—*Paridæ*.

Genus—*Parus*.	*P. major*.	The Great Tit, or Oxeye.
	P. ater.	Coal Tit.
	P. palustris.	Marsh Tit.
	P. cæruleus.	Blue Tit.
	P. cristatus.	Crested Tit (rare).
	P. caudatus.	Long-tailed Tit.

Great Tit, or Oxeye.—Bill black; upper part of head glossy black, joining the black throat by a line of the same colour, bordering and forming a marked contrast to the white of the face; the nape is yellow, with a green tinge; the back olive, and the rump pale ashen grey. The breast and belly are yellowish green, divided down the centre by a black line. The female is smaller, and of a duller shade throughout; the breast line, too, is shorter and narrower than in the case of the male. Length, nearly 6 inches; tail, 2½.

Coal Tit.—Upper part of head and neck black; back of the head and nape, also cheeks and sides of neck, white; under surface bluish ashen grey; darker towards the vent. Length, $4\frac{3}{4}$ inches; tail, $1\frac{3}{4}$.

MARSH TIT.—Much like the last, but has no white on

FIG. 8.—*The Great Tit.*

nape, and the throat is black. In the female there is less of this colour. Length, $4\frac{1}{3}$ inches; tail, $1\frac{3}{4}$.

BLUE TIT, or TOMTIT.—Front of head and cheeks white;

top of head blue ; a black line crosses the eye and a white one surmounts it ; upper surface blue ; under, greenish-yellow ; bill, legs, and feet, slate blue. Length, 4½ inches : tail, 2.

CRESTED TIT.—Top of head and crest white, with black centres to each feather ; face and a line running half round the back of the head white, shaded with minute black lines ; back of head, nape, and throat black ; breast and belly white, with a fawn tinge at sides, and vent dark

FIG. 9.—*The Blue Tit.*

brownish green ; wings brownish blue ; under tail coverts and root of tail reddish brown ; remainder of tail brown ; bill dark grey ; legs and feet slate blue. Length, 4½ inches ; tail, 2.

LONG-TAILED TIT.—Head and face white, with black shading ; a black line crosses the eye and joins the black of the nape, neck, and back ; reddish brown back, irregularly mottled with black ; wings black, but coverts and secondaries have a wide, white border ; the long tail has the four central feathers black, but the rest are white. The breast is greyish white with a shade of blue. The small, stunted bill is black, and the legs and feet dark slate grey. Length, 5½ inches; tail, 3.

It is found throughout the British Isles, where it frequents woods and plantations. Insects, and possibly a few small seeds, are its diet.

All the tits eat insects during the spring, summer, and the greater part of the autumn, when they begin to feed on various kinds of seed, evincing a marked preference for those of the sunflower, which they will travel a long distance to obtain, even penetrating to the heart of London to regale themselves on this dainty of theirs. Other seeds eaten are hemp, and those of the larch and other coniferæ, the alder, birch, and willow.

The five first species nest in holes in trees, where they rear numerous families of sometimes as many as eight or nine, and they usually have two broods during the season.

The long-tailed tit, however, differs from the others in weaving an admirably constructed nest about the size of a cricket ball, which it suspends from the lower branch of a fir or some other tree in a quiet place; it is made of moss and lichens fastened together with fibre and cobwebs, and lined with small feathers; so beautifully built is this cosy habitation, and so securely fastened to the branch, that it seldom gives way, even after the little family have left it, and keeps swinging on with every breeze until far into the following year.

The tits are much persecuted by horticulturists under the mistaken notion that they damage fruit trees by knocking off the buds.

They certainly do remove some in their quest after insects, and especially the hibernating pupæ and the eggs of destructive moths, or, rather, moths, the caterpillars of which do such mischief in orchards; but if a little attention is paid to the matter, it will be seen that the bird's visits are followed by good and not by bad results. For instance, they do not strip a bough of *all* its buds, but merely thin these out, which is exactly what the experienced gardener does in his greenhouse; but out of doors he lops away an entire bough. Then every bud on a branch would not result in a fruit, and by knocking off some the tit favours the development of those that are left.

If it were not for the visits of these active little birds, every egg laid by a moth would in the spring hatch into a caterpillar; that repeated by millions would soon devastate an orchard; but the tits eat the eggs and prevent all this. In severe weather it is a good plan to hang a piece of suet in some convenient part of a garden, and the tits will flock to it, and become objects of much interest to the onlookers by their agility and activity.

All these birds can be brought up quite easily by hand on ants' eggs, insects, and a little bread and milk; but they are too active for confinement, in which they seldom live long, and everyone who destroys a tit is an encourager of insects.

THE NUT-HATCH.

Another small family now engages our attention, namely that of the nut-hatches, which is represented in this country (Britain) by one genus of a single species only.

Family—*Sittidæ*.
Genus—*Sitta*. *S. cæsia*. Common Nut-Hatch.

Upper parts bluish grey, brighter on the forehead: cheeks and throat white; a black line, rising at the insertion of the bill, crosses the eye and reaches to the back of the neck; the under parts are greyish orange. Length, 6½ inches; tail, 1½; bill, ¾.

It is found in woods and plantations throughout Great Britain and Ireland, and is resident all the year round, though frequently changing its quarters during the winter from one wood to another.

The food consists of insects, nuts, beech-mast, acorns, and berries; the latter more particularly during the winter season. In the house it should be provided with the same diet; but is too active and restless for a cage, though it does better in a garden aviary, but never, in any case, survives very long in confinement. It makes a nest in a hole of some tree, and lays six or seven white eggs, sparingly spotted with dull red. The young can be reared on ants' eggs, small meal worms, and other insects, and a little bread and milk; and if it be desired to keep them, they should be taken from the nest and hand fed.

The very difficulty of preserving it makes the nut-hatch attractive in the eyes of some people; but it should not be taken in hand lightly. Occasionally, in severe winters, some of these birds will come near a house and feed with the tits and robins.

THE WAGTAILS AND THE PIPITS.

The next family on our list is a much more numerous one than the last, and probably better known to the general public; two British genera are included in it, as well as one Australian one.

Family—*Motacillidæ.*

Genus—1. *Motacilla.*	*M. lugubris.*	Pied Wagtail.
	M. alba.	White Wagtail.
	M. melanope.	Grey Wagtail.
	M. raii.	Yellow Wagtail
2. *Anthus.*	*A. arboreus.*	Tree Pipit.
	A. pratensis.	Meadow Pipit.

The Pied Wagtail is only found, out of Britain, in the Scandinavian peninsula. Like the rest of its family it is

Fig. 10.—*The Pied Wagtail.*

an elegant bird, the upper surface of which is black, except the forehead, which is white, and the wing coverts and secondaries, which are edged with the same colour. The face and line running down the side of neck are also white, as are the lower breast, belly, and outer tail feathers. The bill, legs, and feet are dark slate grey. Length, 7 inches; tail, 3½.

White Wagtail.—Notwithstanding its name, this bird is by no means an albino, but rejoices in a variety of colours. The bill is black; the top of the head, face, belly, under tail coverts, and outer tail feathers are white; the back of the head, nape, chin, and throat black, faintly edged as to each feather with grey; central tail feathers dark blackish brown; the back is lavender grey, shaded with a darker hue; the wings are dark brown; the greater and lesser wing coverts and secondaries are edged broadly with yellowish brown; the breast greyish white; the bill and legs and feet dark slate colour. Same size as the last.

Grey Wagtail.—This species is handsomer even than the last; its upper surface is dark lavender colour, except the rump and upper tail coverts, which are greyish yellow, and the tail, which is black; over the eye is a narrow white line, and the black throat is separated from the grey cheek by another narrow band of white; the wings are brown, edged with yellow on the secondaries only; the outer tail feathers are white, and the remaining parts bright yellow: the legs, feet, and bill are greyish brown. It is the same size as the two preceding species.

The Yellow, or Ray's Wagtail might be taken for an undersized specimen of the former, than which it is altogether lighter in colour, the back having a yellowish green tinge, and the wings and tail being browner, while there is no black on the throat, and the yellow surface is much more extensive. Length, 6¼ inches; tail not quite 3.

Tree Pipit.—Upper surface brown; darker on head and neck than on wings, where the coverts have dark centres and whitish yellow edges; throat, upper breast, and lores tawny yellow, with black spots; breast bluish grey, speckled with black; belly, vent, and under tail coverts tawny yellow without spots; tail brown, except two outer pairs, which are white; bill, upper mandible horn, lower yellow; legs and feet yellowish grey. Length, $5\frac{1}{2}$ inches; tail, $2\frac{1}{2}$.

Meadow Pipit.—Upper surface greyish brown, lighter towards tail, spotted sparely with narrow dark lines; over the eye is a white line, also spotted with black: the wings have an olive tinge that almost masks the brown; the outer edge of the coverts and secondaries darker than the inner; under surface white spotted with black marks; bill yellowish; legs and feet yellowish grey.

THE SHRIKES.

Three species are met with in Britain, the two first being of frequent, and the third of rare, occurrence, and all are summer visitors only.

Family—*Lanidæ.*		
Genus—*Lanius.*	*L. excubitor.*	Great Grey Shrike.
	L. collurio.	Red-backed Shrike.
	L. rufus.	Woodchat.

Great Grey Shrike, or Butcher Bird.—This is the largest species of the three shrikes that come under the notice of the British aviculturist; it is a fine, bold-looking bird of a light slate blue colour on all the upper parts except the tail, the two central feathers of which are black, and the remainder, except the outer pair, which are all white, are black with white ends; the wings are black, with a patch of white on the centre of the primaries, and a small edging of the same colour on the three or four inner secondaries. The strong notched and hooked bill, the lores, and a narrow oval patch extending beyond the eye, are jet black, and the under parts white, with a faint tinge of buff on the breast and belly. The legs and feet are dark slate. The length of the bird is about 10 inches, of which the tail measures 3.

RED-BACKED SHRIKE.—This is a handsomer bird than the last. The top of the head is lavender grey; the back chestnut brown, changing to grey on the upper tail coverts. The tail is blackish brown inside, but the outer feathers have their basal ends white. The bill is strongly hooked and black, a narrow black line runs round its base, and, crossing the eye, extends beyond it into a broad patch over and a little further back than the ear coverts; the sides of the neck and of the body are pale, ruddy chestnut; and the throat, breast, and belly whitish grey: the legs and feet are greyish black. Length, 7½ inches, of which the tail measures nearly 3.

WOODCHAT.—This bird, which is of rare occurrence in Britain, has a narrow white line at the base of the upper mandible, followed as far as the eye, surrounding the latter and extending along the sides of the neck, where it expands into a large patch on the upper part of the back, by a band of intense black. The lower back, rump, and upper tail coverts grey; the wings are brown, with a white spot on the centre of the outer primaries, and a white band on the lesser coverts. The under parts are white, with a ruddy tinge, fading to grey at the vent. The two middle tail feathers black, the next three grey blue, and the remainder white. The bill is grey, and the legs and feet a darker shade of the same colour. Length, 7½ inches.

In the case of all these birds the female is larger than

the male, measuring nearly an inch more, and weighing considerably heavier.

The shrikes all feed on insects, small birds, and reptiles, and are consequently of much use to farmers and gardeners, for they are not strong enough to attack the young of the domestic poultry successfully, or, at least, of the larger kinds of game, though they may occasionally secure a very young quail or partridge.

A curious fact connected with their feeding is that they all have a habit of transfixing on a sharp thorn any prey they do not require for immediate consumption, a custom of theirs that has won for them the name of butcher-birds.

The grey shrike frequents groves and woods of small extent, and builds in the fork of a tree, laying four or five eggs. Sometimes it remains in the spot it has selected all the year through; but the flusher, or red-backed shrike, is migratory, arriving in spring, and taking its departure in autumn.

All three can be easily tamed, and have a sufficiently agreeable song, but they cannot be kept in the company of other birds even larger than themselves.

In the house they may be fed on the offal of poultry with an occasional mouse, but if beetles and meal worms can also be freely given, the change will have a beneficial effect.

THE WAXWING.

This can scarcely be called a British bird, seeing that it does not visit us regularly, but only occasionally in the winter time. However, as it is classed with our native birds, it has been decided to include a brief notice of it in the present work. It is the sole representative of its family, and comes here from its true home in the distant north.

Family—*Ampelidæ.*
Genus—*Ampelis.* *A. garrulus.*

A stout, plump bird, thickly clad in long soft feathers that effectually protect it from the cold; those on the head are especially long, and can be raised into a conspicuous crest at their owner's pleasure. The upper surface is reddish ash colour, changing to grey at the upper tail coverts. The middle wing coverts are dark grey, almost black, and about six of them are tipped with white, as are the last four or five of the secondaries, which have affixed to their tips little excrescences of a red colour that have the appearance of wax. The other secondaries and the primaries are edged on their outer aspect with yellow, and on the inner with bluish grey. The tail is the same colour as the wings, and has all the feathers composing it bordered at the free extremities with yellow. The chin and upper part of the throat, as well as a spot surrounding the eye, are black. The remaining under parts are grey, with a ruddy tinge especially on the breast. The bill is brown, and the legs and feet dark slate.

This bird feeds on berries and seeds and also on insects, but as few of these are about when it comes to Great Britain, it is probable that while here its diet is mainly frugivorous.

Though often called the Bohemian Chatterer, it is seldom met with in the south, and is rather a silent bird than otherwise. It is to a certain extent gregarious, that is to say, it is usually met with in small parties of eight or ten, consisting of individuals of both sexes, the females being known by the smaller extent of the black spot under the chin, as well as by being somewhat less. The length of the male is 8½ inches.

The waxwing is easily tamed, but, like most of the birds

whose habitat is within the Arctic circle, it does not survive very long in confinement, for the heat of summer tries it greatly, and it usually succumbs to disease of the liver. If it could be kept cool enough it would probably do well, as the appetite is very accommodating.

In its manner of flying and walking it bears considerable resemblance to the starling. The nest has not been found in Great Britain.

THE FLYCATCHERS.

These birds form a distinct family, of which, at least, two species are found in Great Britain, while a third is an occasional visitor.

Family—*Muscicapidæ.*

Genus—*Muscicapa.*	*M. atricapilla.*	Pied Flycatcher.
	M. grisola.	Spotted Flycatcher.
	M. parva.	Red-breasted Flycatcher.

The Pied Flycatcher.—Although abundant on the Continent of Europe, this species is rare in Great Britain, and it is a moot point whether it is of migratory habits here or stays with us throughout the winter. The forehead is white, and the head, face, back, lesser wing coverts and tail are black, with a tinge of blue. The greater wing coverts and the secondaries are white, but the primaries are black, with a faint tinge of brown. All the under parts, including the last pair of the tail feathers, are white, with a greyish blue tinge on the breast and belly. The length is about 6 inches, and the wing expanse 8. Sexes very much alike outwardly, but the female has a faint yellowish tinge on the breast, perhaps contracted during incubation. The young are plentifully spotted with white on the back, and with brown on the breast.

SPOTTED FLYCATCHER.—This is a much more inconspicuous bird than the last. The upper surface is brown, with a dull olive tinge, and the under part is whitish grey on the throat and breast, and faintly tawny on the belly; the vent is greyish white; from the bill to the thighs the surface is thickly dotted with yellowish brown spots. Male and female are alike. The bill is yellowish grey, and is surrounded by many short bristles at its base. The legs and feet are yellowish grey. It is the same size as the last.

RED-BREASTED FLYCATCHER.—This is a rare summer visitor, and might, at first sight, be mistaken for a small robin; but it differs from that bird by the whiter colour of its under parts below the tail, by the white bases of the outer tail feathers, and by the absence of the characteristic orange red on the head and face. The wings are dark brown, and the wing coverts and secondaries are outwardly edged with greenish brown. The female resembles the male, but is smaller. Length, about $4\frac{1}{2}$ inches.

All the flycatchers feed entirely on insects, which they capture for the most part on the wing. They are very shy birds, and may exist in a given locality without their presence being suspected, until accidentally seen feeding a newly-flown young one, or flitting silently from tree to tree.

The nests of all three species are built in holes of trees or buildings, and if the entrance to the cavity is too large to suit the builder, it is plastered up with mud until a convenient entrance has been contrived.

The small white eggs are rather numerous, as many as seven and eight having been found in one nest. Incubation lasts thirteen or fourteen days, and the young are fed on minute insects, aphides, and small dipterous flies.

It is possible, of course, to preserve these birds in the house, but even when reared by hand they do not seem happy or satisfied in confinement, which is only natural on account of their exceedingly shy and retiring disposition; and, being so exceedingly useful, it seems a pity to disturb them.

Whether kept in cage or aviary, they should always be provided with a snug box or covered basket to sleep in, for they never roost of their own accord in the open, and are exceedingly impatient of cold.

THE SWALLOWS.

All the species belonging to this family are migratory, arriving in Britain from warmer climates in spring to breed, and returning to their southern home when that important function has been accomplished.

Family—*Hirundinidæ.*

Genus—*Hirundo.*	*H. rustica.*	Swallow.
	H. urbica.	Martin.
	H. riparia.	Sand-martin.

Swallow.—This exceedingly handsome and most graceful bird is of a steel blue colour on all the upper surface of the body, except the forehead, which, with the throat, is chestnut brown; the breast is white, with a ruddy tinge in the centre, which deepens towards the vent and under the tail coverts; the wings are long and narrow, and the long tail is deeply forked; the feet are very short and small, of a leaden grey colour, and have small prehensible power; the bill is black. Length, 8$\frac{3}{4}$ inches. The wings expand to a width of 14 inches, and reach to the middle of the tail.

The female resembles the male, but her plumage is not as lustrous as his, and her tail is shorter.

MARTIN, or HOUSE-MARTIN.—Upper parts steel blue, except rump, which is white; all the under surface is of the latter colour; the tail is but slightly forked, and the wings, when folded, reach almost to the end of it; the legs and feet are stronger than in the last species, and of a paler grey; the bill is black. The female resembles the male, but her plumage is not so bright. Length, 5¼ inches; expanse of wings, 12 inches.

SAND-MARTIN.—Upper surface brownish grey, the same colour forming a band between the throat and breast, except which all the under surface is white; bill, legs, and feet, black. Length, from tip of bill to end of tail, 4¾ inches; expanse of wings, which reach beyond tail, about 12 inches. The female exactly resembles her mate.

All these birds are migratory, and are supposed to winter in Africa. They feed entirely on insects, which they capture only when on the wing.

They vary a good deal in their mode of nidification. The swallow makes an open, cup-like nest, which it places on a beam in a barn or other building, as well as in many other convenient resting-places which afford a foundation and covering for the structure, which is made of mud.

The martin makes its mud nest under the eaves of a house generally, but occasionally in caves by the sea-shore, which are also sometimes frequented by the swallow. It is rounded, and has an aperture at the top.

The sand-martin excavates itself a dwelling in a sandy cliff or bank, scooping out with its bill a tunnel three or four feet in length, at the end of which it cuts out the nesting chamber, which it lines with grass, hair, bits of string, and similar materials, as do its congeners also.

The eggs of the swallow are four or five in number, of a

white colour, but speckled red or brown. It has two broods in the season as a rule. The martin lays white

FIG. 11.—*Sand Martins.*

eggs, and so does the sand-martin, and they also have two broods; but the martin occasionally hatches a third, which, however, is very often deserted, if not sufficiently advanced to accompany the parents when they migrate about the middle of October.

It seems a thousand pities that such eminently useful birds should be destroyed for the ornamentation (?) of ladies' hats and bonnets, to which they are affixed in their unsophisticated natural tints, or dyed almost past recognition in every colour of the rainbow. So terrible is the persecution to which they have been subjected on this account, more particularly on the Continent, that their numbers of late years have sensibly diminished, to the manifest delight of the gnats and objectionable insects of that kind.

It is unquestionable that a nestful of young house martins make a considerable mess on the ground underneath their birth-place, hence, some people prevent the birds from building on their premises; but a board affixed to the wall, some little distance below the nest, would entirely obviate the trifling inconvenience.

THE FINCHES.

We now come to a rather nondescript family, made up of, at least, half-a-dozen distinct ones, while its genera are multipied in the most diffuse and perplexing manner; however, thus it has been decreed by zoological authorities, and thus, for the present, we are constrained to leave it.

Family—*Fringillidæ*.

Genus	Species	Name
Genus—1. *Passer*.	*P. domesticus*.	House Sparrow.
	P. montanus.	Tree Sparrow.
2. *Coccothraustes*.	*C. vulgaris*.	Hawfinch.
3. *Ligurinus*.	*L. chloris*.	Greenfinch.
4. *Fringilla*.	*F. cœlebs*.	Chaffinch.
	F. montifringilla.	Brambling.

5. *Carduelis.*	*C. elegans.*	Goldfinch.
6. *Chrysomitris.*	*C. spinus.*	Siskin.
7. *Linota.*	*L. cannabina.*	Linnet.
	L. flavirostris.	Twite.
	L. rufescens.	Lesser Redpoll.
	L. linaria.	Mealy Redpoll.
8. *Pyrrhula.*	*P. europæa.*	Bullfinch.
9. *Pinicola.*	*P. enucleator.*	Pine Grossbeak
10. *Loxia.*	*P. curvirostra.*	Crossbill.
11. *Plectrophanes.*	*P. nivalis.*	Snow Bunting.
12. *Calcarius.*	*C. lapponicus.*	Lapland Bunting.
13. *Emberiza.*	*E. miliaria.*	Corn Bunting.
	E. citrinella.	Yellow Hammer.
	E. cirlus.	Cirl Bunting.
	E. schœniclus.	Reed Bunting.

HOUSE SPARROW.—It is almost superfluous to describe this well-known bird, now acclimatised, and not always a welcome acquisition, wherever the British race has effected a settlement. However, to complete our description we may say that the upper surface is brown, shaded with grey on the head, and dark brown on the back, and that a bar of yellowish white marks the lesser wing coverts; the throat to the middle of the breast is marked by an irregular line of deep black; the cheeks are whitish grey, and the remaining under parts are bluish grey; the bill is brown, and the legs and feet greyish brown. The female is brownish grey, and is smaller than the male, which, when newly moulted, is a handsome bird. Length of male, 6 inches; female, 5½.

The very vexed question of the food of this species is, nevertheless, a very simple one. The sparrow itself lives chiefly on seeds of various kinds, though it also eats many insects; but the young, at first, are fed entirely on the latter, and until they leave the nest and are able to cater for themselves their parents give them little else. The sparrow is often accused of destroying the farmer's corn, and there is no doubt that he does help himself to some, but the damage effected is much less than is often supposed, but even when put to its utmost, the harm he does is more than balanced by the good he effects by the destruction of insects, and the devouring, wholesale, of the seeds of some of our most obnoxious weeds. When it is remembered that it is only during a week or two that he visits the corn-fields and does harm, and that during all the rest of the year he is doing positive good to the farmer, his mischief should be condoned. In the garden, too, he is accused of doing an incalculable amount of harm; but it is easily prevented by netting fruit and vegetables, or by supplying the birds with some more readily accessible food.

Of course where, owing to the destruction, the absolutely senseless destruction, of the minor birds of prey, the sparrows have increased beyond due bounds, their numbers must be reduced by legitimate means; but to compass their extermination, or even wholesale slaughter, is an economical error that is much to be deprecated.

The nest of the sparrow is variously placed—in holes of trees or of buildings, or among the boughs of a tree, or some creeper, such as ivy, growing against a wall. In the first place, the cavity is simply lined with grass stems and feathers, but in every other position the large, clumsy construction is domed. The eggs, which vary from three to five in number, are greyish white, speckled and streaked with brownish grey; there is usually two broods in the season, but occasionally three. The "observers," who credit these birds with eight or more eggs to the nest, and five or six broods in the season, are either "romancing," or do not know what they are talking about.

Tree Sparrow.—Is not unlike the last in appearance,

Fig. 12.—*The House Sparrow.*

but he has some black on the face as well as on the throat, and is greyer on the back and lower parts; he is also a little smaller. The nest is usually placed in the hole of a tree, but it is surely a mistake to say that they build in the thatch of barns and out-houses, as Morris affirms they do; but, failing suitable trees with convenient cavities, they may, and sometimes do, nest in a hedge or bush. Length, $5\frac{1}{2}$ inches; female, a little less.

It is curious that the female should almost exactly resemble the male in plumage, seeing that the common sparrows differ so immensely in outward appearance.

The eggs of this species are usually five in number, of a dull white, specked with brown of several shades. There are two broods in the season, and the young have no black on the throat or face until after their first moult.

The tree sparrow is not a common bird anywhere, and in many parts of the British Islands it is quite unknown. It is more susceptible of domestication than the last, and readily learns to come and go if brought up by hand on the nest, which it is not difficult to do on ants' eggs and bread and milk. There are several instances on record where the tree sparrow has nested successfully in an aviary; but it does not appear ever to have cross-paired with the ordinary house sparrow, notwithstanding the strong resemblance that exists between the two species.

HAWFINCH.—The forehead is yellowish brown, which unites with the light chestnut on the top of the head and cheeks; the circle of the head is black, and forms, under the chin, a large square spot; the nape of the neck and upper part of the back are of a fine ash grey; the lower part is of a dark brown, with some shades of grey on the back. In the female, the cheeks, head, and upper tail coverts are of a greyish chestnut colour: the throat, wings, and tail rather brown than black, the spot on the wings greyish; the under part of the body reddish grey, shading to white on the belly. Length, 7 inches; tail, $2\frac{1}{2}$.

The bill, which seems disproportionately large, is dark blue in summer, and flesh-coloured with the tip black in winter.

In its wild state, it feeds on berries of all kinds, and some insects. In the house, it may be readily kept, if a due proportion of its natural food is added to the ordinary bird seed of the aviary. It builds a compact nest, and lays from three to five greenish grey eggs, spotted with brown, and streaked with bluish black. In England the hawfinch is mainly migratory, but a few pairs remain here and there through the summer to breed in suitable localities, and no doubt more would do so but for the inveterate persecution they are subjected to. The young are very easily reared by hand on soaked bruised seed, and bread, or biscuit.

Greenfinch.—Why this familiar bird should have been constituted a separate genus does not readily appear, for it is one of the true finches, feeding its young and mate with food prepared in and regurgitated from the crop.

The prevailing colour of the plumage is yellowish green, lighter on the lower part of the body, and still more so on the rump and breast, shading to white on the belly. A patch of brilliant canary yellow decorates each wing.

The female is browner above, and ash-coloured on the lower surface, so that she presents, at a distance, a strong resemblance to a female house sparrow, for the yellow patch on her wings is not very noticeable except at close quarters.

The young are curiously speckled, so that ignorant

people who believe in wild "mixed marriages" very often take them for hybrids; but they soon moult, and the wonder vanishes.

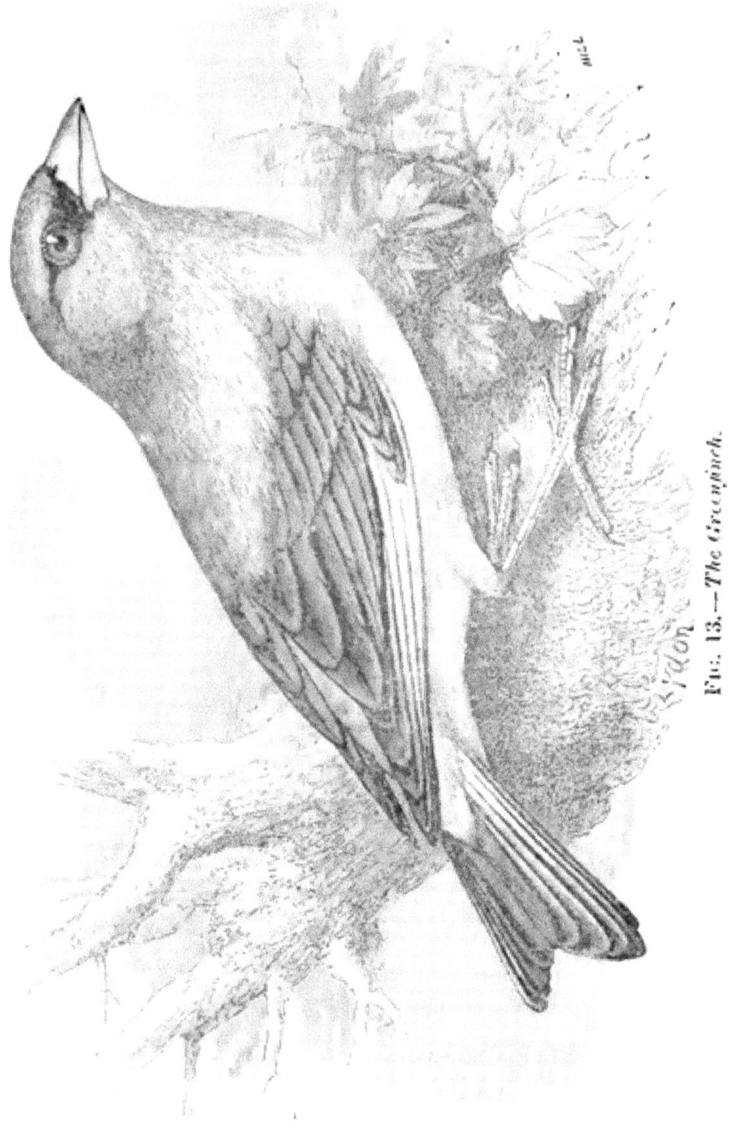

FIG. 13.—*The Greenfinch.*

The nest is compactly built of grass and moss, and is

very like that of the canary, the eggs also resembling those of the latter bird, except in point of size, for they are larger. Two or three broods of four or five are produced every season, and the young are easily reared on bread and milk.

These birds breed very freely among themselves, and with allied species in both cage and aviary, but have nothing much to recommend them to the notice of amateurs, for the song is a croaking squeal that is most unpleasant: but, strange to say, the call note is musical and pleasing.

The food consists of seeds, buds of trees, and the succulent portion of various plants. Much of the damage done in gardens and elsewhere, and attributed to the sparrow, should, in reality, be laid to the charge of the greenfinch, which has very few redeeming qualities, if any, to compensate the horticulturist and farmer for the damage done to their crops. Length, 6 inches; tail, 2½.

FIG. 14.—*The Chaffinch.*

CHAFFINCH.—The scientific name for this and the following species were not very happily selected, for there is nothing of the finch about either of them.

The forehead of the male is black; the top of the head and the nape of the neck are greyish blue—in very old subjects, deep blue; the breast is reddish brown, and there is a conspicuous white mark on the wing; the head is ornamented with a crest, which the bird can raise and depress at pleasure.

The female is smaller, greyish brown above, and greyish white on the under parts.

The bill of the male is blue in summer, when that of the female is greyish brown; but both turn to horn-colour in the winter.

The young are like their mother until after the first moult, and are easily brought up from the nest on bread and milk, and a few ants' eggs, small meal worms, or other insects.

When wild, these birds feed about equally on seeds and insects, and are wrongfully accused of destroying buds in their eager search for the latter; that they knock some off is probable, but the damage done is inappreciable, for those that remain are all the stronger for the thinning out, and more likely to come to maturity.

The nest of the chaffinch is the most beautiful of those built by British birds. It is variously placed, sometimes in a fruit tree, but generally where there are a good many lichens about, with which the outside of the nest is thickly covered, so that it is difficult to see, especially when placed against a wall on an espalier, or against the trunk of a gnarled apple tree. The eggs are about five in number, of a pale bluish grey, streaked and splashed with purplish brown.

There are two broods each season, the first of which consists, for the most part, of males, and the second of females. They are easily reared from the nest, and will then breed freely in cage and aviary.

It has long been a subject of contention whether the chaffinch will, or will not, pair and produce mules with the canary, and after protracted experimentation with them, the writer is enabled to say that it is not at all uncommon for the union to take place, but the eggs (whether of chaffinch or canary) are invariably barren. Length, $6\frac{1}{4}$ inches; tail, $2\frac{3}{4}$.

Fig. 15.—*The Bramblings.*

Brambling.—This bird, in habits and general configuration, bears a strong resemblance to the last, but instead of being partially migratory, it is entirely so, arriving in the autumn from the north, sometimes in large flocks, and departing in greatly reduced numbers in the spring.

The nest is stated to have been occasionally found in the northern counties of England, and in Scotland.

It should be fed and treated like the chaffinch, that is, on a mixed diet of seed and insect food. It is asserted to have bred in several aviaries, and even to have produced in one a mixed offspring with the chaffinch.

Fig. 16.—*The Goldfinch.*

The colour of the bird is black on the head and neck, variously spotted and streaked with chestnut brown, the rest of the plumage being similar in character.

The female is smaller, and has no black about her.

GOLDFINCH.—This bird is a true finch, and the handsomest one we have got; indeed, his brilliant colouring gives him a foreign appearance, which he soon will possess in reality, for he is fast being exterminated in Britain, which is a great pity, for he is as sweet a songster as he is bright, not to say gaudy, in his person.

The bill of the goldfinch is long, and terminates in a fine point: it is horn-colour in winter, and white in summer. The forehead, or rather a circle round the bill, is deep crimson or scarlet, varying in depth; the sides of the head, or bridle, are black, which is also the colour of the top of the head; the cheeks and a spot on the back of the neck are white; the breast is white, and the sides brownish grey: a line of the same colour sometimes descends from the chin to the lower part of the breast, or beyond it: the under parts are light grey. The shoulder joint and the lesser wing coverts are black, as are the quills of the tail and wings, but the latter are ornamented with a broad patch of yellow, and are tipped with yellowish greyish white; the back and hinder parts are brown.

The female is smaller, has less yellow and red, and the small wing coverts are black, edged with brown.

The young are very dissimilar, having grey heads, and bearing but little resemblance to their parents.

The nest is very compactly built, and is considered second in point of elegance to that of the chaffinch. It is often placed in a fruit tree in an orchard, among the upper or terminal branches. The eggs are usually five, and bear a considerable likeness to those of the canary, but are smaller.

There are two broods, as a rule, in the season, and the young are easily reared on crushed biscuit and milk, which should be given warm every ten or twelve minutes from dawn to dusk, one or two mouthfuls at a time; when able to pick, crushed hemp is the best feeding for them.

These birds will breed among themselves in cage or aviary, and pairing with allied species, will produce hybrids freely; crosses have been obtained with the canary, bullfinch, linnet, redpoll, siskin, greenfinch, and some of the foreign finches, but the two first are those ordinarily met with. Length, $5\frac{1}{2}$ inches; tail, 2.

SISKIN.—While the goldfinch resides in Great Britain throughout the year, the siskin only visits us during the winter, though a few pairs may remain and breed in the north.

The top of the head and the throat are black in the male; the cheeks, back of the neck, and the back are green, streaked with black in the last situation; the rump, breast, under part of the neck, and a line that passes over each eye, yellow. The flights are black, and the wing coverts and secondaries are tipped with yellow.

The food consists of seeds of all kinds, those of the birch, alder, fir, and pine, being first favourites; in the winter it will eat any small seeds of weeds it can find, as well as a few buds of trees.

The female has no black, and is greyer than the male.

The siskin is readily domesticated, and breeds freely in the house, where its natural tameness makes it a favourite.

LINNET.—The adult male is a beautiful chestnut brown on the upper surface, and the breast, as well as the forehead, rosy red. The flights and tail are black, the former tipped with greyish yellowish white, and the four outer feathers of the latter have white edges.

The female is brownish grey, with darker streaks and spots; the under parts are lighter than the upper, and have darker spots; there is no trace of red about her.

The young resemble their mother until the first moult,

when the males assume the adult plumage, but are neither as brown or rosy as their elders.

They are easily brought up by hand on bread and milk, and when they begin to feed they should have their seed soaked till soft. In the house they never assume the distinctive red of the wild bird, but are brown and grey.

In confinement they breed freely in cage and aviary among themselves and with allied species.

The agreeable, brilliant, and flute-like notes of the linnet consisting of several strains, succeeding each other very harmoniously, make the birds general favourites, and it is surely a great mistake on the part of the trappers to destroy the females that they catch; the practice has led to the extirpation of the species in many parts of the country.

The nest of the linnet is built of grass and lined with hair; it is very compactly put together, usually in a clump of furze, and the eggs, which are very like those of the canary, are usually five in number. The length of the linnet is 5½ inches; tail, 2¼.

TWITE, or MOUNTAIN LINNET.—This species is quite distinct from the last, and is brownish grey all over, but darker above than below, mottled and streaked with black and yellow; there is no red on the forehead or breast, but the rump is of a dull reddish brown colour, which is less apparent in the female, which otherwise closely resembles the male. The bill is yellow. Length of the bird, about 5 inches; tail, 2¼.

LESSER REDPOLL.—The etymology of the name being so apparent, it seems strange that Morris should have spelled it as if the bird had some connection with poles: but he has, and offers no explanation of his motive for having done so.

Reddish brown is the colour of the male, but the head (poll) is fiery red, which is not always lost in confinement:

the chin is black, and the throat and breast, as well as the rump, crimson.

FIG. 17.—*The Redpoll.*

The female has no red on the breast, but has on the forehead.

The nest, like that of the preceding species, is compactly built, and is usually placed in a dense bush; it does not habitually breed in England, but does so freely in Scotland and Ireland.

The eggs are four or five in number; the first batch is laid in May, and the second about the beginning of July.

These little birds breed freely in confinement, even rearing their young in a cage.

They are often chained to a stand, and taught to open a seed box and draw up water in a miniature bucket from a little well. Length, 4½ inches: tail, 2.

MEALY REDPOLL.—This is a migratory species from the north. Its forehead is crimson, and the top and nape of the neck, as well as the upper part of the back, are brown, spotted with a darker shade of brownish black; the rump, also spotted, is greyish white, with a yellow tinge, and the under parts are the same. The wing coverts, flights, and tail feathers are blackish brown, edged with yellowish white; a circle round the bill is black, and the bill itself yellow, with a black tip: the legs and feet are grey.

The female has no red, and is smaller than the male, which measures 5 inches in full length, of which the tail makes 2¼.

All the members of the genus *Linota* feed exclusively on seeds, chiefly of grass, and in the house are best dieted on canary seed, with groundsel and plaintain for green food.

BULLFINCH.—This handsome bird is of stouter build than any of the preceding, and has a thick head, with a short, stout bill, which, together with the head, is jet black; the wings and tail are also black, with a steel blue reflection; the back is slate grey: the rump white; the face, neck, and breast bright crimson red in the male, but brownish grey with a subdued reddish tinge in the female and the young of both sexes. The legs and feet are dark slate; the small wing coverts have a brownish tinge, and the greater have white tips, making a conspicuous line across the middle of the wing.

This beautiful bird, in spite of its handsome appearance, charming song, and extreme tameness, is much persecuted by gardeners, who have completely exterminated it in many places where it used formerly to be abundant; and the reason given for this mistaken policy is that it destroys their fruit trees by knocking off and eating the buds.

FIG. 18.—*The Bullfinch.*

That it does so to a certain extent is undeniable, but the damage effected by it has been greatly exaggerated.

To give an example:—The writer is acquainted with an extensive orchard, containing apple, pear, and plum trees, covering many acres of ground, from which the owner in one season removed 3,000 cartloads of branches by pruning.

There were a few buds destroyed then! The writer picked up an average-sized bough that had been cut off, and counted the buds on it; they numbered 1,003.

In each load there were between 200 and 300 branches, but say 250 for an average, that is to say, 250,000 buds to the load, or a total of 752,250,000 (seven hundred and fifty-two millions, two hundred and fifty thousand) buds, which it would require a whole army of bullfinches to knock off, and that the trees would have received no harm.

A bullfinch, from observations made, will eat about 120 buds a day, that is, 43,800 in twelve months, and if that number is multiplied by 100 bullfinches (scarcely so many exist in a county), we arrive at a total of 4,380,000 buds, an insignificant number compared with that of the buds deliberately destroyed by the horticulturist himself for the benefit of his trees.

If the birds were left alone, he would be spared the labour of pruning, and have far healthier trees, for the proper way to prune a tree is to rub off superfluous buds, not to lop off an entire bough, a most mistaken policy, which Nature resents by growing three or four branches from the stop, and so weakening the tree to a corresponding extent: but she takes no notice of the removal of buds, if, indeed, she does not actually approve of it by producing a finer crop of fruit on every branch or tree thus treated.

Moral.—Do not shoot the bullfinches, for they do good, not harm, and a discharge of lead among the branches does a great deal of mischief.

If the bullfinches, from one cause or another, should become too numerous (which is extremely unlikely), their numbers can be easily kept within due bounds by taking and hand-rearing the young, which, when well trained to pipe a tune, sell for various sums from 10s. to £20 each.

The nest of the bullfinch is usually built of roots, and is lined with hair. There are two broods in the season, the young of the first being mostly males, and those of the second mostly females; but the latter sing almost as well as their brothers, if they do not fetch quite so much money.

The young are easily reared on bread and milk, and

when they are able to pick, they should have soaked canary seed and crushed hemp, but not too much of the last, which turns them dusky, and destroys the brightness of their beautiful red breast.

A small twig of some fruit or forest tree is also conducive to their happiness and health.

PINE GROSSBEAK.—This bird, which may be called the cousin-german of the last, is not, like it, a resident in Britain all the year round, but comes over in winter only from the far north. It is of a reddish brown colour, except the wings and tail, which are black. The former have the wing coverts broadly edged with grey, and the back feathers have dark centres; the under surface is of a lighter shade than the upper, and is not spotted: the bill is short, thick, and black. The female is rather of an olive brown colour than red. The young resemble her.

These birds feed chiefly on the seeds of the various coniferæ that grow in the countries they frequent. In Britain they are partial to the seeds of the larch and the beech, but will eat any others they can find. Length, 8½ inches; tail, 3.

CROSSBILL.—These curious birds are winter visitors only to Great Britain, and then but occasionally. They vary greatly in size as well as in colour, scarcely two in a flock being alike in either respect. The prevailing tints are green, olive, orange, red, scarlet, and yellow. The upper and lower mandibles cross each other, but also vary a good deal in length and in the amount of curvature they present. The young are dark green, with blackish spots and streaks.

These birds feed principally on the seeds of fir and pine trees, but are very partial to those of the cypress and arborvitæ. They very seldom nest in Britain, but instances are, nevertheless, recorded in which they have done so, the nest being placed in the fork of a tree at varying elevations from the ground. The eggs are four or five, of a faint green colour, streaked and spotted with purple and brown.

SNOW BUNTING.—This winter visitor also varies a good deal in size and colouring. It is stoutly built and densely covered with feathers, which are generally of a buffish brown, lighter on the under than on the upper surface of the body. The female is smaller, but bears a general resemblance to her mate. Like the rest of the buntings, they have a bony tubercle at the palate, and feed on a mixed diet of seed and insects.

It is quite exceptional for any of them to remain in this country during the summer, and those that are kept in cage or aviary appear to suffer very much from the heat, which generally throws them into a decline. Eggs have, however, been laid occasionally. They are greenish blue white, with dark brown spots at the thicker end, and others, distributed all over the surface, of greyish purple. Length, $6\frac{3}{4}$ inches, or 7 inches; tail, $2\frac{3}{8}$.

LAPLAND BUNTING.—This is a smaller bird than the last, and, like it, visits Britain in the winter only. It is rather a handsome creature, at least the male is. His head, neck, face, and breast are jet black; nape chestnut brown; back brown, with a dark centre to each feather; rump and outer edges of tail feathers yellowish brown. Backwards from the eye is a white streak, which descends, broadening to the under parts, where it merges into faint bluish grey; the head portions of the band are grizzled by a number of fine white hair-like lines, and the sides are spotted with brown: the wing coverts are edged whitish grey, with a blue tinge.

The female is smaller, has no black, and is greyer on the back. Hind nail long; legs and feet yellowish grey. Length of bird, $6\frac{1}{2}$ inches.

CORN BUNTING.—This is a British species, pretty generally distributed, but seldom noticed on account of its shy and retiring habits.

It is of a brownish grey colour, darker above than below, and heavily spotted with blackish brown in both situations; there is a faint rusty red tinge on the wings, and a bluish one on the breast and belly; the bill and legs and feet are yellowish grey.

The female is indistinguishable outwardly from her mate.

The nest is generally placed on the ground among grass. It is loosely put together, and made of grass, roots, and moss, lined with hair. The eggs are four or five in number, are grey, speckled and streaked with chestnut and black.

They are easily tamed, and will even build in a garden aviary.

The food consists about equally of seeds and insects. Length, 7¼ inches; tail, 3.

YELLOWHAMMER.—This well-known species, like the last, is resident throughout Britain, but wanders about a good deal during the winter. Its coloration is very variable, that of an adult male being as follows:—Head, neck, and all lower parts bright yellow, shaded with chestnut on the crown and face; along the sides are a number of elongated reddish black spots; the upper parts are brown, with light lacing to the different feathers, especially the wing coverts.

The female has very little yellow about her, and her back and wings are rather greyish than reddish brown.

The nest is built generally in a low bush, or among brambles. It is compactly put together, and, as a rule, fairly well concealed. The eggs are generally five, of a pale purplish white, spotted with brown, and marked with a number of zigzag lines of a greyish colour.

They are readily brought up by hand on biscuit and milk, with some ants' eggs and flies added. A certain amount of insect food must be added to their dietary in confinement, or they are apt to fall into a decline ; this is especially so in summer.

It is singular that nine out of ten cuckoos place their egg, or eggs, in the nest of a yellow bunting. Length, 7 inches ; tail, $2\frac{3}{4}$.

CIRL BUNTING.—This species very strongly resembles the last, but is distinguished by a triangular-shaped patch of dark feathers under the chin, which is wanting, or nearly so, in the female : there is a bluish band across the middle of the breast, and a yellow streak above the eye.

It feeds on a mixed diet of seeds and insects like its congeners, and is often seen in company with the yellow-hammer, than which it is a little smaller, measuring $6\frac{1}{2}$ inches, of which the tail takes up $2\frac{1}{2}$.

REED BUNTING.—Like the last, this species is of partial distribution only in Britain, and is chiefly met with in localities where the rush, from which it derives its trivial name, is found, and there it may occur in considerable numbers. The head and throat of the male are black, and the lower parts white, spotted with brown at the sides, which are also tinged with slate blue. The upper parts are dark brown, with black centre and dark edges to every feather.

The female is without the black on head and throat, and a shade of olive dominates the brown of the face. She has the spots distributed all over the lower parts of her body. Length, $6\frac{1}{2}$ inches ; tail, $2\frac{1}{4}$.

THE STARLINGS.

We now pass on to a somewhat large family, that of the starlings, of which but one species is a native of the British Isles, namely the Common Starling.

Family—*Sturnidæ*.
Genus—*Sturnus*. *S. vulgaris*.

This well-known bird is black, reflecting various shades of blue, purple, and bronze, and more or less covered with small white spots, that impart a pepper-and-salt appearance to the plumage. The bill, which is pointed, and of a yellowish colour, is about an inch in length, and is used for probing after the maggots and grubs, on which the bird mainly subsists.

Fig. 19.—*The Starling.*

The female much resembles the male, but her plumage is much less lustrous, and the spots on her body are larger, as well as more numerous.

The nest is made in holes of trees and buildings, under

eaves, and in dovecotes, or where the bird can find a convenient place for its purpose. The eggs are five or six in number, of a greenish blue colour, mostly without, but sometimes with, a few small black spots sparsely scattered about the longer end.

The young are easily reared on biscuit soaked in milk, ants' eggs, meal worms, maggots, and other insects, and get very tame, learning to repeat words and airs that are whistled or played to them.

The favourite food of the starling is the grub of the fly known by the name of daddy-long-legs, which is so destructive in pasture lands, where it eats the roots of the grass, and sometimes leaves the ground bare for acres; for when the roots have been destroyed, the blades, of course, wither away; and yet, because when driven by stress of weather during the winter, this most useful bird picks up a little corn from the stack-yards, he is remorselessly persecuted in some parts, and a price is put upon his head.

There are two nests in the season, as a rule, and it is not uncommon for white and cream-coloured or buff specimens to be met with, which are generally shot or captured. In the aviary these breed freely, but the young are usually of the ordinary kind, which shows that albinism is not necessarily hereditary.

The starling is gifted with great powers of imitation, which he exercises even in the wild state, but more especially in captivity, when he will learn to repeat not only all kinds of domestic sounds, such as coughing and sneezing, sawing wood, pouring out water, etc., but he will learn to say tolerably long sentences in a wonderfully natural manner, so as to deceive persons unacquainted with his talent.

As the bill of this bird grows very fast, and is kept ground down to a suitable length by constantly poking it into the soil and rooting about for grubs and worms, it is a good plan to put some of the latter under a sod of grass in his cage, which he will at once commence to bare in search of them, and thus keep his beak in good order.

He may be taught to go and come, and although he may disappear during the summer he will be sure, if alive, to return when winter has sealed Nature's fountains with its icy hand.

Too much flesh meat is not good for these birds, but they are fond of picking a bone, and may have one. Neither can they live on a diet of farinaceous matters alone, but require a free supply of insects if they are to remain in health.

THE CROWS.

The Crow family is a very numerous one, and has no less than eight representatives in Britain.

Family—*Corvidæ*.

Genus—1. *Corvus*.	*C. corax*.	Raven.
	C. corone.	Carrion Crow.
	C. cornix.	Hooded Crow.
	C. frugilegus.	Rook.
	C. monedula.	Jackdaw.
2. *Pica*.	*P. rustica*.	Magpie.
3. *Garrulus*.	*G. glandarius*.	Jay.
4. *Pyrrhocorax*.	*P. graculus*.	Chough.

Raven.—The colour of this bird is jet black, with steel blue, violet, and purple reflections, also a green tinge on the under parts; the throat is more of a dingy black. The female presents but little difference, but she is slightly smaller than her mate, and the metallic reflections of her plumage are less conspicuous than in his case.

FIG. 20.—*The Raven.*

The nest is large and made of sticks, lined with hair and wool. It is variously placed, sometimes on a tree, sometimes on a ruined building, a church tower, or some similar position, including precipitous cliffs and precipices. The eggs are four or five in number, say some authorities, but, according to others, only two or three, and, considering the voracious appetites of the young ones, and the difficulty of finding them an adequate supply of suitable food, the latter is more frequently the number than the former. The ground colour is bluish green, which is spotted with a darker shade of the same and with brown. The young are covered at first with greyish down. The old birds breed freely in confinement.

Carrion Crow.—This bird is a miniature raven, and is often confounded with the rook, from which it differs mainly in point of size, being a little larger than the latter, but is much less than the raven, which measures 26 inches in length, and the carrion crow only 20 or 21. From the rook it is distinguished by having feathers close up to the base of the bill, and by flying about in pairs, or, at most, in little parties of four or six, probably the old birds and the young of the year, also by building singly, each pair in a separate locality, and never in company.

The nest is large, made of sticks, and is placed among the topmost boughs of a tree, where it forms a very conspicuous object until the leaves come out. The eggs are three or four in number, rarely more. They are pale bluish green, spotted and speckled with brown and grey, but they vary a good deal both as to the ground colour and the markings on them. There are two broods in the season, the first in March, and the second in May or June. As soon as the young can feed themselves the old ones drive them away.

Both the raven and the carrion crow feed on small animals, such as moles, rats, etc., and birds. They also eat any dead animal of larger size they may find lying about, and the crows especially are often to be seen on the sea-shore searching for offal cast up by the waves, or for molluscs and crabs left there by the receding tide. Like the raven, they are very easily tamed, and will live a long time, and breed in confinement.

HOODED CROW.—Many naturalists are of opinion that this bird is merely a local variety of the last, and assert that the two interbreed and produce a fertile offspring, not piebald, but exactly resembling one or other of the parents. If that be so, then there can be no doubt as to their specific identity. The bill, head, and neck of the hooded crow are black; the back, breast, and lower parts dark slate grey; but the wings and tail are black, with a bright blue tinge. In size this bird equals the carrion crow, which it closely resembles in its habits.

FIG. 21.—*The Hooded Crow.*

ROOK.—The well-known rook is one of the "common objects" of the country, nor is it even unknown in towns—witness the colonies that still maintain their ground in several parts of London. It is of a bluish black colour all over, and is known by a bare circle round its bill, where the skin is of a dull earthy colour, and much wrinkled or corrugated, a peculiarity that was long supposed to be due to the bird's habit of constantly digging in the ground for worms and grubs, as the nestlings have feathers in the same part.

The idea, however, is now quite disproved by the fact that young rooks, reared in confinement and supplied with an abundance of food, so that they have not to work for their living, and do not, also lose their feathers round the base of the bill when they moult for the second time, which is, or should be, conclusive that the denudation is natural, and not the result of abrasion.

The rook, as is well known, builds in companies among the upper branches of lofty trees. The eggs are two or three in number, very rarely more; they are of a pale green ground colour, spotted with blotches of brown and greenish grey, but vary greatly, even in the same nest.

It is curious that the rooks begin to repair their old nests, or build new ones, on the first of March regularly every year, as the writer has ascertained from observation in a variety of places extending over a number of years. There is rarely a second brood, never, indeed, unless some accident has befallen the first.

The rook is more vegetarian in its tastes than the preceding species, but, nevertheless, it consumes an immense quantity of earthworms, grubs, and other injurious creatures, also small frogs and other reptiles, and occasionally a stray or injured small bird.

It is easily tamed, and is very amusing, but inclined to be mischievous; indeed, a lady, well known for her appreciation of all the feathered tribes, assured the writer that a tame rook of hers could get through more mischief in a given time than any other creature she had ever met with.

It is a pity that so much misapprehension as to the habits of the rook and its value to the agriculturist should still exist; that some farmers should continue to poison them wholesale, forgetting the amount of vermin they destroy, and only noting the comparatively small quantity of grain and vegetables consumed by them in severe weather, when the ordinary supplies are cut off. It would surely be worth while to feed them at such times. Length, about 20 inches.

JACKDAW.—This is the smallest of the true crows that inhabit Great Britain. It has a kind of crest, the back

FIG. 22.—*The Jackdaw.*

part of which, as well as the back of the head and the nape, are grey; the remainder of the plumage is black, with steel blue shading; the legs, toes, and nails are burnished black.

The female is smaller than the male, has much less crest, and very little grey on her head.

Pied and pure white individuals are not uncommon:

sometimes the latter have blue eyes, but more often they are clear red, as happens in the case of most albinos.

The nest is usually placed under cover in a building, such as a church tower, but occasionally in trees, or among the statuary on the front of public edifices: for the jackdaw often frequents towns. The eggs are three or four, rarely more, though Morris says seven; they are of a pale greenish blue, spotted with brown and grey, chiefly at the larger end.

The jackdaw feeds on offal of all kinds, as well as on mice, young birds, and small reptiles and insects, also worms and grubs, for the possession of which he may often be seen disputing with the starlings.

In confinement, and he is easily domesticated, too much butcher's meat will cause him to have fits. His diet should be varied in accordance with the nature of what he eats in the wild state; he will then be healthy and very amusing, but he is as mischievous and as great a thief as the other members of the family to which he belongs. Nothing of a bright or glittering appearance should be left in his way. Full length, 14 inches.

Magpie.—This is a beautiful bird, the glistening glories of whose plumage rival those of the inhabitants of the inter-tropical forests, to which we shall advert when treating of our colonial and Indian birds.

The head, neck, breast, and back are black, with a shade of deep blue; the belly, sides, and wing coverts white: the wings black, with bright steel blue reflections; the inner web of the primaries white to within half-an-inch of the tip, which is blue, with a shading of green; the long central tail feathers and the secondaries are black, with blue green shading, the others black. The bill and the legs and feet are black.

The female is smaller than the male, and her plumage is

less lustrous than his. Length, 18 inches, of which the tail measures 10.

The nest is built in tall trees, and, failing these, in bushes. It is made of twigs and domed with thorns; it

Fig. 23.—The Magpie.

has two openings opposite to each other, from one end of which may be seen projecting the bill and from the other the tail of the owner.

The eggs are four or five in number (Morris again says seven or eight!), and of a pale greenish colour, spotted with grey and olive brown; but they vary a good deal in appearance.

Two broods are usually hatched in the season, and the young are easily reared on table scraps (not too much meat), ants' eggs, meal worms, and other insects.

They make good talkers and mimics, and will learn to come and go, especially in the country.

FIG. 24.—*The Jay.*

The magpie is accused of sucking eggs and killing young game, chickens, and ducklings, and not, it must be confessed, without foundation; but he is a great enemy to rats, moles, and mice.

JAY.—This most handsome bird is counted vermin by every gamekeeper and most farmers and country gardeners.

the consequence being that it has been almost everywhere exterminated, or so reduced in numbers as to call forth an exclamation of wonder when one is accidently seen.

It is about the size of the jackdaw, and, like that bird, has a handsome crest, which it raises and depresses at pleasure. It is white, with a reddish shade, and has a number of narrow black lines running through it. The head, neck, and back are reddish grey, the rump white, and the tail blackish grey. A long, black line runs backwards from the bill, and looks like a moustache; the chin and upper throat are white; the breast and belly pale reddish grey; the vent and under tail coverts white. The wings are blackish grey, but the outer web of the primaries is white, so is the centre of the first four secondaries; but the "thumb" and the first wing coverts are blue, barred with black; the bill is blackish grey, and the legs and feet yellowish grey with a red tinge.

In the female the crest is less conspicuous, and the red of her back and breast is greyer than happens in the male.

The flight of the jay, says Morris, is very observable, as heavy and irregular, effected with some degree of apparent difficulty, and in a scurrying sort of manner, as if conscious that it was a proscribed bird, and doomed to destruction for real or supposed faults; it is a series of quick beats, with occasional short cessations. They seldom settle on the ground; they glide cleverly through woods and thickets, and keep flitting along hedge sides; to which we add, screaming loudly as they go.

The nest is placed in various situations, but, where such a site is available, among the thick young growth of a tree that has been lopped during the previous year, though it is sometimes found in an old hedge or a thick bush, but always where there is plenty of cover. It is built of sticks, lined with fibre, roots, grass, horse-hair, and other materials of a like kind. The nests differ a good deal in finish and construction.

The eggs, four or five in number (Morris says five or six), are pale bluish green, thickly spotted with purple and brown; they differ a good deal in appearance as well as size.

The female resembles the male, but her crest is smaller, and the vinous red of her breast less pronounced.

Length from extremity of bill to end of tail, 14 inches.

The jay eats insects, young birds, and eggs, also snails, worms, fruit, and does some harm in country gardens; but he also does much good, as a careful watching of his ways must undoubtedly prove. He is an extremely vigilant creature, the watch-bird, indeed, of wood and copse, and is invariably the first to warn the feathered inhabitants of the approach of an enemy, bipedal or quadrupedal, for which reason, as well as for his undoubted partiality for game eggs *au naturel*, he is abhorred by shooters, whom he often baulks of an expected prey by uttering his harsh cry of "wrak wrak" in time to enable the intended victim to effect its escape.

Fishermen also use the blue wing feathers in the construction of "flies," but it is chiefly to gamekeepers that the almost complete extermination of this beautiful, and, on the whole, useful bird is due.

The CHOUGH, or CORNISH CHOUGH, as it is sometimes called, is, at first sight, very unlike a crow; but a closer acquaintance soon demonstrates the fact that his habits and proclivities are decidedly corvine.

The general colour of the plumage is black, but shaded with brilliant reflections of green and blue and purple. The long bill and the legs and feet are reddish orange.

The female resembles the male, but is a little smaller and less brilliant in colour.

The chough is essentially a shore bird, seeking its food chiefly among the refuse cast up on the beach by the tide, but occasionally searching for worms and insects, such as grasshoppers, in adjacent fields.

The nest is built in the most inaccessible cliffs, to which fact alone the species so far owes its exemption from complete extermination in Britain, where at one time it was fairly abundant, but at present it is only met with in a few favourable situations on the south and west coasts. The eggs are four or five in number, of a dull white colour, spotted, chiefly at the larger end, with dull brown and grey.

The young are easily reared on table scraps and insects, but should not have much meat or they get cramp, and lose the use of their feet and legs.

When brought up by hand they become very tame, and are very inquisitive and mischievous, like all the other members of the crow family. Though they will sometimes imitate various domestic sounds, there is no recorded instance of any of them learning to speak. Length, about 16 inches, 3 of which is included in the bill.

THE LARKS.

The larks next claim our attention. The British species include two favourites that remain all the year round, and one that has its principal habitat in America, but, nevertheless, pays an occasional visit to Great Britain.

Family—*Alaudidæ.*

Genus—1. *Alauda.*	*A. arvensis.*	Skylark.
	A. arborea.	Woodlark.
2. *Otocorys.*	*O. alpestris.*	Shorelark.

SKYLARK.—Upper surface brownish grey, every feather

edged with a lighter shade than its centre. The head is ornamented with a crest, which the bird raises and de-

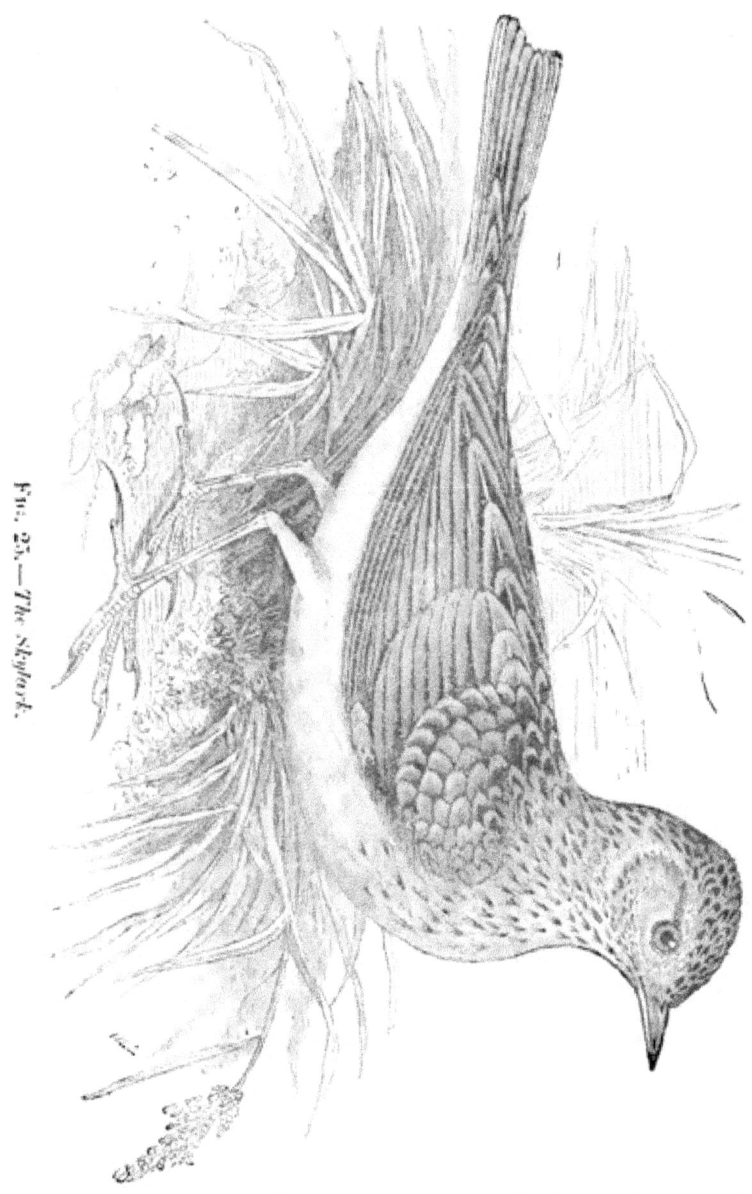

FIG. 25.—*The Skylark.*

presses at pleasure. A line running back from the eye is of a tawny colour, and merges into the fawn of the throat, which is thickly spotted with long, blackish brown marks; under the eye is a white line; the breast is whitish grey; the belly grey, with a slight greenish tinge; the under tail coverts and the outer feathers of the tail itself are white; the bill is horn-colour, but there is a yellowish spot about the middle of the lower mandible: the legs and feet are greyish flesh colour: the hind toe is armed with a long nail or spur.

The skylark does not perch on branches of trees, though it will on a gate or the top of a hedge; its favourite resting-place, however, is a clod of earth or a clump of coarse grass.

The female closely resembles the male in outward appearance, but, as a rule, is more spotted on the breast, and greyer on the back. The young are of a lighter colour than either parent.

The nest is made of grass, and lined with finer portions of the same; it is placed on the ground among long grass or corn, and many nests are destroyed yearly by the mowing machines when the grass is cut for hay. The eggs are four or five in number, and differ greatly in appearance; the general colour is whitish grey, spotted and streaked with darker grey or brown.

The song of the skylark, which is seldom uttered from the ground, but almost invariably from mid-air, is well known as one of the harmonies of Nature, and it is sad to think that so perfect a performer should be growing scarce in consequence of the demand for it by a certain class of people, who ought to know better, as a delicacy (?) for the table, apropos of which it may be mentioned that although a cat will readily kill a lark if she can, she will rarely eat it, but, if she should do so, it will make her violently sick in a few minutes afterwards.

The food consists in about equal parts of grass seeds,

blades of grass, and insects, a diet that must be provided for it if it is wished to preserve it in confinement, where oats, soaked to the point of germination, are much relished by the bird, which also eats soaked oatmeal, as well as ants' eggs and meal worms.

The song, though extremely pleasing when heard out of doors beneath the free canopy of heaven, is rather too loud for the house, and is much more enjoyable in the open.

The young are easily reared on oatmeal and milk, with ants' eggs and small insects. These birds will sometimes breed in an aviary.

WOODLARK.—This bird differs in several respects from the last. For example, it does not soar to nearly such a height when singing, but it has a sweeter and less penetrating song; it also perches on trees, and sings from that elevation.

It is much the same colour as the skylark, but has rather a yellower tinge throughout. It has no crest, a very short tail, and also a shorter spur. The nest and eggs have a general resemblance to those of the preceding species, but the latter vary a good deal. While the skylark measures from $7\frac{1}{2}$ to $7\frac{3}{4}$ inches in full length, the length of the woodlark is little more than 6 inches, of which the tail includes less than 2. It is a more delicate bird than the last, and more difficult to preserve in the house; but with strict attention to cleanliness, else it will speedily contract sore feet, and a liberal supply of insect food, it may be preserved for eight or ten years, which is probably as long as it would live out of doors, or longer.

It is a good plan to have the cage in which it is kept provided with a canvas top to keep the bird from hurting its head when it rises, and the same remark applies, even more forcibly, to the skylark. The woodlark's cage should be provided with a perch, but this is unnecessary in the case of its congener. Both birds roll in the dust, like poultry, rather than wash themselves in water; but the woodlark occasionally "tubs," and no doubt in its wild state often wets itself in the damp grass it is in the habit of frequenting. Food, both when wild and tame, the same as the last.

SHORELARK.—This is rather a pretty bird, and, at first sight, reminds one somewhat of the cirl bunting. The head is ornamented with a double crest, that is, a narrow pencil of almost black feathers starts from the front of the head, and reaches back past the ears on either side. The forehead and the face, except a black "moustache," is yellow, with a reddish tinge in the centre. The chin also is yellow, and the upper part of the neck black. The breast and other lower parts have a purplish pink tinge, and the former is slightly speckled with spots of a darker shade of the ground colour. The bill, legs, and feet are dark horn-colour.

It is a northern species, but individuals occur in Britain every winter; but it is not known to breed there. The young are said to be hatched in July (Audubon), and to leave the nest before they are able to fly. The eggs, four or five in number, are greyish white, spotted with pale blue and brown spots.

The food consists of seeds, insects, blades of grass, and the succulent parts of the leaves of other plants. They are easily kept in confinement if a similar diet is provided for them, but they require a good deal of gritty sand to enable them to fully digest their food.

The shorelark, as its name implies, is met with on the beach, where it catches and eats marine insects, small molluscs, and crustacea.

The male soars, but to no great elevation, when singing his sweet and plaintive song, and in the cage should be provided with a flat stone or a log of wood to sit on, rather than a thin perch, which it seldom makes use of. Length, about 7 inches.

THE SWIFT.

Family—*Cypselidæ.*
Genus—*Cypselus. C. apus.*

It seems a refinement of differentiation that is quite superfluous to separate this bird from the swallows, and constitute it a family and genus by itself. But it has pleased certain authorities to do so, and what are we that we should run counter to their decision, and kick against the pricks?

Migratory, like all the British *Hirundinæ*, the swift comes over later than the others—about May—and departs again in August. This is the rule, wrote Morris; but exceptions to it, as a matter of course, have occurred, do occur, and will occur.

The legs of this bird are extremely short, and its wings proportionately long, so that it rises with difficulty from the ground, and never alights upon it of its own free will; but in the air it never seems to tire, and is comparable with the albatross for its extraordinary power of flight.

The note or cry of the swift is a harsh scream, "Kee-skree, skree-kee," uttered frequently while the birds are gyrating, especially during showery weather, round a church steeple or some other elevated building, where the nest is usually placed in some convenient crevice. The materials are collected by the bird while on the wing, and are agglutinated together by its saliva, for, unlike the other swallows, it does not pick up mud wherewith to construct a foundation for its nest.

The eggs are usually two in number, rarely three, but, where more have been found, they were, doubtless, the

Fig. 26.—*Swifts in Mid Air.*

production of more than one female. They are white, and of an elongated form.

The diet consists entirely of flies, gnats for the most part, though it is partial to the small caterpillars that dangle in thousands by an invisible thread from the leaves and branches of trees, poplars especially, during the summer time. The bill is very short, and of a black colour, but the gape of the mouth is considerable, resembling that of the next species in that respect. With the exception of a small patch of greyish white under the chin, the whole plumage is blackish brown, with a shade of purple and green. The length of the bird is about 7½ or 8 inches; but the wings expand to a width of a foot and a half.

The female is indistinguishable from the male, but have some of their back feathers edged with white.

Provided with food resembling that of which it partakes in a state of nature, the swift can be kept alive for a long time in the house; but no bird is more unfitted for a life of inactivity in a cage, and it never ought to be so kept.

White specimens have been occasionally seen, and, of course, shot; but they were albinos, and by no means a variety, or even very rare.

The ALPINE SWIFT is a much larger bird than the bird under consideration, but it is very doubtful whether it has ever really occurred in Britain, an extra large specimen of the ordinary species having probably been mistaken for it.

THE GOAT-SUCKERS.

Family—*Caprimulgidæ*.
Genus—*Caprimulgus*. *C. europæus*.

This is a more extensive family than the last, for it has

representatives in almost every part of the world; but only one species occurs in England (the one named above).

The COMMON GOAT-SUCKER in its general appearance is not unlike a cuckoo, and has often been mistaken for one, even by persons with some pretension to ornithological knowledge. It differs from that bird, however, in many essential points.

The head is very large, and the gape prodigious; the sides of the mouth are armed with long bristles, which are supposed to be of use in retaining the insects it collects, as it flies open-mouthed during the crepuscule.

Like all the members of its family, its plumage is handsome, if not as gaudy as that of some of its relations; and it is especially soft and downy, as becomes a night-flyer, who must needs glide about on noiseless wing in order to effect the capture of its sleeping prey, which it swoops upon, but without settling, while it is secure, or fancies itself secure, in the darkness; for, if report speak the truth, many a small bird disappears down the capacious throat of the prowling night-jar, as this bird is also called, from the season in which it emits its jarring note.

The general colour above is brown, abundantly waved by narrow black lines, and spotted with dark brown and yellow spots; the wing coverts are broadly edged with yellow or brownish yellow, and the three outer flights have each a spot of white about their outer third; the outer tail feathers are also tipped with white.

The female is duller and darker as to her plumage, and she has no white either on wings or tail. She makes no nest, but lays her two long, narrow eggs on the bare ground. They are greyish white, marked heavily with dark grey spots; but they vary a good deal, both as regards shape and colour. When surprised on her eggs, she will sit very closely, and almost allow herself to be trodden on before she attempts to escape. When thus suddenly rising, she is almost always taken for a cuckoo; hence the story, credited in quarters where one might have looked for more enlightenment, that that usurper of other birds' nests occasionally incubates her own eggs, which, needless to say, is a mistake.

The food of the night-jar consists of insects of all kinds, and no doubt an occasional little bird, such as a wren, or a regulus, or even a tit, if such venture abroad before the goat-sucker (what a ridiculous appellation!) has retired for the day; and as it is an especial foe to the cockchafer and the goat moth (*Cossa ligniperda*) it should receive all possible protection, and its murder, as well as the abstraction of its eggs, be severely punished.

The night-jar has one remarkable peculiarity, namely, that of not perching on a branch in the fashion common to most birds, but of resting lengthwise upon it, so as more effectually to conceal its presence from any lurking foe beneath. Length, about 10½ or 11 inches, of which the tail measures at least a third. It cannot be preserved in confinement for more than a month or two. Migratory.

THE WOODPECKERS.

These birds are the subject of much misapprehension in many quarters, which in the following paragraphs it will be our purpose to try and dispel.

Family—*Picidæ.*

Genus—1. *Dendrocopus.*	*D. major.*	Greater Spotted Woodpecker.
	D. minor.	Lesser Spotted Woodpecker.
2. *Gecinus.*	*G. auratus.*	Green Woodpecker.

GREATER SPOTTED WOODPECKER.—Crown and upper parts black, a crimson patch on the back of the head, a white spot on each side of the neck; scapulars, lesser wing coverts, and under parts white; belly and under tail coverts crimson; female without crimson on head. Length, $9\frac{1}{2}$ inches; tail, 4 inches.

LESSER SPOTTED WOODPECKER. — Forehead and lower parts greyish white; crown, bright red; nape, back and wings black, with white bars; tail black, the outer feathers

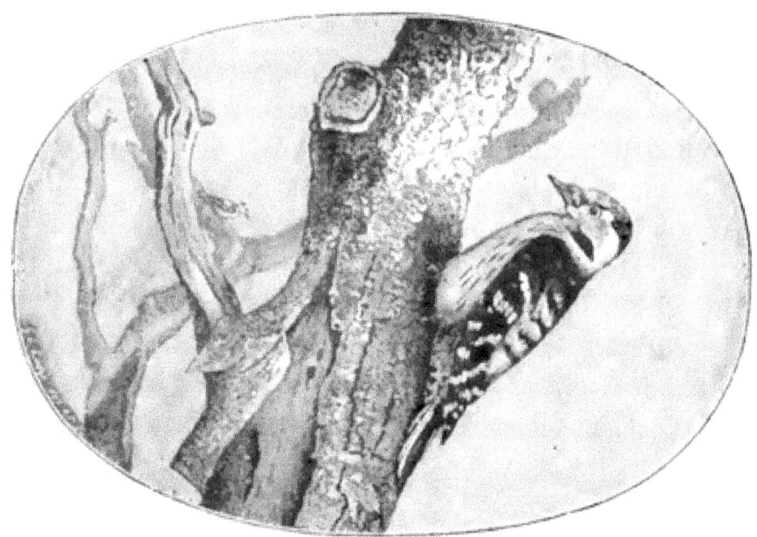

FIG. 27.—*The Lesser Spotted Woodpecker.*

tipped with white and barred with black; iris red; female without crimson on head. Length, $5\frac{3}{4}$ inches; tail, $2\frac{1}{2}$.

GREEN WOODPECKER.—Upper parts olive green; rump yellow; under parts greenish grey; crown, back of head, and moustaches crimson; face black. Female less crimson on the head; moustaches black. Length, 13 inches; tail, $4\frac{1}{2}$.

All three species are found throughout the British Islands, but rarely in the northern counties of England, in Scotland, and in Ireland. All three are resident.

The food consists principally of insects found in the crevices of the bark on decayed or decaying trees; also nuts, acorns, and occasionally fruit and seed. The green woodpecker also feeds largely on ants and their "eggs," (pupae).

The woodpeckers are shy, restless birds, frequenting groves and wooded districts, where they may be seen flying from tree to tree, examining the bark or tapping the decayed branches in search of their insect food. They nest in holes, which they excavate in soft-wooded trees, and deposit pure white, very glossy eggs, which are slightly pyriform in shape.

There is no more trustworthy herald of spring than the green woodpecker or yaffle; as soon as his laughing note is heard, one may be sure that the sap is rightly astir, and that presently the grove will be dim with new greenery. The jay, harshly garrulous at other times, falls cunningly silent in the nesting season; but the yaffle cannot hold his tongue in the honeymoon.

Admirable as is the tongue of the green woodpecker, as an example of consummate adaptation of structure to requirements, it is by no means the only organ which has been modified to suit this bird's peculiar mode of getting its livelihood. The foot is zygodactylic, that is, arranged with two toes before and two behind, to enable it to climb the better. The breast bone, too, has been pared away in a remarkable manner, so as to clear the tree trunk in ascending, for the yaffle never climbs down. The resulting shallowness of the pectoral muscles renders the breast almost devoid of flesh, so that even in France nobody has yet concocted a dish of *Piverts*.

The female of *Dendrocopus major* and *minor* is started in

life with a red cap, but the bright colours disappear at the first moult. (Abridged from Sir H. Maxwell's account of the woodpecker in the Tracts of the Society for the Protection of Birds.)

THE WRYNECK.

This bird differs in a few respects from the woodpeckers, but scarcely enough to be constituted a family, genus, and species all in one, as certain authorities have done; however, as we have elected to follow them for the present, we proceed.

Family—*Iyngidæ.*
Genus—*Iynx.* *I. torquilla.*

The general colour is brown, but diversified with numerous markings of black, dark brown, and brownish yellow, which gives it a speckled appearance; the throat is yellowish buff, mottled with dark grey; the lower breast white, spotted with small black "arrow-heads" pointing downwards; these are continued more thickly on the belly, which has a yellowish tinge. The tail has a slate-blue ground colour, thickly covered with minute black spots, and is crossed by three brown bands tipped with black. The bills, legs, and feet are yellowish grey. The female resembles the male, but her colouring is not so bright. Length, 7 inches; tail, $3\frac{1}{2}$.

The wryneck is migratory, arriving in April and departing in August or September. It occurs, sparsely, in Great Britain, but has not been reported from Ireland.

It feeds exclusively on insects, chiefly ants, for collecting which its long tongue, the end of which is covered with a glutinous secretion, is extremely useful; it is also an adept at snaring with the same instrument any fly that chances to alight near it.

The disposition of the toes is zygodactylous.

The nest is placed in a hole of a tree, which is lined with various soft substances, and the eggs are white, and six or seven in number, though Morris says as many as nine or ten!

The young are easily reared with flies and ants' eggs, and become very tame and amusing.

THE CUCKOO.

This well-known bird, whose peculiar note has provided a name for it in every country that it frequents, is the only representative in Britain of the

Family—*Cuculidæ.*
Genus—*Cuculus.* *C. canorus.*

Its general colour is greyish blue, and the lower parts ash colour or rufous brown; but the belly is white, and the vent yellowish; the wings and tail dark brown, inclining to black; the breast and vent are covered with numerous black curved lines, and the tail has white tips, and a row of round white spots down the centre of each feather; the short shanks and long zygodactylous toes are yellow, but the nails are black; the long, slightly-curved tail is dusky yellow, with a black tip to each feather, and the iris is dull orange; the wings are long and pointed, and reach to the lower third of the tail. The female is smaller and browner in colour than the male. Length, 13 or 14 inches; tail, 5.

The cuckoo is migratory, arriving in April and departing from Great Britain in August.

The food consists almost entirely of insects, many of which the bird catches on the wing; in autumn it appears to take a few berries.

The egg varies a good deal in appearance, but it is an error to say that the bird has the power to assimilate it, as to colour, with that of the eggs in the nest where she places it, and it is a wonder how such a statement can have been made, in the first instance, unless a double-yolked egg was mistaken for one laid by a cuckoo.

It is well known, of course, that the cuckoo does not incubate her own eggs, and that the young of the bird on which she has intruded are not reared; but is it correct to suppose that the young cuckoo wilfully destroys them? The fact of their perishing is easily accounted for by the superior size, strength, voracity, and activity of the changeling: but to credit the latter with their deliberate murder by hoisting them up on his back and tossing them out of the nest is so absurd that it is a wonder how it can have gained credit.

The notion was first promulgated by "Vaccination" Jenner, but that worthy had been imposed upon by a nephew whom he had set to watch; for the young fellow was idle, and went off amusing himself, afterwards inventing the tale, which his uncle accepted, and subsequently related to the Royal Society as the result of his own actual experience. Afterwards the youth confessed the imposture, which is, nevertheless, credited by many so-called naturalists of the present day, whom no amount of evidence would convince that what they have accepted as the truth is nothing but a clumsy fable.

The cuckoo, however, is a veritable ornithological puzzle, for in addition to the stories about its young, it is said to swallow its foster-parents, and to lay but one egg, not to speak of its being credited with spoiling the horticulturist's crops, which no cuckoo ever did. But it is really a puzzle, nevertheless, for no one knows exactly where it goes when it leaves this country, or from whence it comes to us. It is pretty sure to announce its arrival by its note, but the exact time of its departure is a mystery.

It is curious, too, that it should never, or hardly ever, make the mistake of entrusting one of its valuable eggs to a hard-billed, seed-eating bird, though the semi-insectivorous chaffinch is sometimes, and the yellowhammer very often, selected to nurse its offspring.

THE KINGFISHER.

Family—*Alcedinæ.*
Genus—*Alcedo.* *A. ispida.*

The Kingfisher is perhaps the most brilliantly-coloured of any real British bird, for some others, included in Morris's work, surpass it in gaudy attire, but can scarcely be considered British on the strength of a specimen or two escaped from some aviary, and, of course, shot by some Briton on the rampage, gun in hand.

The top of the head and the wing coverts are a fine shade of green, the one with transverse and the other with oval spots of sky blue; the back and shoulders are turquoise blue. The lores, and a circle round the eyes, are black; below this is a patch of orange, succeeded by one of pure white; the rump and tail coverts are light blue, the tail a very dark shade of the same colour; the chin is white, shading to light buff, which deepens on the breast and under parts to orange; the bill is greyish black above, but yellowish underneath; the legs and feet dull red. The length is 7 inches, of which the tail measures 1½, and the bill 1½. The female is less vivid in all her colours. In the young the whole bill is black.

It is a resident species, and is always found in the vicinity of water, where at one time it was fairly common, but owing to the persecution to which it has been subjected by the cockney sportsman, the taxidermist, the angler and his minions, and by Tom, Dick, and Harry, it has become so scarce that its occurrence in a locality is deemed of sufficient interest to be chronicled by the press. There is no doubt that in a few years it will, as a British species, be extinct.

To the above enemies may be added another—the hunter after prizes for "rare specimens" at shows, who traps two or three kingfishers, cages them, and sends them off to a big show, where they are judged and "put in the money," to die, as a rule, before the exhibition is over, and always in a few days afterwards; but what does the prizemonger care? he has gained the object he had in view—a few paltry shillings—and he is quite ready to begin again for the next, and send off one day the poor bird he had captured, perhaps from her nest, on the day before.

The kingfisher feeds almost entirely on small fish, to catch which it plunges boldly into the stream, rarely missing its aim. It is thought to destroy much trout and salmon fry, and no doubt it does take some; but it preys on other kinds as well, and, fish being scarce, is said not to disdain tadpoles, small frogs and newts, or even water beetles and dragon-flies.

It is a shy bird, and a patient, persistent hunter, remaining fixed, sometimes for hours, on a branch, from which it darts into the stream at sight of the first passing fish of convenient size, returning, to kill and swallow its prey, to the spot from which it had started. The nest is placed at the end of a tunnel, a yard or two in depth, bored by the bird itself, or more often by a water-rat, in the bank of a stream. The eggs, six or so in number, are rounded and white, but are quickly soiled by the bird's feet and the wet necessarily carried into the hole, which, from the nature of the food used by the occupants, generally emits an abominable smell.

If the kingfisher must be kept in confinement, it should have an abode specially constructed for its accommodation along a sunny wall facing south or south-west, through which a little stream, broadening into a small pond, should be conducted. A bank and some willows overhanging the brook must not be forgotten, and a constant supply of small fish, minnows, and sticklebacks, must be arranged for, and, failing these, a few dead sprats of small size, or even morsels of fish cut up, must be thrown into the water; but live food is undoubtedly the best. In such a place a pair of kingfishers would be fairly happy, and might breed, but it is hopeless to attempt to keep them successfully in any other manner.

The wire covering the aviary, and all bars and posts connected therewith, must be painted black, so as to show off the beauty of the kingfishers to the best advantage.

These birds, in many places, are now strictly protected by legislative enactment, and need all the help they can get to save them from extermination. Whatever their shortcomings, it is quite sure that they do not touch fish-spawn, for in their natural conditions they never take anything that they do not see move. Sometimes a fisher, when about to throw an artificial minnow, will, to his surprise, find that he has hooked a kingfisher.

In severe weather, when stream and mere are frozen over, these birds will descend to the seashore in search of fish or something else that they consider edible.

The brilliant colours of the kingfisher have brought him

into great request with the plume trade, which our gentle ladies, by their passive obedience to despotic milliners, so deplorably encourage. There are signs, however—welcome signs—that in proportion as they are becoming better informed of the nature and effects of this trade, so lady customers are showing discrimination and forbearance in the matter of hat and bonnet decoration. This, thinks Sir H. Maxwell, to whom this concluding paragraph is due, is no more than might have been reasonably expected, for nobody believed that Englishwomen would consciously encourage cruelty.

THE OWLS.

We now come to a very useful and much misrepresented, as well as little understood, class of birds.

Family—*Strigidæ*.

Genus—1. *Strix.*	*S. flammea.*	Barn or White Owl.
2. *Syrnium.*	*S. aluco.*	Wood, Brown, or Tawny Owl.
3. *Asio.*	*A. brachyotus.*	Short-eared Owl.
	A. otus.	Long-eared Owl.

The Barn or White Owl has its upper parts of a buff colour, shaded with orange, and finely marked with grey, and spotted with white and dark grey; the face and under parts are white; the bill is pale yellow, and the feet, which are usually covered with bristles, are dark. Length, 13 inches, of which the tail measures 5.

The Tawny or Wood Owl has the upper parts reddish brown, spotted with brown of a darker shade, and black; the lower parts are pale buff, mottled with brown, and streaked with a darker shade of the same colour; the legs are feathered. Length, 18 inches, of which the tail measures 7.

The LONG-EARED OWL has its upper parts buff, mottled with various shades of brown; the ear tufts are long, and consist of black feathers, margined with buff. The under parts of the body are of a lighter shade than the upper, and are broadly marked with brown of two shades; the bill is dark horn-colour, and the eyes brilliant orange yellow. Length, 14 inches, of which the tail takes $5\frac{3}{4}$.

FIG. 28.—*The Barn Owl.*

The SHORT-EARED OWL is dark buff above and below, but the wings and tail are traversed by bands of dark brown; the rest of the plumage is spotted with blackish brown; the eyes are yellow. Length, 14 inches, $5\frac{3}{4}$ of which are included in the tail.

The long-eared owl is of a dark buff colour throughout, the wings and tail are barred with dark brown; the rest of the plumage, except the thighs and under tail coverts, which are plain, are streaked and spotted with blackish brown; the eyes are bright yellow. Length, 15 inches, of which the tail measures $5\frac{3}{4}$.

The barn or white owl is pretty generally distributed

throughout the British Isles, or rather was until recently, but of late it has been extirpated from many localities, to the intense satisfaction of the rats and mice.

The tawny or wood owl, as well as the last, is resident, but incessant persecution is slowly producing its extermination, to the encouragement of all the small rodents.

The long-eared owl is migratory, and partial in its occurrence; and so is the short-eared owl, which is more frequently met with in Scotland and the northern counties of England than elsewhere. It prefers moors and marshes to woodlands.

All four species prey on bats, small birds, dormice, mice, voles, moles, shrews, rats; and, in addition, beetles, cockchafers, and occasionally a young game bird or rabbit. Any misdeeds are small in comparison with the good practical work done by these birds.

In common with other birds of prey, owls have the habit of ejecting from the mouth pellets containing the indigestible portions of the food they have swallowed. They are nocturnal in their habits, see better by night than by day, and possess a gliding, noiseless flight, necessary on account of the keen sense of hearing possessed by their prey—rats, mice, etc. The note is a screech, hoot, or snore.

The long-eared owl is more frequently seen in the daytime than any of the others.

Of all birds, from a farmer's stand-point, owls are the most useful, and are placed in the highest class by the economist, yet they are destroyed wholesale by the game preservers and their minions, and the loss of their services to the agricultural interest is great.

(Condensed from report by Mr. Montagu Sharpe, to Society for the Protection of Birds.)

Charles Waterton, the well-known naturalist, made a retreat for owls near his house, and it was soon taken possession of by a pair of barn owls, when Waterton "threatened to strangle the keeper if ever afterwards he molested either the old birds or the young ones."

Owls should be as common as rooks; they should be tempted in every way to live among us, and a reward should be given to every farmer that reported a nest on his ground.

Owls are lynx-eyed cats with wings, and it has been computed that an owl, when it has young, will bring a mouse to its nest every quarter of an hour from dusk to dawn.

An examination of pellets from the barn, tawny, and long-eared owls, give, according to Mr. Montagu Sharpe, the following results :—

REMAINS FOUND.

	No. of Pellets Examined.	Bats.	Rats.	Mice.	Voles.	Shrews.	Small Birds.
Barn Owl,	706	16	3	237	693	1,590	22 (*a*)
Tawny Owl,	210	0	6	42	269	33 (*c*)	18 (*b*)
Long-eared Owl,	25	0	0	6	35		2

(*a*) Nineteen sparrows, a greenfinch, and two swifts.

(*b*) Fifteen small species undetermined, a wagtail, a tree creeper, and a yellow bunting.

(*c*) A countless number of cockchafers.

Owls are frequently attracted to game coverts by the number of rats and mice to be found there, in consequence of the food laid down for the birds. Therefore, from the game preserver's stand-point, the destruction of birds of prey—owls especially—is a short-sighted policy.

THE FALCONS.

The next family on the list is the deposed one of the eagles, hawks, etc., which, until recently, held the foremost rank in all systems of ornithological classification, but have now to take a back seat, and give up their place to the musicians.

Family—*Falconidæ*.

Genus			
Genus—1.	*Pandion.*	*P. haliaetus.*	Osprey.
2.	*Circus.*	*C. cyaneus.*	Hen Harrier.
		C. æruginosus.	Marsh Harrier.
		C. cineraceus.	Montagu's Harrier.
3.	*Buteo.*	*B. vulgaris.*	Buzzard.
4.	*Archibuteo.*	*A. lagopus.*	Rough-legged Buzzard.
5.	*Pernis.*	*P. apivarus.*	Honey Buzzard.
6.	*Haliaetus.*	*H. albicilla.*	White-tailed Eagle.
7.	*Aquila.*	*A. chrysaetus.*	Golden Eagle.
8.	*Accipiter.*	*A. nisus.*	Sparrow-Hawk.
9.	*Astur.*	*A. palumbarius.*	Goshawk.
10.	*Falco.*	*F. peregrinus.*	Peregrine Falcon.
		F. subbuteo.	Hobby.
		F. æsalon.	Merlin.
11.	*Tinnunculus.*	*T. alaudarias.*	Kestrel.
12.	*Milvus.*	*M. ictinus.*	Kite.

OSPREY, or SEA-EAGLE.—Unless in the extreme north of Scotland, this fine-looking and most interesting species may be said to be practically extinct. The bill, which is strong and curved, is bluish; the top of the head, a line above the eye, and another surrounding and extending

FIG. 29.—*The Sea-Eagle.*

in a backward direction beyond it, are brown, as also is the whole of the upper surface, every feather having a dark edge and centre; a line above the eye is greyish white, as are also the lower half of the face, the throat, and all the lower parts, every feather having a darker edge and centre; at the junction of the neck and breast are two patches of brown feathers with black lines and white edges; the feet are slate blue, and the under surface of the tail of the same colour, with two bands and tips of brown. In length, the male measures 1 foot 10 or 11 inches; but the female is considerably larger, measuring as much as 2 feet 3 inches in total length. Variations in point of colour and size are frequently met with.

HEN HARRIER.—In this species, the head is bluish grey, and is surrounded by a ring of short, stiff feathers, which are white at the base, and slightly tipped with grey; the neck is grey, sometimes shaded with brown; the chin and throat bluish grey, with a black edge to each feather; the under parts are white, with a tinge of grey: the back is grey, with or without a tinge of brown: wing coverts grey; primaries black, or very dark brown; under surface of wings grey, with many darker round spots; tail blue grey on outer pair; next pair crossed by narrow brown bands; remaining tail feathers white, with similar bars, forming five lines at regular intervals when the tail is spread out; bill grey; cere and legs and feet yellow. Length of male, 18 inches; of female, 21 or 22 inches.

This bird is also known by the name of RINGTAIL.

MARSH HARRIER.—This is a very handsome bird. Head and neck yellowish grey, with numerous narrow dark lines; other upper parts, except wing coverts and tail, which are greyish blue, dark brown, with a shade of red on the shoulder; face and chin grey; breast whitish grey, with many long pointed dark lines, which are continued on the remainder of the under plumage which at the belly, hocks, and vent has a ruddy tinge; the bill is very dark horn, the cere yellow, and the legs and feet yellowish brown. The female resembles the male

FIG. 30.—*The Hen Harrier.*

in colour, but is considerably larger, her length being 2 feet, while the male only measures 19 or 20 inches.

These birds vary considerably in appearance.

MONTAGU'S HARRIER.—This bird bears a general resemblance to the hen harrier, but is altogether of darker plumage; it has a white line extending round the front part of the neck; the white of the under parts has a bluish grey tinge, and the spots on it, as well as those on the tail, are rufous brown; the bill is grey, the cere yellow, and the legs and feet yellowish grey. Length of male, 1 foot 5 or 6 inches; of female, 1 foot 7 or 8 inches. In appearance like her mate, but shows a general tinge of brown.

BUZZARD.—The colouring of this species is brown above, and white, with a buff or fawn tinge, below; the latter parts are heavily spotted with light brown. The brown tail is traversed by numerous bands of a darker shade of the same colour. The female is much the larger of the two. Length, 1 foot 9 or 10 inches; that of the male, 1 foot 6 or 7 inches.

ROUGH-LEGGED BUZZARD.—This species is altogether of lighter colour than the last. The upper parts are cinnamon brown, except the flights, which are nearly black, and the tips of the great wing coverts, which are white, as also is the basal two-thirds of the tail, the remainder is blackish grey. The under parts are whitish, with a rufous tinge and a band of dark brownish grey across the belly, the whole plentifully marked with large dark brown elongated spots; the shanks are clothed with buff hair like feathers. The female is the larger, measuring 2 feet, and the male 22 inches. They vary exceedingly in appearance. The belt on the abdomen and the white on the tail being the most constant; but even in these parts considerable differences are to be met with in different individuals.

Specimens have occasionally been met with that were more or less white. It does not breed in Britain.

HONEY BUZZARD.—This fine bird is of rare occurrence in England, and only a very few examples of it have been met with in Scotland. The general colour of the upper parts is a fine dark brown, touched with grey on the fore part of the head, and yellowish brown on the long rounded tail, which is traversed by many narrow bands of a light greyish black colour. The under parts are greyish white, thickly spotted with brownish black. The bill is horn-colour, the cere bluish, and the legs and feet yellow. The female is larger than her mate, and her under parts are light yellowish red, spotted with brownish red. The male is about 2 feet in full length, and the female measures 2 or 3 inches more. Both sexes, however, vary a good deal both in point of size and colouring.

FIG. 31.—The Honey Buzzard.

WHITE-TAILED EAGLE, or ERNE.—This bird is also called the sea eagle, and used formerly to be abundant in Britain ;

but, thanks to game-preservers, it is now but rarely met with there. The whole of the plumage is brown, except the rather short, broad tail, which is pure white. The bill is yellow, as are also the feet and legs, but the cere is orange. Male and female are much alike, even as regards size, which is about 3 feet in total length.

Golden Eagle.—This fine bird is not unlike the last, but its brown colour is tinged with a golden yellow in some lights, especially on the upper parts; and the tail is bluish, barred, and broadly tipped with black. The bill is grey, but the feet and cere are yellow. The shanks are covered down to the toes with brown, hair-like feathers. The female closely resembles the male, except in size. He measures nearly 3 feet in length, and she nearly 6 inches more.

Fig. 32.—*The Golden Eagle.*

Sparrow Hawk.—This eminently useful bird has been practically exterminated in Great Britain, much to the comfort of the small birds and mammals on which it was accustomed to prey. The upper parts are dark brown, lighter on the wings and tail, which last is crossed by four broad black bands. The cheeks and sides of the neck are chestnut, and the lower parts white, tinged with grey and marked with wavy brown lines. The bill is slate blue, and the cere and long legs yellow. The male weighs from 5 to 6 ounces, and measures 11½ inches in total length, while the female weighs about 9 ounces, and measures from 14 to 16 inches in length. Both sexes vary a good deal in appearance, the female having more or less white about the head.

FIG. 33.—*The Sparrow Hawk.*

GOSHAWK.—Unlike the last, which is resident, or was, the goshawk can only be called an occasional visitor to Britain. Its general colour is dark slate colour above, and whitish grey on the under surface, which is thickly marked with butterfly marks of a grey colour. The cere, legs, and feet, and the eyes are yellow. The female is much larger than the male, but otherwise closely resembles him. Length, nearly 2 feet; male, 1 foot 9 or 10 inches.

PEREGRINE FALCON.—Head bluish, greyish, or brownish black; neck blackish behind and white in front, sometimes with and sometimes without spots; back deep slate colour, more or less barred with blackish grey, the bars becoming narrower with age. The female is considerably larger than the male, and is darker in colour. She measures about 23 inches in full length, while the length of the male is 19 inches; but both sexes vary in the most remarkable manner, both as regards size and plumage.

HOBBY.—Head, dark slate colour, white line over eye, black under; throat whitish, and remaining lower parts buff, or light chestnut, spotted with black; bill bluish black; cere and legs and feet yellow. Female head feathers edged with brown. Her length is about 14 inches; that of the male $12\frac{1}{2}$ to 13.

FIG. 31.—*The Peregrine Falcon.*

MERLIN.—This small hawk is a winter visitor to Britain, or the most part, though it has occasionally nested. Upper surface slate colour, with brownish black quills; tail spotted and broadly tipped with black; cere and legs and feet yellow; bill bluish black. The female is larger than the male, but both vary in size. He measures about $12\frac{1}{2}$ inches; she 13 or 14.

KESTREL.—A very beautiful hawk. The head, neck, and tail are slate blue; the back and wing coverts ruddy chestnut, the latter spotted with black; the tail near its free end, which is white, is broadly barred with black; and the flights are brownish grey black, spotted with a darker shade of the same; the legs and feet are yellow. Male length about 14 inches; female about 15.

KITE.—This species is distinguished from the rest of the hawks by its forked tail. Its upper surface is generally reddish brown, lighter on the neck, and almost grey on the head; the under parts are light reddish grey, deepening backwards; the flights are brownish black; cere, eyes, legs, and feet yellow; bill bluish grey. The female is much larger than the male, and her plumage is rather orange and grey than brown and white. The length of the male is 2 feet 2 inches, and that of the female 2 feet 4 inches. For their size these birds are light, the weight of the male being about $2\frac{1}{2}$ pounds, and that of the female $2\frac{1}{4}$.

FIG. 35.—*The Hobby.*

The food of the larger species of the hawk family consists of birds and mammals, namely, hares, rabbits, and even small lambs, as well as partridge, ptarmigan, and grouse. Some of them eat "carrion," but they mostly capture their prey alive, and kill it either by a stroke of the bill, or the pressure of their formidable feet.

The osprey and erne, however, feed mainly on fish, which they plunge into the water to obtain.

The medium-sized hawks kill small birds and mammals, such as sparrows, buntings, etc., also rats, mice, moles, voles, etc., while many of them consume quantities of insects, such as beetles, moths, and especially cockchafers.

FIG. 36.—*The Kite.*

Some of the smallest of the members of the family feed principally on insects, and all may be said to be useful birds, unless, of course, when, from some cause or other, their numbers increase out of due proportion.

They are most bold and even audacious in their bearing, and few of them hesitate to attack animals as large as themselves. Spallanzani relates an instance of a large mastiff that was attacked and killed by a golden eagle.

The nests are mostly built of sticks in lofty trees, but some of them breed on ledges of rocks, and resort to the same place for many years in succession.

The eggs are two for the larger species, and three or four for the smaller; mostly with a white ground colour, more or less spotted and marked with red, which latter colour, in the case of the merlin and kestrel, almost obscures the former. As a rule, the eggs are rather rotund in form, but a few are elliptical. They all pair for life, and the couples are very affectionate together.

Many of them have bred in captivity, in which they endure very well when correctly treated, living to a great age.

It is a great mistake to so ruthlessly persecute these fine birds, for even granting that they destroy a head or two of game here and there, they certainly do good by preventing the undue increase of small birds, and the various rodents, which become so mischievous when their multiplication (fostered by supplies of artificial food) remains unchecked.

Then, if it be permissible to refer to æsthetics in this connection, what a charm is added to the landscape by the soaring eagle or the graceful and rapidly gliding hawk. At once they attract the eye, so buoyant and airy is their flight, and so elegant and well adapted for their mode of life is their form. It is a positive loss to everyone, even the farmer and the game preserver, to exterminate them, and in some places this has been discovered when it was too late, and vast hordes of mice, voles, and rats have devastated the country, for the balance of Nature had been destroyed by the destruction of the winged police that were made to keep the vermin in order.

In former days, when the sport of "hawking" was more

in vogue than it is at present, many of the members of this family were trained, and quite an elaborate code built up to regulate the pursuit. The peregrine falcon was perhaps the most frequently employed, but the merlin, sparrow-hawk, and goshawk, were frequently trained, and the merlin is recommended as the best for "a beginner" by the author of "Hints on the Management of Hawks."

THE CORMORANTS.

Passing from the terrestrial birds of prey to those that are more or less aquatic in their habits, we come to the

Family—*Phalacrocoracidæ*.

Genus—1.	*Sula.*	*S. bassana.*	Gannet.
2.	*Phalacrocorax.*	*P. carbo.*	Cormorant.
		P. graculus.	Shag.

GANNET.—This bird, also known as the solan goose, has the head and neck of a pale buff colour, but a bare place round the eye is dull blue, which is also the colour of the lower mandible; the iris is pale yellow, the flight feathers greyish black, and all the remaining parts white, except the legs and the webbed feet, which are dark green. The female resembles the male, but the young are different from their parents, having the eyes of a dusky slate blue, and the head and neck of the same shade, darker or lighter according to age, each feather tipped with a white spot of triangular shape; the under parts are grey, mottled with white, and the back black or slate, according to each, with white mottlings. The full white plumage is not acquired until the bird has attained its fourth year. Length, nearly 3 feet.

Cormorant.—The hooked bill is greenish in colour, and a round bare portion of skin surrounding the lower mandible is yellow; succeeding this is a border of short, black, bristle-like feathers, a patch of the same covering the top of the head; the rest of the head and neck are covered with feathers of a similar description, but of a grey colour; the remainder of the plumage is black, with a bronzed reflection on the back and wings, blue on the breast, and green towards and on the tail; there is a round white spot on the thigh, and the legs and feet are dark grey; the eye has a greenish tinge. In the winter the plumage generally has a much duller appearance. Length, about 3 feet.

Shag.—This bird is also known as the green cormorant, and is chiefly distinguished from the last by a tuft of upstanding greenish black feathers on the forehead, the tips of which have a forward inclination; in colouring it is much like the last, but is rather more bronzed; the eye is green, and the bill very dark orange; the legs and feet are black, and there is no white above the thigh. Length, 2 feet 3 or 4 inches; female somewhat less.

All three are resident species. The gannet makes a nest of sea-weed on a ledge of rock, lays two large white eggs, elliptical in form, and the young are covered with yellowish white down.

The cormorant makes a nest of sticks on a cliff, or among the top branches of a tall tree. The eggs, two or three in number, are greenish blue, of an oblong shape, and rather rough in appearance.

The green cormorant, however, makes its nest on a ledge of rock, using sea-weed in its construction, and lining it with grass; the eggs, which are white, but soon get stained and discoloured, are from three to five in number.

Fish is the natural food of all the members of this family, and they catch it by diving and even swimming under water. It is said that they assist each other in the capture of large fish; but Morris doubts this, and says he is not inclined to think that there is much disinterested generosity in the nature of the cormorant.

THE HERONS.

The British species are classified as follows:—

Family—*Ardeidæ*.

Genus—1.	*Ardea*.	*A. cinerea*.	Heron.
2.	*Botaurus*.	*B. stellaris*.	Bittern.

Heron.—This well-known British bird is resident, and at one time was fairly common, but fish preservers have greatly thinned its numbers of late years. Upper surface blue grey, with two white lines on head, and a long crest, divided into two, of a deep black colour; the flights and tail feathers are deep blue black; the under parts white, with elongated black lines on the sides of the throat and breast, in which latter situation, as well as on the saddle and flanks, the plumes are long and lanceolated, like those on a cock; the long legs are greenish, and the bill yellow. The female resembles the male, but is of duller tinting. The young are greyer, and do not attain their adult colours until they are two years old. Length, 3 feet 2½ inches; the wings expand to a width of 5 feet.

Bittern.—Unlike the last species, which is resident all the year round in Britain, this bird is usually met with during the winter only; though instances are on record of its having remained to breed; bill greenish yellow, with darker point; from its base proceed two black lines—technically, moustaches; eye yellow; head, which is flat, black, with tinge of purple and metallic green; the feathers at the back of the head are brown, barred with black and mixed with white; this is the general colour; the long, strong legs and feet are green. The female is exactly similar to the male.

The food of the heron and of the bittern consists of fish, reptiles, snails, and insects, especially such as have an aquatic origin; and there is no doubt if they existed in large numbers they would do a good deal of mischief by devouring both the spawn and fry of useful fish.

They are very shy and timid, and the bittern is nocturnal in its habits, hiding during the day in the reeds of the marshes it frequents and whin. When it does breed in Britain, it makes its nest on the ground, heaping together sticks, reeds, and other rough materials for the purpose. The eggs, from three to four in number, are elliptical in figure, and pale brown, without spot or mark of any kind.

The heron, on the other hand, builds a nest not unlike that of a rook among the topmost branches of high trees, and as it always nests in companies, the assemblage is called a "heronry," which is generally protected by the proprietor on whose ground it is placed. The eggs are three or four, of a greenish ground colour, sometimes blotched with patches of a darker or lighter shade of the same, but usually plain. Incubation lasts about three weeks, and in five or six more the young are able to fly. The ground under a large heronry exhales during the breeding season an odour resembling nothing so much as that of a fish-manure manufactory, and can scarcely be described as ambrosial.

There are two broods in the season.

At one time the heron was much used for hawking purposes, but since that "sport" has gone out of fashion they have diminished.

The attitude of repose conveys the idea of dejection, but the heron is rather a lively bird than otherwise.

THE SPOONBILL.

This bird is another instance of minute specification, for it is the sole representative in Britain, or elsewhere, of the

Family—*Plataleidæ*.
Genus—*Platalea*. *P. leucorodia*.

General colour white, with a buff tinge on the back of the neck and the lower parts, and a bluish grey shade on the back and wings. The long, peculiarly-shaped bill, which is made something in the shape of a spoon, is black, except at the broadened extremity, where it is dull yellow, with a few small spots of a black colour. The eye is red; a small orange line proceeds back for about half-an-inch from the corners of the mouth; the long legs and the semi-palmated feet are dark blackish grey.

At one time it was a regular summer visitor, and bred here in communities like the heron; but of late years it has become very rare, partly owing to the reclamation of its favourite haunts, and latterly to the persecution it receives at the hands of "sportsmen," and collectors on the prowl.

The food consists of small fish, aquatic insects, grasses, and aquatic plants.

It is not particularly shy, nests in trees, or on the stump of a willow or alder, near water. The nest is made of sticks, rushes, and grass, and the eggs are three, sometimes four in number, white in colour, with pale red or brown spots, but sometimes plain.

The young remain in the nest until able to fly; if taken early, it is easy to bring them up by hand, but if captured when adult they do not usually live very long.

The head feathers can be raised into a kind of crest.

THE DUCKS.

This is a large family, one, indeed, of the most numerous, and well represented in Britain; the Goose, Swan, and others have been incorporated with it. The following is an enumeration of the British species:—

Family—*Anatidæ*.

Genus	Species	Common name
Genus—1. *Anser*.	*A. cinereus*.	Grey Lag Goose.
	A. brachyrhynchus.	Pink-footed Goose.
	A. segetum.	Bean Goose.
2. *Bernicla*.	*B. leucopsis*.	Bernicle Goose.
	B. brenta.	Brent Goose.
3. *Cygnus*.	*C. olor*.	Mute Swan.
4. *Tadorna*.	*T. vulpanser*.	Sheldrake.
	T. casarca.	Ruddy Sheldrake.
5. *Chaulalasmus*.	*C. streperus*.	Gadwall.
6. *Querquedula*.	*Q. crecca*.	Teal.
	Q. circia.	Garganey.
7. *Dafila*.	*D. acuta*.	Pintail.
8. *Mareca*.	*M. penelope*.	Wigeon.
9. *Spatula*.	*S. clypeata*.	Shoveller.
10. *Fuligula*.	*F. cristata*.	Tufted Duck.
	F. marila.	Scaup.
	F. ferina.	Pochard.
11. *Clangula*.	*C. glaucion*.	Golden-eye.
12. *Œdemia*.	*Œ. nigra*.	Scoter.
13. *Somateria*.	*S. mollissima*.	Eider Duck.
14. *Mergus*.	*M. merganser*.	Goosander.
	M. serrator.	Red-breasted Goosander.

GREY LAG, or WILD GOOSE.—This species is of greyish brown colour on the upper surface and lighter on the lower, merging into white at the vent; the bill is orange, and the legs and feet a greyer shade of the same. Length of male, nearly 3 feet. The female is smaller and of duller colour; length, about 2 feet 6 inches.

PINK-FOOTED GOOSE.—Dark grey on upper parts, except head and neck, which are pale brown. The great wing coverts and secondaries are broadly edged with greyish white, and the rump is of the same colour, but the tail and flights are very dark slate blue; the under surface is greyish white, with dark base and light tips to each feather, especially towards the sides; the vent nearly white; the bill is black, with an orange tip; the feet are yellowish grey, with a pink tinge in the webs. Length, 2 feet 4 inches.

BEAN GOOSE.—This bird is very much like the last in appearance, but the end of the bill is distinguished by a black mark, in size and shape like a bean, hence the name. Length, 2 feet 8 inches to 3 feet; female a little smaller.

BERNICLE GOOSE.—This is a much more striking-looking bird than any of the preceding. The bill, and a line proceeding from it to and a little beyond the eye, black; the neck, breast, and upper part of the back black, with a leaden shade or tinge; wings slate grey, with black marks on each feather; face, throat, and rump white; breast whitish grey; belly the same, but every feather slightly edged with grey; legs and feet very dark slate. Male and female are alike. Length, 2 feet 1 inch; weight, 4 or 5 pounds.

BRENT GOOSE.—Like the last, but altogether darker; has a small white patch on both sides of the upper third of the neck; face black. Length, 1 foot 9 inches; weight, under 3 pounds.

The two last species are migratory, and occasionally visit Great Britain, but more especially Scotland. They are all susceptible of domestication, especially if the eggs are hatched by a barn-door fowl, or a duck, or an ordinary goose.

SWAN, or MUTE SWAN.—This bird, as everybody knows, is of snow-white plumage, but the bill is orange yellow, and the knob and parts surrounding it black; the legs, toes, and webs black. The female is smaller, and her knob is much less conspicuous than that of the male. The young are ashen grey, but by the end of their first year they have put on the adult livery, and cannot be distinguished from their parents. Length, from 4 feet 6 inches to 5 feet.

It is doubtful if the swan now occurs in Britain in a wild state; but there is no question that the numerous specimens which are found on the Thames, and many ponds and small private lakes, are the direct descendants of ancestors that were at one time wild.

The swan feeds on aquatic plants entirely, and, if a few molluscs and insects are swallowed, it is along with the former, and not intentionally. It is, therefore, absurd to credit, as some have done, these noble birds with the destruction of fish spawn and fry.

Few birds have a more majestic appearance than the swan when, with plumes displayed to their full extent, he grandly moves along upon the placid surface of a lake; but, when flying with his long neck stretched out to its full extent before him, and his short round wings flapping laboriously to keep him up, he looks a little bit ridiculous. Nor is he much more graceful on dry land, where his walk is a waddle, and his long neck seems to be in his way. The water is evidently his element, and he ought to leave the air and the earth alone.

The swan lays her four, five, or six white eggs near the water's edge on a bed or nest made of reeds, sedges, and water flags. At first it is very small, but she keeps on adding to it, and, by the time the young are hatched, it is a huge affair indeed. Incubation lasts between five and six weeks, but she never seems to tire of her task. The young take almost immediately to the water, and, when fatigued, rest upon their mother's back, which is flat, and, when her wings are raised, keeps them comfortably snug and warm.

The male swan is very courageous in defence of his young family, for those birds are monogamous, and will attack both man and beast if they venture to approach too near, instances being on record in which he has successfully repulsed a fox; a blow from his pinion is so powerful that it has been known to break a man's leg.

Except when attending to their young brood, the swans are very gentle birds, and scarcely ever drive away the ducks and other small swimming birds that rush in to devour the food that is thrown to their larger companions.

At one time the swan was considered to be excellent eating, but it is very seldom utilised for the table now, though, as a full-grown male weighs about thirty pounds, and a young one close on twenty, it is somewhat curious that the swan should be thus overlooked by domestic economists; and, as it is quite as exclusive a vegetable feeder as the goose, its flesh ought to be good; but perhaps it is thought to be too beautiful for killing.

Several other swans are reported as occasionally visiting this country, but they can scarcely be considered British birds.

SHELDRAKE.—Bill orange, with a black tip; head and upper part of neck blue black, with a metallic gloss:

remainder of neck white; breast and beginning of back chestnut, forming a ring round the body; first wing

FIG. 37. *The Mute Swan.*

coverts white, second glossy green; secondaries white, with yellowish brown edge, their coverts dark green; rest of body white; tail slightly tipped with black; legs and feet yellowish red. Female much like the male, but the knob at the base of the upper mandible not so prominent. Length, from 2 feet to 2 feet 2 inches.

This species occurs, but sparingly, in the north of Ireland and Scotland, as well as in the Scottish Isles, but only as a straggler occasionally in England. They are found in pairs, and are resident.

The food of the sheldrake consists of marine vegetables, crustacea, molluscs, etc., but they will also eat corn and vegetable seeds when their more relished diet cannot be had.

They are handsome birds, walking, swimming, and flying in an easy and graceful manner. They nest in old rabbit-burrows, sometimes at a considerable distance from the surface. Both sexes share the task of incubation. The eggs are from nine to twelve in number, white, with a faint greenish tinge, and very smooth and shining.

They are easily reared in captivity if the eggs are procured and hatched by a hen or a common duck, although their natural home is in the vicinity of the sea.

These handsome birds are devoted to their young, and will feign lameness to draw off an intruder. Occasionally they breed among themselves in confinement.

Ruddy Sheldrake.—Bill black, and destitute of knob; head and neck to middle ruddy buff; a narrow black ring separates the neck from the breast; and the tail, its upper coverts, and the primaries are black; greater and less wing coverts white, with a faint tinge of buff; the outer webs of the secondaries rich bronzed green; the rest of the plumage orange brown, with a golden yellow sub-tinge; legs and feet dark greyish black.

The ruddy sheldrake is of rare occurrence in Britain, and seldom breeds here.

The food is the same as in the case of the last species, but they seem more partial to grain and vegetable matters, frequenting stubble fields at a distance from water.

They are shy birds, and keep in pairs, which seem much attached to each other; but when the breeding season is over, they assemble in small flocks. They breed in holes in banks of natural occurrence, or formed by rabbits or other animals. The eggs, eight or ten in number, are white, but soon become soiled.

In confinement, these birds will breed more freely than the common sheldrake, providing they have a suitable burrow to nest in.

They occur upon, and near to, inland waters rather than in the neighbourhood of the sea; and if it be desired to keep them for ornament, the eggs should be hatched as advised for the allied species, as adult birds, when captured, rarely become tame.

The cry or call is shrill, and is described by Yarrell as not unlike the tone of a clarionet when the bird is on the wing; but, at other times, it calls like a peacock, and occasionally "clucks" like a domestic hen.

GADWALL.—This bird has somewhat the appearance of the famous American canvas-backed duck. It is rather a difficult bird to describe, but the general effect is grey, with a ruddy sub-tinge on the head and neck, which parts are plentifully dotted with small round black spots; the breast feathers are black, with distinct bluish grey edges; the back, sides, and part of the belly are bluish grey, indistinctly margined with black; the lesser wing coverts are bright chestnut; the greater, dark green, with a metallic lustre; the outer webs of the first secondaries are white, and the remaining wing feathers, as well as the tail, ashen grey; the under tail coverts, dark bluish black; the breast, pale bluish grey; the bill is black, with a greenish line towards the tip; the legs and feet orange. The female has a white streak over the eye. Length, 1 foot 7 inches.

The gadwall is of rare occurrence in Britain, but is occasionally met with in the north, where it is a winter visitant, migrating during the night in September or October, and March or April.

The food consists of aquatic insects, the spawn and fry of fish, also plants and seeds.

The nest is placed among reeds and rushes, and the eggs, which are from five to seven in number, are of a uniform pale buff colour.

It is found on inland lakes, bogs, and ponds, furnished with an abundance of cover, for it is a shy bird, keeping close during the day, but coming out at night to feed. It seldom occurs on the sea-shore.

FIG. 58.—*The Teal.*

These birds succeed very well in confinement, and occasionally breed there. The note is "quack, quack," repeated a few times in succession.

TEAL.—This pretty little bird has the bill of a dark leaden colour with a black tip. The feathers next the bill are green, and darker underneath, where they form an almost black patch. A band of buff stretches round this, along the chestnut of the head over the eye. Another stripe of the same colour passes in front of the eye, and becomes white on the ear coverts. The head and part of the neck are rich chestnut brown, which is also the colour of the throat and neck in front; breast whitish yellow, with black spots. The wing coverts are brown; the outermost three have white edges, and so have the three last secondaries; the others are bright green. The wings are brownish grey, and the rest of the body grey, with wavy black lines. The bill and the legs and feet are greenish grey. The female is of the ordinary duck colour, and, except during the breeding season, the male resembles her. Length, 1 foot 2 or 3 inches; female rather less.

It is a migratory species, arriving in Britain in September, and departing in March; but towards the north many are resident all the year through.

The food consists of grain, aquatic plants, and insects: but the greater portion of the diet is collected in or close to water.

The nest is usually placed among rushes by the waterside, but occasionally among rocks and loose stones on or near the seashore. The eggs are eleven or twelve in number, and are cream or very light buff colour.

They are readily domesticated, and form a handsome addition to the avifauna of ornamental waters. They are reputed to be excellent eating.

Garganey.—This very elegant species is dark brown above, and lighter on the under surface. The head and neck are almost black, and there is a whitish grey line over the eye, extending down on either side to the middle of the neck, where it terminates in a point. The back, including the flight, feathers, and the tail, are very dark brown, but each feather has a lighter border. The face and throat are very dark brown, but slightly mottled with a lighter shade of the same colour; the breast is lighter, with a yellowish brown border to each feather; the belly is light grey, with irregular grey black markings, and the vent and under tail coverts white with dark spots. From the sides some long lanceolate feathers, with black edges and broad white edges, hang over the wings, the coverts of which are light leaden blue; the outer secondaries are tipped with white; the bill and legs and feet are dusky. Length, 1 foot 5 inches; the female less; in her the eye streak is pale brown, and the breast greyish white.

The garganey is migratory, and occurs sparingly in Scotland, where the nest has been occasionally met with.

The food, like that of the other members of the family, consists of aquatic insects, frogs, fish and their spawn, grain, etc., but the last is always taken to and eaten in the water.

The buff-coloured eggs are from ten to twelve in number, occasionally more.

The garganey is easily tamed, and is a very ornamental bird, although not so brilliantly coloured as some other members of its family. It is accounted by connoisseurs to be excellent eating.

Wild Duck.—In his summer dress the male has the head and neck of a steel blue colour, with green reflections. This is succeeded by a narrow band of white that almost encircles the neck. The breast is rich purple, the back brown, the rump and tail blue. The first wing coverts are brown, succeeded by a band of white, then one of blue, one of very dark steel blue, and another of white. The rest of the wing is dark brown; the sides and the under parts grey, finely peppered with a darker shade. The bill is orange, with a black tip; the eye greyish yellow; and the legs and feet yellowish grey, with a shade of green. The female, and the male while out of colour, brown, with streaks of black and darker brown. The wing spot is small, and the breast dull yellowish brown. Length, 2 feet 2 inches; female, 1 foot 10 inches.

They migrate in the spring and autumn, occurring in

greater numbers during severe winters, but many couples remain in suitable localities to breed.

The food is similar to that indicated for the other ducks already mentioned. The nest is usually made in April of reeds and grass among rushes and sedges. The eggs are eleven or twelve in number; they are pale green in colour, and are usually covered with down by the mother.

The wild duck is monogamous in a state of nature, but becomes polygamous in captivity, to which it is easily reconciled, some even voluntarily taking up their abode on ornamental waters, which they never afterwards quit. Aged females sometimes assume the male plumage.

PINTAIL.—Bill leaden blue; head and neck brown; breast white; back and sides whitish grey, with numerous undulating dark grey lines; the central feathers of the tail are twice as long as the others, and of a steely blue colour, the rest are white; the abdomen is white, with a tinge of buff; and the under tail coverts blue; the wing coverts are brown, edged with buff, then follows a steel blue broad band and a narrow white one; the flights are bluish black; the long pointed saddle feathers are dark blue, with white edges.

It is of rare occurrence in Britain, and is migratory in its habits, changing its quarters in October and March.

The food consists of aquatic plants and insects, worms, snails, etc., and grain.

It is readily domesticated, and is esteemed to furnish an excellent dish for the table.

WIGEON.—Head pale buff; face and upper part of neck brown, with dark spots; back and sides grey, with wavy black lines; rump white; tail and under tail coverts very dark blue; breast reddish buff, with grey edging to feathers; under parts white; flights grey; secondaries bright steel blue; wing coverts white; innermost secondaries, which are nearly as long as the flights, black, with broad white outer edges; bill lead colour; legs and feet greenish grey. Female browner and mottled. Length, 1 foot 8 inches.

It is a winter visitor, frequenting the sea-coast, also rivers and inland waters. Food same as the other ducks.

The nest is placed among rushes, etc., near water, and contains from five to nine eggs of clear cream colour.

It is readily domesticated, and breeds freely in confinement.

SHOVELLER.—Bill very large and dull black; top of neck and head steel blue; back brown, every feather with dark centre and light edge; breast and sides of back white; wing coverts pale greenish blue; outer secondaries steel blue; inner long and pointed, blue, with dark grey edges; belly deep chestnut brown; vent buff; under tail coverts blue; tail white: legs and feet orange; eye pale yellow. Length, 1 foot 8 inches.

Has bred in Norfolk, Scotland, and elsewhere in Great Britain, frequenting marshes and inland waters. More numerous in winter than summer. Food—grass, aquatic insects and plants; but their diet is obtained for the most part on land.

The eggs are eight or ten in number, of a pale buff colour, with a green tinge. Incubation lasts three weeks, and the young take at once to the water.

The shoveller, or shoveler, is readily domesticated, and breeds freely in confinement. It is esteemed good eating by connoisseurs.

TUFTED DUCK.—General colour above, black, with blue reflections, particularly on the head and neck; the former part is decorated with a tuft of long narrow blue feathers that hang over the neck; the back and wings are shaded with brown; the under parts are white; and a bar of white occurs on the centre of each wing; the bill is blue; the eye pale yellow; and the legs and feet bluish green. Length, 1 foot 5 inches. The female is dull brown.

They are winter visitors in Northern Britain, and feed on aquatic plants and insects, fish, etc.

The nest is placed among grass or rushes, and contains eight or nine buff-coloured eggs, with a greenish tinge.

It breeds in confinement, and is readily domesticated.

In the summer the male assumes a brown plumage, but the middle part of the breast is white, and the vent dull yellow.

SCAUP.—Bill blue; head, neck, upper part of breast and of back dark blue, with metallic lustre: back and lesser wing coverts grey, with a brown tinge in the former and a bluish one in the latter, all thickly marked with narrow, black, undulating lines: the upper and lower tail coverts have a greenish tinge; the tail is grey, and the rest of the plumage white. Female darker. Length, 1 foot 9 inches. They are compact and thickset, and are much esteemed for the table. Food much the same as other ducks.

As they are winter visitors to Britain, not much is known of their breeding habits, but the eggs are said to be covered with down, and to number from six to eight, of a dull brownish yellow colour.

POCHARD.—Bill parti-coloured, black at base and tip, and lead blue in centre; head and upper part of neck rufous brown, with small black pencillings; lower half of neck and breast blackish blue; rump and over and under tail coverts black; lower breast white; back grey, shaded with brown, marked with numerous grey undulating lines; belly and sides the same, but the undulations lighter. Length, 1 foot 7^1 inches. The female has the bill black, and is altogether browner in appearance.

The pochard is a winter visitor to Britain, and occurs

rather in the north than any other part. The food is the same as that of the other ducks, but obtains most of it by diving.

The eggs are from twelve to fifteen in number, of a whitish buff colour.

These birds are readily domesticated, and pair among themselves, as well as with allied species, very freely. They are strong swimmers and good divers, keeping under water for a long time. They also fly well.

Golden-Eye.—This duck has a dark, horn-coloured bill, at the lower part of the base of which is a round white spot; the rest of the head, which is large and round, and the upper part of the neck are steel blue: the back and upper tail coverts are blackish blue, with a metallic gloss; the under parts are pure white, except the sides of the belly, which are thickly spotted with black; the tail and the flights are dark grey, but the wing coverts and part of the secondaries are white; the legs and toes are greyish yellow, but the webs are black. The female is browner, and her breast is flecked with grey. Length, 1 foot 7 inches.

The golden-eye is a winter visitor only, breeding in Lapland and other northern parts.

The eggs are said to be about fourteen in number, and to have a greenish hue.

Scoter, or Common Scoter.—The bill is black, with a spot of orange surrounding the nostrils; the whole of the plumage is black, with green and blue reflections. The female is greyer. Length, 1 foot 6 inches. A winter visitor only.

Eider Duck.—Bill greenish grey; top of head black; face white; back of head bluish grey; back of neck to between shoulders grey; back and upper wing coverts white; the side feathers are long, and hang below the wings, which are dark brown, with green and chestnut narrow edges; the lower belly and the rest of the under parts are dark bluish green; legs and feet grey. Length, 2 feet 2 inches. The female is pale brown.

This bird, so well known on account of the beautiful down, with which (plucked from the breast of the female) the eggs are covered, is a resident in Scotland, and especially the Scottish Isles, where it is almost domesticated.

It feeds like the other ducks, and can remain under water for a long time.

GOOSANDER.—The bill is long, narrow, curved at the tip, which is black, and the rest yellow; the eye orange; the head and upper neck, as well as the back and the greater wing coverts, greenish blue black; the lower half of the neck tinged with pale pink; the rump, tail, and lesser wing coverts pale bluish grey; legs and feet yellowish. Length, 2 feet 2 inches. The female has the head reddish brown.

It is a native of the north, occurring in Britain in winter only; and then, as a rule, sparingly. It is said sometimes to breed in the Hebrides.

The nest is made on the banks of fresh-water lochs, among long grass, or in a hollow stump of a tree. The eggs, which are long and of an oval shape, are seven or eight in number, and are of a buff or creamy yellow colour. The young swim directly they are hatched.

The goosander is a shy bird, cuts a very poor figure when trying to walk on dry land, but flies, swims, and dives in an easy and rapid manner.

RED-BREASTED MERGANSER.—Bill much the same as that of the last species, without black tip; the head and the beginning of the neck dark greenish blue, with a metallic gloss; the back of the former is ornamented with a tuft of long narrow feathers; the front of the upper part of the neck is white; but the lower part and the breast chestnut red, with long black spots; the back of the neck, the back, and the scapulars deep blue black; the wing coverts white, with broad black edges: secondaries white; primaries dark grey; under parts bluish grey; tail black; legs and feet dark orange. Length, 1 foot 10 inches.

Winter visitors only, these birds are, nevertheless, extremely shy, and swim low in the water, often with the nostrils only above the surface.

Occasionally they breed in the north of Scotland, and their principal food is small fish.

Both this bird and the last seem to form a kind of connecting link between the Ducks and the Gulls.

THE DOVES, OR PIGEONS.

Passing from what may be described as amphibious birds, namely, the Duck family, which, for the most part, are equally at home on land and water, we come to one, the members of which are terrestrial and arboreal, namely, the Doves, or Pigeons, of which there are four representatives in Britain, but a great number in her dependencies.

Family—*Columbidæ.*

Genus—1. *Columba.*	*C. œnas.*	Stock-Dove.
	C. livia.	Rock Pigeon.
	C. palumbus.	Ring-Dove.
2. *Turtur*	*T. communis.*	Turtle-Dove.

Stock-Dove.—Bill long, straight, pale brownish red, with yellowish edges: cere yellowish red; eye bright orange red; head bluish grey; sides of neck iridescent green and reddish purple; nape and back bluish grey;

breast, upper part, purple red, shading away to greyish blue; the wings are long, and measure, when expanded, 2 feet 2 inches from tip to tip; wing coverts bluish grey; primaries leaden grey, with pale outer margins; secondaries light greyish blue, with dark ends, the three inside have a large spot of black on the outer web; tail bluish grey for two-thirds, then a band of light grey, and a dark, almost black, tip; tail coverts grey; legs and toes carmine. Female differs little from male, but has less iridescence on neck. Length, 1 foot 2 inches, male; 1 foot $1\frac{1}{2}$ inches, female.

This is the least numerous of the four species of British doves, but is evenly distributed. Resident.

It feeds on seeds and leaves and succulent plants, also small snails and worms, acorns, beech-mast, etc.

The eggs are two, white, and rounded. The nest is on the ground, or in a hole in a tree. Incubation lasts seventeen days.

Rock Pigeon.—Bill horn-colour; cere white; head greyish blue; neck greenish blue above, and reddish purple on its lower half, both parts glitter with iridescent hues; back and wing coverts dull leaden blue; secondaries black, with a band of lead blue about the middle; primaries dark grey; rump white; upper tail coverts dark lead blue; tail same, with broad end of a deep black; legs and feet carmine; eye orange red.

Female similar, but less iridescence on neck.

More abundant on the coast than inland. Resident throughout the year.

Its food consists of seeds, berries, snails, and the succulent leaves of various plants.

These birds, and the last, pair for life, but if one be killed or dies, the survivor does not waste much time in lamenting it, but quickly sets to work to find it a successor, and is generally successful.

The nest is made of sticks, and is placed on a ledge of rock, or in a cave. The eggs are two, and there are two broods in the season, sometimes three.

This bird is believed to be the original of all our domesticated varieties, which it resembles in its preference for stones and rocks as roosting places to trees. It has bred and produced a fertile progeny with the common pigeon, especially that variety known as the blue rock, which it greatly resembles in appearance, but the latter is the larger. However, domestic pigeons decrease in size, and show a tendency to revert to the ancestral plumage, when neglected by their owners. Length, 1 foot $1\frac{1}{2}$ or 2 inches. It is frequently found breeding in companies, like the domesticated breeds that are descended from it.

RING-DOVE, or WOOD PIGEON; also known as CUSHAT, and QUEST, or WOOD QUEST.—Bluish grey above, a vinous red breast, and light grey on the under surface; on the neck are a number of iridescent colours—red, purple, blue, and green—and a large patch of white, technically known as the ring: the tail is terminated by a broad band of black; the bill is orange yellow, with a tinge of red, and has two little knobs that swell out in the breeding season, and almost disappear during the winter; the legs and feet are yellowish carmine. The female is smaller than the male, has less iridescence, and the knobs on her upper mandible are hardly perceptible. Length, 1 foot 6 inches.

The ring-dove has increased in numbers of late years, in spite of the persistent manner in which it is shot. It is resident, and collects in flocks in the winter, which flocks, at that time, are often augmented by the stock-dove, the only other pigeon with which it voluntarily consorts in a state of nature. It is thought that the native companies are strengthened during the winter by migrants from the Continent.

Food—seeds of weeds, acorns, beech-mast, chestnuts even —for this bird has a most capacious swallow—and the succulent parts of vegetables, as well as snails and worms.

The nest consists merely of a few sticks put together on a flat bough at varying heights from the ground. The eggs, roundish and white, are generally two, but sometimes only one. There are usually three broods in the season. The eggs are deserted for the slightest cause; but the old birds are not so ready to desert the young. There are very few authentic instances of this bird pairing with the domestic pigeon, with which no hybrids have, as yet, been produced.

TURTLE-DOVE.—Bill slender, and of a pale bluish shade: the eye is orange red, and a bare circle round the eye has a pink tinge; the legs and feet are carmine, with a purple tint; the forehead is whitish grey; the head and upper part of the neck light blue; then onward to the tail the blue is of a duller shade, and on each side of the neck is a black spot, crossed by several narrow, crescentic, white lines. Length, 11 inches.

The female much resembles the male, but is duller in appearance.

The turtle-dove is migratory in Britain, arriving in April or May, and departing in September to the beginning of November.

The nest is often placed among the young growth of a pollard, or where branches have been cut off at the side of a tree and Nature has attempted to repair the injury by pushing forth a number of shoots. It is also more compactly put together than those of the other members of the family, but is not a very pretentious structure for all that.

The turtle-doves will breed in confinement among themselves and with allied species, but Bechstein's statement that the mixed progeny will be fruitful when one of the parents is a Barbary turtle has not been borne out by sub-

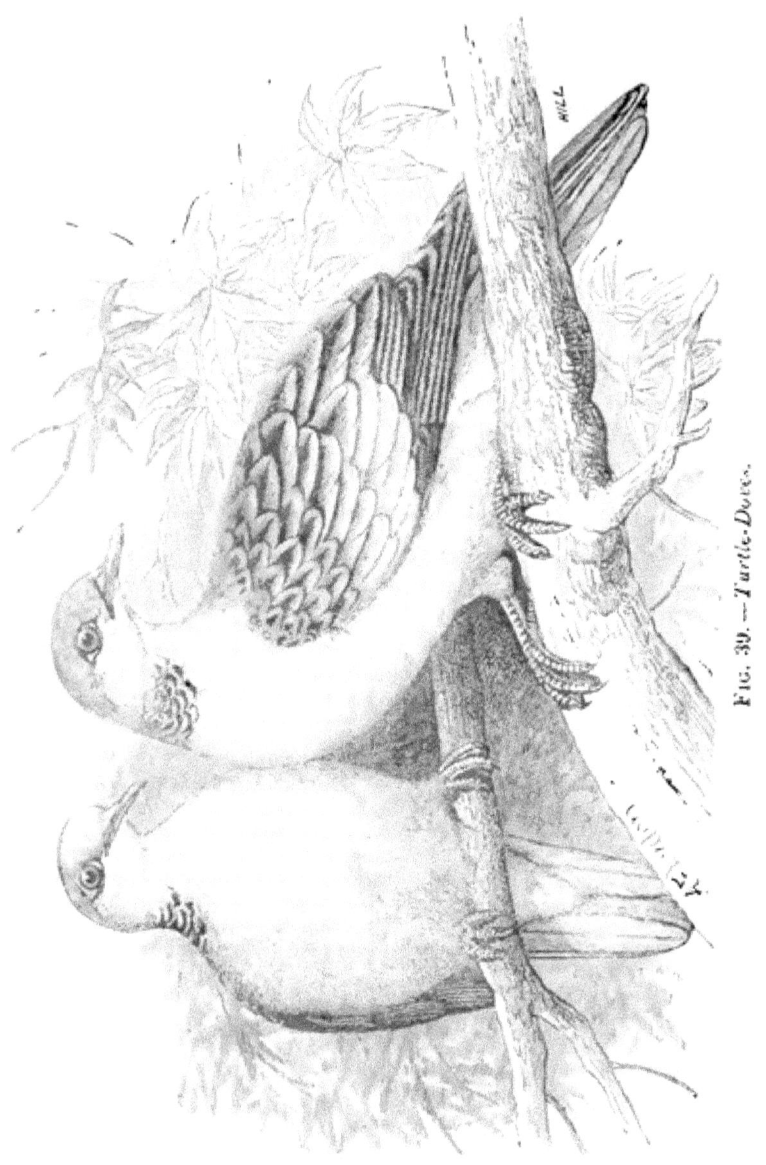

Fig. 39.—*Turtle-Dove.*

sequent observations, and no doubt originated in a mistake as to the identity of the bird.

The food consists of seeds of all kinds, and the succulent

leaves and other parts of growing plants. They also consume considerable quantities of small snails and various insects, especially coleopterous ones of small size, for which, in confinement, they evince much partiality.

As the males arrive before the females, it is probable that these much belauded birds only pair for the season, and that their reputed conjugal fidelity is a pleasing myth.

THE GROUSE.

The Grouse family next engages our attention, and comprises some notable genera and species resident in Britain, and many others that occur in different parts of the Empire, though, of course, at present we are only concerned with the former.

Family—*Tetraonidæ.*

Genus—1. *Tetrao.*	*T. tetrix.*	Black Grouse.
	T. urogallus.	Capercaillie.
2. *Lagopus.*	*L. scoticus.*	Red Grouse.

Black Grouse.—In this species the sexes differ very much from each other in appearance. The male, the head of which, as well as the nape, is dark glossy purple; the chin, throat, and breast have a brownish tinge, and on the lower part of the latter the feathers a lighter coloured border. The back is deep purple, glossy, and shading to black; the greater and lesser wing coverts are black, with white base; primaries dark blackish brown, with lighter shafts, the innermost of which have the base white; the secondaries and tertiaries have white tips, and the tail, which consists of eighteen feathers, of which the outer four are elongated and expand into the form of a lyre, are black; the under tail coverts are white; the legs, which are short, are covered with hair-like feathers in front, and the toes are dark horn-colour. The length of the male black grouse is 1 foot 11½ inches.

The female is smaller than the male, is of a general greyish brown colour, most of her feathers having a lighter border than base. The red mark over her eye is much duller than the same feature in the male, and she also has a similar white spot on the shoulder. The length of the female is about 1 foot 6½ inches.

The food of the black grouse consists of berries, the tender shoots of plants, grain, and insects, and the young are fed entirely on the latter at the beginning of their existence; they run about almost as soon as hatched.

The nest is merely a shallow hole scratched, or a natural depression, in the ground, slightly lined with bits of the surrounding herbage; and the eggs, which are six or eight in number, are buff coloured, irregularly spotted with brownish red. It is usually situated at no great distance from water, of which these birds drink a good deal. Incubation, which lasts about twenty-four days, is begun about the middle of May.

The black grouse seems to have lost a good deal of the natural instinct that keeps wild birds from forming a *mésalliance* with others of an analogous kind, and hybrids between it and the pheasant, red grouse, capercaillie, ptarmigan, and even the domestic fowl, have been met with, both sexes erring equally in this respect. It is not a pleasing feature in their character, and shows that they have fallen very considerably away from Nature's standard under the domination of man.

These birds, however, are not easily kept in confinement, but have borne transportation to the south and west of England very well.

They are polygamous, and, except during the actual pairing season, the sexes live apart in separate companies, the females harbouring with the young of both sexes.

The black grouse is reputed to be good eating, but the flesh is dark, and opinions vary as to its excellence.

CAPERCAILLIE.—This bird at first sight resembles a "big brother" of the last, but a closer inspection shows some difference, especially in the formation of the tail, which in the one now under consideration is long, broad, and rounded at the end. The long upper tail coverts, as well as the lower side ones and the tips of the secondaries, have greyish wide borders, the ear coverts are brown, and the bill yellowish whitish grey, except at the tip, which is black. The red mark over the eye is more arched, and there is a narrow white line at the lower part of the eye; the legs are thickly covered with brownish, hair-like feathers. The female is brown, barred and spotted with yellowish brown and black. In full length the male measures 3 feet 4 inches; the female, 2 feet 10 inches.

This bird was formerly abundant in Scotland and the north of England, but towards the end of the last century became extinct; of late years, however, it has been successfully re-introduced, and is now fairly abundant in several parts, but more especially in the north.

While the black grouse passes the night on the ground, the capercaillie perches in trees during the prevalence of snow. In habit it is shy, but prefers to escape from its enemies by running among the brushwood to taking wing.

Though indifferent eating itself, the eggs are a much vaunted delicacy; they vary in number from nine to twelve, and are pale yellowish brown in colour, spotted with a darker shade of the same.

They are polygamous in habit, but the male "keeps an eye" on his harem till the young ones in each nest escape from the shell.

The food is the same as in the case of the last.

RED GROUSE.—The general colour of this bird is reddish brown, with numerous black markings all over its person, and a few white ones on the breast and wing coverts. There is also a very small white moustache; and a white ring surrounds each eye, the upper one being surmounted with a red mark; the bill is dark horn; and legs and feet are encased in a thick covering of white, hair-like feathers, which also prevail on the thighs; the nails are greyish black. Length, 1 foot 4½ inches. The female is considerably smaller.

The red grouse has the distinction of being the only exclusively British bird known; a certain number of them occur in Ireland, more especially in the Wicklow Mountains; but these have almost certainly been introduced. All attempts to acclimatise it in other countries have failed, and yet it can be kept pretty well in confinement, and will sometimes breed freely in an aviary.

The food consists for the most part of the tops and tender shoots of heather, and, no doubt, such insects, chiefly coleopterous, and ants, as abound in the localities it frequents.

Red Grouse are monogamous, at least for the most part; both parents attend to the young, though the duty of incubation is performed by the female only, who sits very closely, and has even suffered herself to be taken in the hand rather than desert her charge.

A slight hollow among the heather serves for a nest, and there from seven to eleven eggs, of different shades of yellowish brown, spotted and speckled with darker brown, are deposited, incubation lasting nearly four weeks; the young are able to run about at once, and at first feed mainly on ants and their eggs.

THE PHEASANTS.

By many naturalists the next family, that of the Pheasants, is not separated from the last, and both are included in that of the gallinaceous birds, of which the domestic poultry is the best known example.

The following is an enumeration of the British species:—

Family—*Phasianidæ.*

Genus			
Genus—1.	*Perdix.*	*P. cinerea.*	Partridge.
2.	*Coturnix.*	*C. communis.*	Quail.
3.	*Caccabis.*	*C. rufa.*	Red-legged Partridge.
4.	*Phasianus.*	*P. colchicus.*	Pheasant.
5.	*Pavo.*	*P. cristatus.*	Peacock.
6.	*Meleagris.*	*M. gallo-pavo.*	Turkey.
7.	*Numida.*	*N. meleagris.*	Guinea Fowl.

Partridge.—The bill, which is strong and rather short, is of a light bluish grey colour, and has the upper mandible rather hooked, and projecting beyond the lower one; the eye is hazel, and surrounded by a ring of bare skin coloured bright red. The general colour is reddish brown above and on the breast, most of the feathers having light yellow shafts. The breast is grey, marked with many wavy dark lines, and the rest of the under parts are yellowish grey. The flights and secondaries are brownish grey, spotted in rows with yellowish brown. The legs and feet are bluish grey. The female is smaller, and the breast feathers browner. The male measures about 12½ inches, and the female 11½ or 12.

These birds are plentifully distributed throughout the British Isles, but are less abundant in some parts of them than they were a few years ago.

The food consists of grain, seeds, berries, insects, especially ants and their eggs, though they also destroy immense quantities of wire-worms and aphides and other insect pests. The leaves, tender shoots, and succulent parts of many plants are also devoured by them.

The nest is merely a hole scraped in the ground, or a natural depression, sparingly lined with fragments of such vegetation as grows near it, and the eggs vary in number from 10 to 15; they are of a uniform olive green colour. Incubation takes about twenty-eight days, and is performed by the female alone, though the male keeps near her when she is sitting, and joins with her in the care and defence of the young brood.

These birds appear to pair for life, and, except during the autumn and winter, are only found in couples.

They can be kept fairly well in confinement, and will sometimes nest and rear young in an aviary, but require a considerable amount of insect food when young.

They seldom drink, merely sipping a few drops of dew from the grass, and are fond of rolling in dust, for which purpose they resort to country roads, where they will often run for a considerable distance before a disturber ere they take wing and pop over a hedge, generally on the left hand side of the pursuer.

Albinos, wholly or in part, are not uncommon.

Partridges pair early, often in February, and the eggs are laid in April or May; but a good deal depends on the state of the weather.

QUAIL.—The general colour of the quail is grey, but starting from the eye are two circular lines of black, that meet under the chin, and outside each is a white line of the same width. Above the eye is a white curved line, and towards the top of the head another; but this last is very narrow. The head itself is dark brown, with many minute yellowish dots; the breast has a reddish tinge, is covered with small hair-like black lines; the under parts are greyish white, a few darker spots appearing at the sides of the belly. All the upper feathers have yellow shafts, and are crossed by two dark grey bars. The primaries are brown, spotted like those of the partridge with dots of a lighter shade. The bill is horn, and the legs and feet grey. The female is paler generally, and destitute of the black and white crescentic lines. Length of male, 8 inches; of the female a little less.

These birds are found sparingly throughout the British Islands, where they are migratory, arriving in May and departing in September.

They are thought to be polygamous, but at any rate the males are extremely pugnacious. The eggs, which vary in number from six or seven to twice the latter number, are of a creamy white colour, more or less spotted with brown; they are laid in June or July.

The food is the same as that of the partridge, in company with which these birds are often found. They are rather impatient of confinement, especially at the migratory seasons, when they often seriously injure themselves by rising and striking their heads violently against the roof of their abode.

Quails are in much request for the table, and extraordinary prices are paid at the commencement of the season, as much as thirty shillings having been given for a single bird.

RED-LEGGED PARTRIDGE.—Bill short, thick, and red; top of head brown, sides grey; a broad black line starts from the corners of the mouth, passes round the eyes, down the sides of the face and neck to about the middle of the throat; the enclosed space under the chin is greyish white; the neck and front of the neck and the breast are grey, the two first parts thickly spotted with black, but the last clear; the side feathers are large, grey, have a black line near the edge, and a chestnut red border; the under parts are buff, the flights reddish brown, and the back, wing coverts, tail, etc., brownish grey; the legs, which are spurred, and the feet are red. Length of male, 1 foot 2 inches. The female has a much less distinctly marked garget than the male, and is browner and smaller. Length, 1 foot 1 inch.

This species is an importation from the Continent, and is so little esteemed in Britain as a table delicacy that in some parts where it has thriven and ousted the native partridge it is voted "vermin," and its nest and eggs are destroyed.

They frequent cultivated grounds, and feed on grain, seeds of weeds, and insects, grass, clover, etc.

The nest is merely a shallow depression, sheltered by long grass or heather; the eggs are ten or twelve in number, and are of a reddish yellow colour, spotted with brownish red. The female alone performs the duty of incubation, but the male keeps near her while it is in progress, and assists her to look after the young, which are able to run about almost as soon as hatched.

These birds are easily domesticated, and breed freely in confinement.

Although mostly found on the ground, they often perch in trees, and are frequently seen on a hedge or rail, where the male emits his call, "cokilekee," with much distinctness in the spring.

PHEASANT.—Bill yellowish horn-colour; head and neck blue, with metallic reflections; naked place round eye scarlet; eye hazel; rest of body brown and grey, with metallic gloss on breast; primaries leaden blue; feet and legs bluish grey; side feathers and wing coverts have yellowish white angular markings. Length of male, 2 feet

FIG. 40.—*Reeves's Pheasant.*

10 or 11 inches. The female is greyish all over, and has none of the metallic gloss so characteristic of the male; she measures about 2 feet 2 inches in full length.

The pheasant is also a naturalised species in Britain, but the date of its introduction is not known; it is doubtful, too, if any really wild specimens exist, but is largely bred for shooting, and strictly preserved, to the detriment of many more useful and handsome native species which are supposed to be detrimental to it.

The natural food consists of seeds, berries, acorns, etc., as well as leaves, shoots, and insects; but English pheasants are usually fed artificially.

They are polygamous, each male having from five to nine hens, which begin to lay in April or May, after which they are deserted by the male, who pays no more attention to them or to their young. The number of eggs produced varies greatly, but an undisturbed nest generally contains ten, which are smooth of surface, and of a light olivaceous colour, thickly spotted with minute pits. Incubation lasts about twenty-six days.

At the present time many of the eggs are hatched in incubators or under hens of the dorking or barn-door types, and but few are left to the hen pheasants to bring up.

These birds are good eating, but the disgusting and unhealthy fashion of not cooking them until they are putrid is losing ground in popular estimation. They have been crossed with Reeves's pheasant.

The Peacock, the Turkey, and the Guinea Fowl are now fairly acclimatised in Britain; but it will be more convenient to consider the first along with the birds of India, the second with those of North America, and the third when we come to treat of those that belong to the British possessions in Western Africa.

THE RAILS.

The following is an enumeration of the British species:—

Family—*Rallidæ*.

Genus—			
1. *Rallus.*	*R. aquaticus.*	Water Rail.
2. *Porzana.*	*P. marinetta.*	Spotted Crake.
3. *Crex.*	*C. pratensis.*	Corn Crake.
4. *Gallinula.*	*G. chloropus.*	Moorhen.
5. *Fulica.*	*F. atra.*	Coot.

Water Rail.—Above, the colour of this bird is brown, but every feather has a dark centre, which gives a mottled appearance; the bill is long and pointed, and of a dark orange colour, which is deeper in the upper than on the lower mandible; the tail is brown and unspotted; the primaries are blackish; the chin is greyish white, but the face, front of the neck, and the breast are pale slate blue; the abdomen is grey in front and buff towards the tail, both parts being marked by numerous large crescentic black marks. The legs and feet, which are very large, are greenish yellow. The eye is red. Length of male, $11\frac{1}{2}$ inches; the female is a little less, and is some paler in colour.

This bird is partly migratory and partly stationary in Britain, where many breed each year in suitable localities; the nest is placed near water, and the eggs, about seven or eight, are cream colour, spotted and speckled with grey and red.

The food consists of aquatic insects and molluscs, tadpoles, small frogs, and fish, and the spawn and fry of the latter; it is very active on its feet, but a poor flyer, and yet it has been met with many miles out at sea making for the nearest land.

The water rail is readily kept in confinement where it is very accommodating in regard to its appetite, which it will appease with anything that is given to it.

It is reckoned good eating by connoisseurs, and perhaps it is; but if a cat eats a portion of one she will often be violently sick.

As these birds frequent the banks of streams and marshes, they suffer a good deal when their haunts are frozen over, and then approach human habitations, evincing great fearlessness, though at other times they are very shy, and not often seen except by those who make it their business to look for them. When surprised, they rarely attempt to escape by flight, but either dive, or run away swiftly through the closest herbage.

White specimens have now and then been met with, and different individuals vary considerably in appearance among themselves.

The young have bars of pale brown on the throat and breast, and are paler in colour than their parents.

A pair of these birds have been known to breed successfully in a suitable aviary, and as they are very graceful in their movements, nodding the head and flirting the tail at every step they take, they are very attractive inmates of such a place.

It is not unusual for a pair or two voluntarily to take up their abode on a piece of ornamental water.

SPOTTED CRAKE.—This bird, in general appearance, is not unlike the last, but its colouring is much more sombre. The bill is greyish yellow; the upper parts of the body are dark grey, with dark centres to the feathers, and white edges to the wing coverts and secondaries, which are also crossed by several wavy white lines; the under parts are greyish blue, paler on the belly, which is not spotted, except a very little at the sides; the middle of the throat has a brownish shade, and is spotted with light grey marks; the breast is crossed by alternate black and white irregular lines; the vent and under tail coverts are thickly barred with broad, crescentic, dark grey markings. The legs and feet are dusky yellowish grey. Length, about 9 inches. Sexes alike.

The nest is compactly built, so that in the case of the water rising it will float. The eggs are whitish grey, speckled with red and brown. Incubation, as with the last species, lasts three weeks, and the young quit the nest very soon after hatching.

The spotted crake is migratory and very local in its distribution, arriving in March and departing in October.

It is of rare occurrence in Scotland and Ireland, and especially in the latter country, where an odd one occurs at long intervals during the summer.

Like the water rail, the spotted crake is easily domesticated, and is esteemed a delicacy on the table; but as it is extremely shy in its habits, and very active in its movements among the thick cover of the places it frequents, it is not often shot, or indeed seen, for although it flies fairly well, it prefers not to unnecessarily expose itself to danger by rising.

Corn Crake.—The bill orange yellow; the head and all the upper parts brown, with a large dark centre to every feather, except the wing coverts, secondaries, and flights, which are unspotted, the last being the darkest. The chin is white, and the face, throat, and breast are bluish grey; but starting from the corners of the mouth are two wavy lines, one on each side, that are prolonged beyond the ear coverts. The remaining under parts are very light bluish grey, broadly marked by numerous crescentic patches of a light buff colour. The legs and feet are yellowish brown. The female is a little smaller than her mate, and her colours are not as bright as his. Length of male, 8½ inches.

Migratory in its habits, the corn crake arrives in Britain in April, and departs in October. It is usually found in pastures and cornfields, and is more frequently heard than seen, for it is extremely active on its feet, and is with difficulty made to take wing.

The nest is merely a slight depression in the ground, lined with bits of the surrounding vegetation. The eggs vary considerably, both in size and colouring, but are generally of a dull cream colour, more or less spotted with grey and red.

The female is very like the male, but perhaps a little smaller.

The young run about soon after being hatched, and at first are covered with dark down, but grow quickly, and in about six weeks are full grown and able to fly. There are usually two broods during the season.

The corn crake is susceptible of domestication, but requires to be protected from extreme cold.

It has been asserted that these birds occasionally hibernate, but the statement lacks modern confirmation.

MOORHEN.—In this species, the first third of the bill is yellow, and the remainder, with a bare place extending along the top of the head to nearly above the eye, orange; the eye is reddish orange; head and back black, with a bluish green gloss; wings brownish black; under parts dark bluish grey, barred across on the belly with clear grey; under tail coverts white; legs and feet dark green; just above the knee is a small orange spot. Length, 1 foot 2 inches for the male; 1 foot 1 inch for the female.

These birds are resident throughout the year, and may be met with wherever there is a pond, large or small, with rushes, flags, or sedges growing round it; on ornamental waters the birds become very tame.

The nest is of rushes, large and compactly put together; the eggs, from eight to twelve in number, are cream, with reddish brown spots. Incubation lasts three weeks, and the young take to the water soon after being hatched. There are usually three broods during the season, the young of the first assisting to feed and take care of their juniors.

The food consists of aquatic insects and molluscs, also slugs, snails, worms, and vegetable matters; they are very fond of grain, if given to them, but rarely seek it for themselves in the fields.

In severe winters they seem to suffer severely from the want of their usual supply of insect food, which proves that they are less granivorous in their habits than has been sometimes supposed.

It has been asserted that they kill the young of game and other birds, and destroy their eggs.

They swim and dive well, but fly badly.

Coot.—General colour black, with bluish shade on head, throat, and back, and a brownish one on the wings; the greater wing coverts have each a white tip, which form a white line across the wing; the bill, and a bald spot on the forehead, are creamy white; the eye is orange red; the legs and toes are green, the former in front only, the back part of the shanks being orange. The toes are long and curiously palmated, with a retraction at each joint; the hind toe has no membrane attached, and is short and slight. Length, from 1 foot 4 inches to 1 foot 6 inches, the female being the larger.

The coot is resident throughout the British Isles, occurring often in considerable numbers in suitable localities, that is, where there are ponds, lakes, or marshes.

The food consists of aquatic and terrestrial plants, insects, molluscs, and worms, also frogs and tadpoles, newts, etc.

The nest is compactly built of rushes and grass, and is not infrequently found floating in the water; but, as a rule, it is attached to the surrounding vegetation, though in such a manner as to permit of its floating should the water rise. Now and then it is placed on the ground. Like the water hen, the coot covers her eggs when she leaves them; they are six or seven in number, and vary in colour from dull yellow to green and stone tint, sparingly speckled with rusty red spots.

The young run about, swim, and dive almost immediately upon leaving the shell, being then covered with greyish black down, except the head, which is orange brown.

The coot is a shy and wary creature, and in severe weather is given to wandering from place to place, but can scarcely be deemed migratory.

THE BUSTARDS.

These birds are practically extinct in Britain, where they used, at one time, to be fairly abundant.

Family—*Otidæ*.
Genus—*Otis*. *O. tarda*.

Head on the centre of the crown chestnut, variegated with black, on the sides white; neck on the back light greyish, on the sides white; about the shoulders a soft grey down takes the place of feathers; nape pale chestnut, barred with black; chin white, underneath it a plume of narrow feathers, about seven inches long, falls backwards, covering a strip of bluish grey skin on the front and sides of the neck; throat above white, below pale chestnut orange, as is the upper part of the breast, which then is white below; the feathers have a pink tinge at the base; back pale chestnut orange, barred and variegated with black; the base of these feathers also is of a delicate rose tint. The wings have the first quill shorter than the second, the second shorter than the third and fourth, which are the longest in the wing; they extend to as much, in the fullest-sized birds, as seven feet three inches: greater and lesser wing coverts partly white and partly chestnut brown, barred with black; primaries blackish brown, the shafts white; secondaries greyish white; tertiaries chestnut brown, barred with black. The tail, rounded at the end, and of twenty feathers, is white at the base, then pale chestnut, tipped with white and barred with black; the two outer feathers greyish white, almost pure white at the base, with two or three small bars of black, near which they are tinted with reddish orange; underneath it is barred with dusky grey; upper tail coverts pale chestnut, barred with black; under tail coverts white. The legs, covered with round scales, toes and claws blackish, the latter, three in number. Length, 3 feet 9 inches; weight, 28 or 30 pounds.

The female is about 3 feet in length; her head and neck are of a deeper grey; nape reddish orange; the chin is without the plume until the bird is of mature age—three or four years old—and then it is said to appear, but less developed than in the male.

The young, at first, are covered with buff-coloured down, barred on the back, wings, and sides, with black.

(The above description is from Morris's "History of British Birds.")

The bustard frequents plains, and was formerly met with

at Newmarket, Salisbury, and similar localities, but as cultivation has advanced it has been driven away, and is now extinct, its last authentic occurrence dating as far back as 1856, when one was "shot" in Wiltshire.

It feeds mainly on vegetable matters, and it is conceivable that a few head of such large birds would do a considerable amount of harm in a field of corn; so perhaps, at least from an agricultural point of view, their disappearance from among the British avifauna is not so much to be deplored.

The female lays two eggs only, on the bare ground; they are olive brown in colour, blotted with red and grey spots.

The young run about directly they are hatched, and are said to feed chiefly upon insects.

The bustard, though naturally shy, is susceptible to a certain extent of domestication; but as in spite of its size and weight, it flies strongly and well, it can only be kept in a covered-in place.

THE STONE CURLEW.

Why this bird, otherwise known as the Thick-Knee, should have been separated from its fellows and constituted a one species, one genus family, is a mystery, the solution of which does not appear upon the surface; but there it is.

Family—*Œdicnemidæ.*
Genus—*Œdicnemus. Œ. scolopax.*

General colour brown, varied as follows: Over the eye a yellow arched line, under it a longer one, blue towards bill, grey at the other end; chin blue; throat grey; middle wing coverts yellowish grey; flights blackish grey; tail, all but central pair of feathers which are brown, black, with white spots; all the feathers, except those of the tail,

Fig. 41.—*The Thick-Knee.*

have dark centres; breast brown, with black, elongated, narrow lines; under parts grey buff, with a few black lines on sides; legs and feet greenish; no hind toe; bill, basal end, yellow; outer half black. The sexes are alike. Length, 1 foot 5 or 6 inches. Eye large and prominent, of a golden yellow colour.

This bird is migratory, arriving in April or May, and departing in September or the beginning of October. It is chiefly found in the eastern English counties, and is mostly seen either singly or in pairs, except when they are about taking their departure, when they assemble in flocks of from seven or eight to forty or more. They frequent open country, commons, heaths, etc., near the coast.

They feed on insects of all kinds, worms, and snails. The eggs, generally two, are laid among loose stones, which they resemble in appearance, and the young run as soon as hatched.

Although naturally very shy, the great, or Norfolk, plover, as this bird is often called, is readily tamed, and lives for a long time in confinement.

THE PLOVERS.

The following is an enumeration of the British species:—

Family—*Charadriidæ*.

Genus—1.	*Charadrius.*	*C. pluvialis.*	Golden Plover.
2.	*Squaterola.*	*S. helvetica.*	Grey Plover.
3.	*Ægitialis.*	*Æ. hiaticula.*	Ringed Plover.
4.	*Eudromias.*	*E. morinellus.*	Dotterel.
5.	*Vanellus.*	*V. vulgaris.*	Lapwing.
6.	*Strepsilas.*	*S. interpres.*	Turnstone.
7.	*Hæmatopus.*	*H. ostralegus.*	Oyster-Catcher.

GOLDEN PLOVER.—Bill dark horn; eye dark yellowish

grey; forehead yellow, with black spots; top of head, back and upper tail coverts dark brown, with black centres to every feather; wing coverts dark grey, the feathers irregularly edged with yellow; flights dark brown, with black outer webs; tail alternately banded with irregular bars of yellow and dark grey; face, chin, throat, breast, and belly, dark velvet black; sides of breast, belly, and under parts greyish white, with a bluish tinge, marked with arrow-headed or blotchy spots of a dark grey colour; legs and feet dark grey. The female resembles the male, but is scarcely as black on the breast. These birds during the winter are mottled with black, white, and yellow in a most diversified fashion.

They are partially migratory, but many remain to breed. They are more numerous towards the north.

Four eggs, of a yellowish grey, spotted with brownish red, are laid on bare ground, and are hatched in seventeen days, the young running immediately.

The food consists of insects, worms, slugs, and snails, and portions of various plants and grass.

GREY PLOVER.—General colour grey and black; above, each feather has a dark, almost black, centre, and a wide margin of grey. The head and tail are white, the latter with black bars, and the former with a number of small black spots. The bill is almost black; the face, below the eye, and the breast and first part of the belly jet black; vent and under tail coverts white; legs and feet blackish grey. Length, 11½ inches. During the winter the plumage is variously mottled.

This species is migratory, and generally occurs in Britain during the winter months; no authentic case of its having bred here being on record.

Like the other members of the family, the grey plover travels during the night, when its weird cry may be heard from a considerable height, for although they appear slow on the wing when suddenly roused from their mid-day nap, they can and do fly excellently well. Notwithstanding their natural shyness, they are susceptible of domestication, and will live for many years in confinement, when their wants are intelligently provided for.

The food consists of insects, snails, slugs, and worms, and the soft parts of various plants. All the plovers are partial to the short blades of growing corn.

The grey, as well as all the other plovers, are in much request for the table, their eggs, especially, being esteemed so great a delicacy as at the beginning of the season to command no less a price than twenty-five, or even thirty shillings each; so that if they would but lay in confinement, it would pay well to keep a few of them.

Ringed Plover.—This bird is also known by the names of Ringed Dotterel and Sea Lark. Its general colour is grey above, and white on the under surface of the body; that is to say, the forehead, cheeks, and a ring or band round the breast, are black. The front part of the head or brow, the chin, and a broad band round the upper part of the neck, and all the other lower parts, are white, shading to grey at the vent and lower tail coverts. The three outer secondaries have a patch of white on their outer webs; the bill is yellow, with a black tip; the eye, which is rather large, is hazel, and the legs and feet are yellowish grey. Length, $7\frac{1}{2}$ inches. The female resembles the male, but the black bands on the head and breast are narrower and of a less intense black.

These birds frequent the coast pretty well all round the island, to which they come in the autumn, departing, for the most part, in the spring, though many couples remain in suitable localities to breed.

The eggs are deposited among stones above high-water

mark. They are four in number, and vary a good deal in appearance, from greenish grey to pale buff and cream colour, spotted and lined with black, brown, and grey.

Both parents assist in the duty of incubation, and the young run about soon after being hatched. Like other members of the family, it will feign lameness to draw off an intruder from the vicinity of its young, which crouch down among the stones in the midst of which they emerged from the shell, and from which it then takes a very practised eye to distinguish them.

They feed on worms, seaside insects, shrimps, and various refuse left upon the beach by the retreating tide, into which they often run in pursuit of some attractive morsel.

DOTTEREL.—Bill dark horn; forehead line grey; top of head very dark brown, with lighter pencillings; from above the eye a creamy white line runs down the face to the back of the neck, and another, narrower, from that in a diagonal fashion across the neck; from the eye a dark brown line runs down to a point to meet the white one just mentioned: the rest of the upper parts are brown, lighter on the wing coverts; the flights are very dark brown, with a greenish tinge; the chin and upper part of the neck thinly marked with minute black spots; the breast is pale slate grey; below it a broad white mark, with indented margins; the lower breast rufous brown; the belly black; and the vent and under tail coverts buff: the legs and feet greenish yellow. Length, 9½ inches.

This species is migratory in part, arriving in April and departing in October, but many pairs remain throughout the year in Britain to breed.

The three or four eggs are deposited among stones, and the nest is difficult to find, in consequence of the grey spotted colour of the eggs. Both sexes seem to share the duty of incubation, which continues for about eighteen or twenty days. The young leave the nest and run about soon after they are hatched.

The dotterels feed on insects of all kinds, worms, slugs, snails, etc., and leaves of various plants.

On the whole, it is a pretty bird, whose wing feathers are in request for artificial fly-making. It has the reputation of being imitative to a foolish extent, hence its name dotterel, and *morinellus*, from *morio* a dotard; but it is doubtful whether this popular estimation of its character is correct, or whether Drayton, the poet, has any real foundation, in fact, for the word picture he draws of it.

LAPWING, or PEEWIT.—Dark green, with a metallic gloss on the upper surface, and black and white on the lower, are the prevailing colours of this well-known bird: but the head and long crest, as well as the chin, throat, and breast, are black, and the belly and under tail coverts buff; the flights and lesser wing coverts have a deep blue shade; and the legs and feet are yellowish grey. Length, about 12 inches.

The lapwing is resident in Britain throughout the year, frequenting marshes, fallow fields, meadows, heaths, and similar localities, especially during the winter, when it assembles in large flocks.

The eggs, which are in immense request for the table, are large for the size of the bird, of a creamy ground colour, but vary greatly in the markings that more or less cover them. They are always four in number, and are placed with the small ends pointing to a common centre. In soft wet ground, they are often deposited on the top of a mole-hill, which the bird tramples down, so as to form a place for them.

When assembled in a flock, these birds have a habit of

wheeling round and round for a long time before settling down again.

They feed morning and evening, as well as on moonlight nights, but keep close during the daytime, unless disturbed, and post sentinels on some adjoining little elevation to give notice of the approach of danger.

The well-known cry of the peewit is a repetition of the syllables that form its popular name. It is also known as the lapwing, in consequence of the way in which it flaps its long broad wings when flying.

The young are covered with a brownish yellow down, and can run directly they are hatched.

TURNSTONE.—The bill, long, with a slight upward tendency, is black; the head is white above, with numerous black spots; the face black and white, and the neck the same; the breast, flights, and tail are black, and the two last tinged with brown; the upper parts, including the wings, are chestnut brown, each feather with a black centre, and the greater wing coverts edged with white; the belly and remaining parts backwards white; legs and feet greyish orange. This bird has a small hind toe. Length, 9½ to 10 inches.

The turnstone is said to occur in all parts of the globe, but it is only a winter visitor in Britain. It derives its English name from the habit it has of turning over stones and other objects for the purpose of obtaining the insects that are sure to be found in such a situation, and a curious anecdote is related by the late Mr. Edward, of Banff, of the sagacity displayed by them under such circumstances; but, as it is much too long for quotation, the reader desirous of perusing the record of a most interesting experience is referred to the "Zoologist," pp. 3077-78-79.

The food of this species consists almost entirely of marine insects and small crustacea, but during high water the turnstone resorts to the fields and banks bordering on the seashore.

OYSTER-CATCHER.—This bird is also called the sea-magpie from its colouring of black and white, the latter below, and the former on the upper surface. The long bill is orange, and the legs and feet yellow; the eye is hazel.

The oyster-catcher is resident, and breeds in many parts of the British Isles, but more especially in the north. It measures 1 foot 4 inches in total length. The female resembles the male.

THE SMALL WADERS.

This group of birds is indeed a motley one, so much so, that it is impossible to guess upon what principle, or want of principle, they have been placed together, or differentiated from many of those that have already been passed in review.

Family—*Scolopacidæ*.

Genus—1.	*Recurvirostra.*	*R. avocetta.*	Avocet.
2.	*Scolopax.*	*S. rusticola.*	Woodcock.
3.	*Gallinago.*	*G. cœlestis.*	Snipe.
4.	*Tringa.*	*T. alpina.*	Dunlin.
		T. canutus.	Knot.
5.	*Machetes.*	*M. pugnax.*	Ruff.
6.	*Calidris.*	*C. arenaria.*	Sanderling.
7.	*Tringoides.*	*T. hypoleucus.*	Sandpiper.
8.	*Totanus.*	*T. caladris.*	Redshank.
9.	*Limosa.*	*L. lapponica.*	Bar-tailed Godwit.
		L. ægrocephala.	Black-tailed Godwit.
10.	*Numenius.*	*N. arquata.*	Curlew.
		N. phæopus.	Whimbrel.

AVOCET.—The long, thin, narrow, upward curving bill is black; so is the top of the head, as well as the back of the neck, wing coverts, flights, and inner secondaries and tertiaries; the remaining parts are white. The long legs and webbed feet are green.

At one time of frequent occurrence, it is now very rare indeed in Britain, the few individuals that straggle over in spring being immediately shot, so that probably not a single one survives to take its departure in September. Length, 1 foot 6 inches, $3\frac{1}{2}$ of which belong to the bill.

The female is a little less, but in every other respect she closely resembles the male.

The food is similar to that of the species belonging to the last family, or rather to that of the turnstone, which it also imitates in its choice of feeding grounds, namely, the seashore.

WOODCOCK.—The general colour of this bird is chestnut brown, darker above than below, mottled with various shades of black, light grey, and buff. The bill is long, and the eye placed very far back in the head; it is large, and of a grey colour; the legs and feet are yellowish brown. The tail is very short, and the general figure of the bird plump. Length, various; some specimens, 1 foot $\frac{3}{4}$ inch to 1 foot 3 or $3\frac{1}{2}$ inches; the weight is equally uncertain, ranging from 7 ounces to 15 ounces, the female being rather larger than the male.

It is, generally speaking, migratory in the British Isles; but a few pairs remain to breed in suitable localities.

The food consists of worms and insects; the former are obtained by boring into the soft ground in the vicinity of water.

The nest is built in plantations and copses near the root of a tree; it is loosely constructed of leaves and grass, and the eggs are, as a rule, four in number; the colour is pale yellowish buff, speckled with chestnut brown. The young can run about as soon as hatched, and it has been observed that the parents carry them in their feet from one place to another. There are two broods in the season. Some are much darker than others.

SNIPE.—The general appearance of this bird bears a strong resemblance to the last, but is of a lighter colour underneath, and much smaller. Like the woodcock, it arrives in England for the winter, though a good many couples remain to breed. It frequents marshy spots and the banks of streams, where it is able to find suitable food, worms and insects of various kinds. The flight of this bird is very swift and erratic, so that it is reckoned good sport, and, like the woodcock, is in much request as a delicacy for the table. The JACK SNIPE is smaller and darker than the common snipe.

DUNLIN.—This bird is brown above, white on the throat and breast, black on the belly, and white again on the vent and under tail coverts. The wing coverts have a tinge of blue grey. The long bill is horn-colour, and the legs and feet green.

It is usually found on the coast, where it feeds on marine insects and small crustacea. The eggs are four in number, and vary much in colour; the nest is placed on the open ground near the sea, and sometimes among long grass or other cover. Length, about 8 inches; female a little larger, but otherwise resembles the male. Resident.

KNOT.—General colour rufous brown, darker above than below, spotted with white on the wing coverts. Bill, legs, and feet greenish; flights and tail dark grey. It is of migratory habits, arriving in August and departing in May; some, however, remain to breed. Food—marine insects, etc. Length, 10 inches. The female is duller in appearance.

RUFF.—The female is called a Reeve. Upper surface brown and grey; lower, white, with brown and red marks on the side. This bird has the power of raising the long feathers of the neck, which then form a kind of ruff, whence its name, that gives it a singular appearance. The female is less than the male, and practically destitute of the ruff. They arrive in April and depart in September, but are much less frequent than formerly. Length of male, 12½ inches; of female, 10 inches. The long legs are yellow. These birds are very pugnacious in the breeding season, but are as easily kept in confinement as the two preceding.

SANDERLING.—This is another shore bird, brownish grey above and on the breast, elsewhere white; the bill and legs and feet dark horn-colour, with a tinge of green; it is destitute of hind toe; across the lower third of the wings is a white bar. The female is larger than the male: it is a winter visitor only.

SANDPIPER.—The common sandpiper (there are a number of other species so called, which consideration of space will not permit to be noticed here) is a small bird of a brownish green colour above, and white beneath; the breast and upper parts are plentifully marked with black; bill, legs, and feet olivaceous green; plumage fine and silky. Length, 7 inches. The sexes are alike in appearance.

It is also called the summer snipe, but has little resemblance to that gastronomic favourite. Migratory in habit, it nests in many parts of Britain, laying four eggs of a creamy white, spotted with brown; they are very large for the size of the bird, and are reputed good to eat.

REDSHANK.—General colour bluish grey, shaded with brown on the wings, darkest on the back, and everywhere plentifully spotted with black and grey, except on the rump, which is plain; the bill, legs, and feet are dull red. Sexes alike, except that the female is rather bigger than her mate. Resident throughout the year in England, Scotland, and Ireland, their numbers are augmented by fresh arrivals during the winter. The eggs, deposited in some marshy spot, are greenish white, spotted with red and brown; they are four in number, and the young, as happens with all birds of this class, run about soon after being hatched.

Food—insects, worms, etc.

BAR-TAILED GODWIT.—This handsome species is grey above, and deep red on the lower parts of the body; the rump, however, is white, sparsely spotted with black; the neck, back, and wings have black centres to the feathers; a bluish bar crosses the wing; the bill is yellow, with a dark tip, and the legs and feet are greenish grey; short hind toe.

It moves north in April, and returns in the autumn when the breeding season is over.

The food is worms, small molluscs, etc. It is usually found on the sands, but retires to adjacent land during high water.

BLACK-TAILED GODWIT.—This bird differs a good deal from the last. It is brown on the breast, and greyish white on the rump and under tail coverts; the back is brown, every feather is centred with black, and numerous crescentic black lines mark the breast and belly; the bill is yellow, with dark tip, and the legs and feet dark greenish grey. Length, 1 foot 4 inches. Food the same as the preceding species.

CURLEW.—General colour grey above, and white on the under parts; in both situations are numerous black and grey spots and lines. Sexes alike in appearance, but the female is much the larger of the two, her length being 2 feet 1 inch, while that of the male is only 22 inches. It is common on moors, heaths, etc., in all three divisions of the

United Kingdom, but in winter is mostly found by the sea. It breeds in the most retired spots it can find, laying four eggs, which, like the birds themselves, differ immensely in size and appearance.

The food consists of insects, slugs, snails, marine creatures, grass, berries, and the tender shoots of growing plants. In France it is esteemed a rare delicacy for the table, but is not held in much esteem in Britain, where the eggs, however, are eaten.

WHIMBREL.—This bird is also called the whaap, and is closely allied to the preceding. It is very widely diffused, visiting England in the winter months, though some remain to breed in the most desolate districts they can find, where the eggs are laid on the bare ground, or among the surrounding vegetation, with little or no attempt at nest-making or concealment; they are four in number, of an olive brown colour, spotted with brown of a darker shade. Length of male, 1 foot 4 inches; of female, 1 foot 6 inches. Like the curlew, the bill of the whimbrel is long, with an abrupt downward curve; it is bluish grey in colour, with a yellow spot at the base of the lower mandible.

THE GULLS.

The British species are fairly numerous, and will be briefly described in the next few pages.

Family—*Laridæ*.

Genus—1.	*Stercorarius.*	*S. catarrhactes.*	Skua.
2.	*Rissa.*	*R. tridactyla.*	Kittiwake.
3.	*Larus.*	*L. glaucus.*	Glaucous Gull.
		L. argentatus.	Herring Gull.
		L. fuscus.	Lesser Black-backed Gull.

	L. canus.	Common Gull.
	L. marinus.	Greater Black-backed Gull.
	L. ridibundus.	Black-headed Gull.
4. *Sterna.*	*S. hirundo.*	Common Tern.
	S. macrura.	Arctic Tern.
5. *Hydrochelidon.*	*H. nigra.*	Black Tern.

SKUA.—This is one of the largest members of the family, measuring 2 feet 2 inches in length. The female is smaller, but otherwise resembles her mate, who may be described as brown, darker above than below; the feathers of the neck are long and pointed, and can be raised by the bird at will. The long narrow wings measure, when extended, nearly 5 feet from tip to tip, so that the skua is extremely powerful on the wing, and is much feared by other birds. It still breeds in a few places in Scotland, but is in great danger of extermination, for during the breeding season it exhibits great fierceness, sparing neither man, beast, or bird that approaches the spot where its large nest is placed in the vicinity of the sea. The two eggs are dark, and the young are at first covered with dark blackish down; there is a white patch on the wing; the bill is very strong and hooked. It flies strongly and for a long time without resting. It attacks other gulls to deprive them of their prey; sometimes they are called "parasitic gulls, because they subsist on the labours of others."

KITTIWAKE.—A very elegant species, white, with a faint bluish tinge on the head, neck, breast, and under parts; pale slate blue on the back and wings; flights black, several of the secondaries have white tips; bill dull orange, shaded with grey; legs dark greenish black; hind toe rudimentary. The eggs are two or three, and differ much in colour and marking. Length, 1 foot 3½ inches. Food—fish, shrimps, and other crustacea.

Glaucous Gull.—Face, throat, breast, and belly, flight feathers and tail, white; top of head, back of neck, back and wing coverts very pale grey blue; bill strong, thick, and pointed, upper mandible white, lower pale orange, darker towards tip. Legs and feet dull yellowish red. Length, 2 feet 8 inches. Predatory birds, they feed on fish and seaside offal, and also rob other gulls; it usually frequents the open sea, but in severe weather ventures inland. The eggs are bluish grey, spotted with brown and purple, but vary considerably. Sometimes they are deposited on the beach above high-water mark, or on ledges of rock; the nest is made of sea-weed and sticks.

Herring Gull.—Head, neck, breast, belly, and tail white; back and wings pale slate blue; primaries black, with a rounded white mark on the first, second, and third. The bill is pale yellow, and the legs and feet are the same colour. Length, 2 feet 1 inch. Makes a nest of grass and sea-weed on ledges of rock and grassy spots along the side of cliffs. They are very gregarious and resident. Flight less graceful than that of the previous species, like which it can be domesticated to a considerable extent.

Lesser Black-Backed Gull.—White on head, neck, and all lower parts, except under tail coverts, which are faintly grey; back and wings black, but the flights and some of the wing coverts are tipped with white. Bill, legs, and feet yellow, but the first a lighter shade. It associates with the last species, which it resembles in its habits and disposition. Length, 1 foot 11 inches.

Common Gull.—Very much like the herring gull, save that the bill is grey with a pale yellow tip, and the legs and feet are lead colour. Length, 1 foot 6 inches.

Greater Black-Backed Gull.—Like the lesser, but

has more white on wings, and the bill is very pale yellow, almost white, and has a blood-red spot near the end of the lower mandible. The legs and feet are grey, with a tinge of flesh colour. Length, 2 feet 1 inch.

BLACK-HEADED GULL.—Bill dull orange, ring round eye reddish orange, eye dark grey, head and upper part of

FIG. 42.—*The Greater Black-Backed Gull.*

neck black; general colour pale slate blue, darker above than below; wing coverts white; first primary black, with white tip; the next is white, edged outside with black. Legs and feet vermilion. This species is easily tamed. Length, 1 foot 5 inches.

COMMON TERN.—The terns are distinguished by their

rather long forked tails, and their long narrow wings, which project beyond the end of the tail when folded; top of head to nape jet black; throat, breast, and belly white; other parts pale slate blue; outer edge of primaries darker. Length, 1 foot 2 inches. The eggs are three in number, and are laid on sand, rocks, shingle, or grass, without any nest. They vary greatly in appearance, being blue, yellow, green, brown, or stone colour, spotted with grey, black, and brown. Both sexes divide the duty of incubation.

ARCTIC TERN.—This bird is scarcely distinguishable from the last, but it has a long tail, the bill is coral red, and the legs and toes deep red. It is common in the north of England, Scotland, and Ireland, where it breeds freely. No two eggs are exactly alike. It measures 1 foot 3 inches in total length. Sexes alike.

BLACK TERN.—It is rather very dark slate blue than black, except on the top of the head and throat; the bill is dark grey, and the legs and feet greyish red. It frequents marshes, bogs, and fens, where it breeds. In Italy it is eaten. Length, 10 inches; female a little less. Food—insects, small frogs, etc.

THE SHEARWATERS AND PETRELS.

None of these birds are very numerous in Britain, and we have only room to notice two of them very briefly here; they have been grouped together to form the

Family—*Procellariidæ.*
Genus—1. *Puffinus.* *P. anglorum.* Manx Shearwater.
2. *Procellaria.* *P. pelagica.* Stormy Petrel.

MANX SHEARWATER.—Very gull-like in form, this bird differs considerably from the LARIDÆ in many respects;

thus it has a much longer rounded tail, is a frequenter of the open sea, except during the breeding season, when it resorts to the grassy or sandy tops of cliffs, where it occupies or makes a burrow in which it deposits a single white egg of considerable size.

The bill is dark brown, with a furrow on the upper mandible; the general colour of the plumage is dark blackish brown above and white underneath; the legs and toes are reddish, but the webs are drab; behind the legs the white feathers are crossed by three or four broad bands of light grey.

The food consists of marine creatures, which the birds capture while swimming in flocks with their heads and bills below the surface, the hindermost of the party every now and then rising and pattering over the water to the front. Length, 1 foot 2 inches.

STORMY PETREL.—This small, inconspicuous bird is best known by the name of MOTHER CAREY'S CHICKEN; it is brownish black, all but the vent and under tail coverts, which are white. It is the smallest web-footed bird known, measuring but 6 inches. One white egg is laid in some disused rabbit burrow at the top of a cliff, and the young one is fed on a kind of oil disgorged by the parent birds.

THE GREBES.

These birds rightly constitute an independent family, for they are separated from all other web-footed birds by marked characteristics.

Family—*Colymbidæ.*

Genus—1. *Tachybaptes.* *T. fluviatilis.* Little Grebe.

2. *Podiceps.*	*P. griseigena.*	Red-necked Grebe.
	P. auritus.	Sclavonian Grebe.
3. *Colymbus.*	*C. glacialis.*	Great Northern Diver.
	C. arcticus.	Black-throated Diver.

LITTLE GREBE, better known, perhaps, as the DABCHICK.—It has the head, back of neck, and back of a dark brown; the face, throat, and upper part of breast bright chestnut brown; the under parts are grey, marbled with darker grey; the bill is horn-colour, and the lores yellowish cream; the legs, placed very far back, are greenish.

It is generally distributed over the British Isles at all seasons. As Morris says: "Its natural home is in the water, both the open lake and the village pond, the gentle flowing river and the still pool, the narrow streamlet, and at times the edge of the open sea. In winter, when the frost has cut off its usual supply of food, it betakes itself to the nearest salt water, and is then to be found in bays and seaside pools."

In extreme length the dabchick measures about 10 inches. The nest is placed near water, among such vegetation as there obtains; the eggs vary from four to six in number, tapering in form, and of a dull white colour. The young take to the water as soon as hatched, and the parents collect food for them until they are able to cater for themselves.

It is a poor flyer, but swims and dives with admirable ease and grace.

RED-NECKED GREBE.—Dark grey above, and red on the neck and breast, the under parts white, except the lower tail coverts, which are grey; the whole of the face is bluish grey, and the feathers, as well as those of the head, can be puffed out to form a kind of hood; the ends of the greater wing coverts are white; eye red.

It is chiefly met with by the sea, but also in ponds, near which it nests.

As the wings are very short, it does not fly much, but can do so fairly well; it is a most proficient performer in the water.

The food consists of small fish and marine insects; and, like the last species, it eats all its own cast feathers. The eggs are white, with a tinge of bluish green. Length, 1 foot 4 inches.

SCLAVONIAN, or GREAT CRESTED-GREBE.—A singular-looking bird when it elevates the long yellow, red, and black feathers of the head and face: the bill is grey; surrounding it is a ring of yellow feathers, followed by another of red, and a third of black, feathers; the neck and under parts are white, the sides buff, and the back and wings dark grey, but there is a patch of white on the latter towards the end; the feet and legs, which are partly webbed, are dark green. Length, 1 foot 10 inches.

This bird is also called the loon, and is but of partial distribution in England, visiting Scotland (Caithness) sometimes in the winter. The eggs are three to five, white, with a green tinge.

The parents are very attentive to the young, which swim directly they leave the shell.

The food consists of fish, tadpoles, frogs, and various water insects.

They are supposed to pair for life, and if the eggs are taken, more will be laid, until the poor bird is quite exhausted.

The GREAT NORTHERN DIVER is of rare occurrence in

the British Isles; it is a sea bird, and frequents the coast only for breeding purposes. It used to nest freely on St. Kilda. The head and neck are deep black, but on the front of the latter are two white patches barred longitudinally with black, which is the arrangement of the rest of the upper part of the body, but the black is replaced by grey; the under parts are white and the flights dark grey. The eye is dull red and the legs, and feet black. Length, 2 feet 9 inches.

Two eggs are laid close to the water's edge; they are dark greenish brown with a few red spots.

The food consists of all kinds of aquatic creatures, fish included, of which they consume a large quantity.

They swim very low in the water, but dive and fly well.

The BLACK-THROATED DIVER.—This bird has the bill, the chin, and the lower part of the face black, as also a patch on the throat; the rest of the neck is white, finely streaked with black; the back is black, and the wings dark grey, both barred with white; breast and under parts white. Both in this species and the last, the legs are placed so far back that on shore the birds adopt a penguin-like attitude.

The black-throated diver is a more numerous species than the last; it breeds in Orkney and comes south in winter. It is very shy and wary. Food same as the last. Length, 2 feet 4 inches.

THE AUKS.

This is the last group of British birds with which we have to deal. The following is on enumeration of the British species:—

Family—*Alcidæ.*

Genus—1.	*Alca.*	*A. torda.*	Razorbill.
2.	*Lomvia.*	*L. troile.*	Guillemot.
3.	*Fratercula.*	*F. arctica.*	Puffin.

RAZORBILL.—Upper parts black, under white; on the bill, which is feathered laterally, is a white line, and another reaches to the eye; there is also a white line across the wings, formed by the edges of the wing coverts. It is purely a marine species, only frequenting land for breeding places, where it lays one egg, the prevailing tint of which is white spotted with brown. Length, 1 feet 5½ inches.

GUILLEMOT.—Bill dark horn, cylindrical, long and pointed. Plumage blackish brown with purple reflections in parts, above, under surface white; broad white line crosses wing. Length, 1 foot 5 or 6 inches. One egg only is laid by each bird; it is very large in proportion, and no two are found alike.

FIG. 43.—*The Puffin.*

PUFFIN.—This bird has a large head and an immense bill, much compressed laterally, and coloured in a remarkable manner; the tip is orange, then come three parallel blue lines on a yellow ground, then a broad triangular blue patch and a yellow line; round the corners of the mouth is a yellow corrugated membrane, and the top of the upper mandible is reddish orange. The back of the neck, top of the head, back and wings are black; the face is white in the centre, shading to light blue grey back and front; a black ring goes round the middle of the neck, and the under parts are white; legs and feet reddish grey. Length, 1 foot 1 inch.

Food—sea creatures of all kinds.

The nest is placed in precipitous places on the coast, at the mouth of a rabbit burrow, or a hole excavated by the birds themselves; one egg only is laid, white with grey shading.

In the foregoing pages an attempt has been made to give a general notice of the more remarkable birds of the mother country; some, no doubt, have been omitted, but, as a rule, these are unimportant, from the infrequency with which they occur, or their doubtfulness as real British species.

PART II.

THE BIRDS OF INDIA.

INDIA, the brightest jewel in England's Imperial Crown, has a large avifauna, for the greater part peculiar to her, but in some cases held in common with adjacent lands. So great, indeed, is the number of the winged inhabitants, that only a selection of them can be given in regard to the demands on the space at the disposal of the writer, who, as he began the history of our British birds by reviewing the Thrushes, proposes to continue upon the same lines with respect to the other portions of the Empire.

THE THRUSHES.

This group is fairly represented in India by no less than five genera and six distinct species, as follows:—

Family—*Turdidæ*.

Genus—1.	*Turdus.*	*T. pœcilopterus.*	Grey-winged Blackbird.
2.	*Geochichla.*	*G. citrina.*	Orange-headed Ground Thrush.
3.	*Miyophonus.*	*M. horsfieldi.*	Horsfield's Whistling Thrush.
4.	*Copsychus.*	*C. saularis.*	Indian Dyal Bird.
		C. seychellarum.	Seychellean Dyal Bird.
5.	*Kittacincla.*	*K. macroura.*	Shamah.

GREY-WINGED BLACKBIRD.—The male is black above, with a large spot of silvery grey on the wing. The female is of brownish black colour, and the young are spotted, especially on the breast.

The male measures $10\frac{1}{4}$ inches in full length, 4 of which belong to the tail.

It is found in considerable numbers throughout the Himalayas, is of shy habits, and is not remarkable as a songster, according to Jerdon. The nest is made of small twigs, roots, and moss, and the eggs, four in number, are pale bluish green, with numerous light brown spots. It bears confinement well.

ORANGE-HEADED GROUND THRUSH.—This bird has the head, neck, lower breast pale orange brown, and the chin and throat whitish; the rest of the upper surface is bluish grey; there is a white spot about the middle of the wing coverts; the primaries and their coverts have black tips; the under tail coverts are white. In length it measures $8\frac{1}{2}$ inches, of which the tail takes 3.

The female is altogether of lighter colour. They frequent the Himalayan Range, and are found in gardens and woods. The food is collected on the ground, and consists of insects of all descriptions.

The nest is placed in the fork of a high tree, and is made of grass, moss, and roots. The eggs are three or four in number, of a pale green colour, marked with reddish spots at the larger end.

The orange-headed ground thrush does well in confinement.

HORSFIELD'S WHISTLING THRUSH, or the MALABAR THRUSH.—Black plumage, tinged with deep blue; on the forehead is a narrow band of the shade of that colour known as cobalt; it measures 11 inches in total length, $4\frac{3}{4}$ of which belong to the tail.

South and Western India, from the summit of the Neilgherries to the sea level is the habitat of this species, especially along the banks of mountain torrents, where it can find an abundance of suitable food, worms, molluscs, insects, etc.

The nest is placed on a shelf of rock, and is made of roots, moss, grass, etc., cemented with earth. The eggs are usually three in number, of a reddish fawn colour, spotted with many dots of a brown tinge.

This species also bears confinement very well.

INDIAN DYAL BIRD.—This bird, locally known as the magpie robin, is found in all the southern parts of India, as well as in China and the Philippines, but is seldom seen in England; it is, nevertheless, readily acclimatised, and has bred in the western aviary of the Zoological Society in Regent's Park, London, in 1873. The general colour is black, with a blue metallic gloss; on the wings are white lines, and all the under parts are the same colour. The bill is black, the eyes hazel, and the feet and legs brown. The female is dull black above, throat grey, belly white, and the sides dull brownish grey.

In size it equals the English song-thrush, or $8\frac{1}{2}$ inches, $3\frac{3}{16}$ of which belong to the tail.

It is found all over India in wooded places. The food consists of insects. The nest is built in thick bushes, and the four eggs are bluish white, with pale brown spots and blotches. Lives well in a cage.

SEYCHELLEAN DYAL BIRD.—Bears much resemblance to the last. The plumage is black, with a glossy blue reflection, and white bands on the wings. It has been represented in the Gardens of the London Zoological Society.

Like the magpie robin, which it closely resembles, it is much esteemed in India as a song bird, and is frequently caged, doing as well in confinement as its congener, and it seems a pity it should be so seldom met with in England, seeing that it is desirable on account of its music and the

FIG. 44.—*The Shamah.*

facility with which it can be preserved, ants' eggs, meal-worms, and other insects, including the familiar black beetle (*Blatta orientalis*), sufficing to keep it in rude health, providing, of course, that its wants in the matter of temperature are understood and attended to, for exposure to cold for any length of time is very injurious to it.

SHAMAH.—The head, neck, back, and wing coverts, as well as the breast and tail are jetty black, but the rump is white; the wings are dull black, and the outermost feathers of the tail have white tips; the breast, belly, and tail are deep chestnut. In length it measures 12 inches, nearly 8 of which belong to the tail.

The female is browner, and her feathers have little gloss; her tail also is somewhat shorter.

The shamah is supposed to be the best of the Indian songsters, and is frequently caged, living very well on a paste made with parched chuma (?) mixed with yolk of hard-boiled eggs, to which maggots and other insects must be added, and, in England, ants' eggs.

The shamah has bred in England, laying four greenish blue eggs, and rearing the young without difficulty; but when these are able to cater for themselves they must be removed from the society of their parents, or they would be killed by the male. There are two broods per season.

THE TITS.

A small group, of which we can only notice the following:—

Family—*Paridæ*.
Genus—*Liothrix*. *L. luteus*.

YELLOW-BELLIED LIOTHRIX.—It is certainly an error to

place this handsome bird along with the tits, for it much more nearly resembles a robin in appearance. The general colour is dark olive green above, the long tail coverts

FIG. 45.—*The Liothrix.*

slightly edged with white; the lores and a patch beyond the eyes, as well as the ear coverts, are grey; from the angle of the mouth on each side there is a black line to the upper part of the breast; the chin and under parts are yellow, and on the middle of the wing is a patch of bright chestnut brown; the bill is orange, the eye full and black and the legs and feet yellowish grey.

THE BULBULS.

The following is an enumeration of the Indian species:—

Family—*Pycnonotidæ.*

Genus—1.	*Pycnonotus.*	*P. pygæus.*	Black Bulbul.
		P. leucotis.	White-eared Bulbul.
		P. leucogenys.	White-cheeked Bulbul.
		P. jocosus.	Red-eared Bulbul.
		P. hæmorrhous.	Red-vented Bulbul.
2.	*Hemixes.*	*H. flavula.*	Brown-eared Bulbul.
3.	*Hypsipetes.*	*H. maclellandi.*	Rufous-bellied Bulbul.
4.	*Phyllornis.*	*P. aurifrons.*	Malabar Green Bulbul.
		P. hardwicki.	Blue-winged Green Bulbul.

Black Bulbul.—The head, which is sub-crested, is of a deep black, while the body and wings are dark ashen grey; the tips of the primaries and the tail feathers are black; the under surface is dull grey; the abdomen and vent paler; and the under tail coverts have a white border each. The bill and the legs and feet are red. The total length is 11 inches, 4¼ of which are taken up by the tail. The sexes are alike in outward appearance.

From Simla to Bootan is the habitat of this noisy, imitative, and gregarious species. It feeds on all manner of insects, the pollen of flowers and their nectar, and also on berries.

The nest, which is very compactly built, is cup-shaped. It is usually placed on a tall tree, and is made of leaves and grass stuck together with spiders' webs. The eggs are usually three in number, and of a rosy white colour, with a few purplish spots and claret red blotches, but vary a great deal in appearance.

The RED-VENTED, or COMMON MADRAS BULBUL.—In this species the head, chin, and throat are black; the nape and back are smoky brown, with a paler edge to each feather, which imparts to the bird a speckled appearance. The rump is cinereous red, and the upper tail coverts white; the under surface is brown, with pale ashen grey edgings, fading posteriorly into white at the vent; the under tail coverts, however, are crimson.

This bird is found in Southern India, where it frequents gardens, cultivated ground, and fields. It is met with in pairs, or small flocks, and feeds chiefly on fruit, buds of trees, vegetables (peas, etc.), and is very destructive to young crops.

The note is a harsh chirp, but at times it has a sweeter trill.

The nest is built in low cover, and the eggs are like those of the black bulbul.

WHITE-EARED BULBUL.—Head and neck black, passing into rich brown on the latter; the ear coverts and a patch below them white, with black edging; the remaining upper parts dull brown; the tail is brown at the base, but terminal part is blackish brown, edges white; the lower parts are whitish brown, and the under tail coverts saffron. The length of this bird is 7 inches, of which the tail measurse 3¼.

White-Cheeked Bulbul.—The top of the head and the nape are brown, and the feathers, which are long, form an erectile occipital crest; a faint white line surmounts the eye on either side; the lores and a ring round the eye black. The upper parts are pale brown, but the primaries are darker; the black tail is tipped with white; the chin and throat are blackish brown, the same colour extending round to the back of the ears; the under surface is paler, and the tail coverts yellow.

The habitat of the white-cheeked bulbul is in the Himalayas, from Cashmere to Bootan. It feeds on seed, fruit, and insects. The eggs are three and sometimes four in number, pinky white with purplish spots. The total length of the male is 8 inches, $3\frac{1}{2}$ of which belong to the tail.

Red-Eared Bulbul.—The head, including the crest, black; ear coverts white, with a tuft of hair-like feathers, of a glossy texture and a bright crimson colour, just over them. The remainder of the plumage above light brown, darker on the quills; the tail feathers, excepting the middle pair, have white tips. Total length, 8 inches; tail, $3\frac{9}{16}$.

This species is found throughout India, but is local in its distribution. In its action it is lively, and it has a pleasant song. It makes a neat cup-shaped nest of moss, grass, and lichen, and lays three or four pinky white eggs. The food consists of fruit, seeds, and insects. It is frequently caged.

Brown-Eared Bulbul.—In this species the long pointed crest and the head are dark grey, and the rest of the upper plumage is ashen grey, darker on the wings and tail; the greater wing coverts and the outer webs of the secondaries are greenish yellow; the lores and the moustache are black, and the ear coverts glossy brown; the throat and under tail coverts are white; and the white breast is tinged with grey. It measures $8\frac{1}{2}$ inches in total length, of which the tail takes up 3½. Its habitat is in the Eastern Himalayas, and its food consists of insects and berries.

In regard to its nidification, the brown-eared bulbul resembles its congeners.

RUFOUS-BELLIED BULBUL.—This species has an inconspicuous crest which, with the head, is of a brown colour, the feathers having purple centres; the remainder of the plumage is olive green, except the ear coverts, which are brown; the chin and the throat white, with dusky edging; and the sides of the neck, breast, and belly light reddish brown, with paler centres; the under tail coverts are yellow. It is found from Nepaul to Bootan, and resembles the rest of its race in regard to its food and mode of nidification. Total length, 9 inches, of which the tail takes 4.

MALABAR GREEN BULBUL.—In the male the plumage generally is bright grass green, but the forehead is golden yellow, and the chin and throat black; it has a small blue moustache, and on the bend of the wing a spot of verditer blue. The female lacks the golden frontlet, and her gorget and maxillary streak are much less conspicuous than in the male.

It is a native of Malabar, where it lives a retired life, going about in pairs, and feeding on fruit and insects, the latter chiefly.

BLUE-WINGED GREEN BULBUL.—The male is green above, where not otherwise stated, but the head and neck have a yellow tinge; the moustache is bright blue, and the shoulder spot cobalt blue; the wings and tail are bluish purple; the throat and the upper part of the neck are black, changing to glossy, dark purple on the breast; the abdomen is clear saffron. The female has no black, her moustache is pale blue, and her lower parts are mixed with green. The total length is 8 inches, 3 of which are taken up by the tail.

THE JAY-THRUSHES.

White-Crested Jay-Thrush.—In this bird the head, including the crest, the nape, the sides of the neck, throat, and breast are pure white, tinged with crimson on the neck, and the remainder of the plumage is rich olivaceous brown. In total length it measures 12 inches, 5 of which belong to the tail.

It is found throughout the Himalayas, has a curious note resembling a discordant laugh, feeds on the ground on insects and berries, and lays three or four white eggs. It is readily tamed, and preserved for years in confinement.

White-Throated Jay-Thrush.—On the upper surface of its body this bird is of a dull brown colour; the lores and a line under the eyes black; the terminal third of the tail feathers white, and the chin and throat also. Length, 12 inches: tail, 5

It frequents the Himalayas, where it is to be seen in small flocks, the cries of which are a trifle less discordant than those of the preceding.

The nest is placed at a height of seven or eight feet from the ground, and contains about three eggs, of a glossy green colour.

Red-Headed Laughing-Thrush.—The head and nape in this bird are of a rich, deep chestnut colour, or ruddy brown; the lores, chin, and throat are black; the ear coverts reddish dark brown: the back part of the neck is olivaceous grey, with black markings; the rest of the neck is ashen grey the shoulders and lesser wing coverts are deep chestnut; the primaries olive, with a brown tinge; on the breast are a number of black spots, and the remaining under parts are olive. The length of this bird, from the point of the bill to the end of the tail, is $11\frac{1}{2}$ inches, of which the tail occupies $5\frac{1}{2}$.

It is found in the North-Western Himalayas. The eggs are usually five in number, of a fine sky blue.

BLACK-HEADED SIBIA.—The head, cheeks, and ear coverts are black; the nape pale reddish brown; the back brownish grey in the middle, but deep rufous posteriorly; the base of the tail feathers is black, the rest rufous. It measures 9 to 10 inches in length, of which the tail takes up about 5 inches.

Its habitat extends from Simla to Bootan, where it frequents tall trees, up the stems and among the branches of which it climbs after the fashion of a European nuthatch or woodpecker. Its food consists in about equal parts of fruit and insects.

The nest is composed of grass, fibre, and wool, with fine roots: and the eggs, which are four or five in number, are pale blue, with irregular red spots or blotches.

GOLDEN-EYED BABBLER.—The plumage is a clear reddish brown above, but the wings are cinnamon brown, the under parts white. The bill is black, and the total length of the bird $6\frac{1}{2}$ inches, 3 of which are taken up by the tail. It occurs universally throughout India, frequenting low jungles. The note is a loud, sibilant whistle, which is heard from a considerable distance. The food consists for the most part of insects.

STRIATED JAY-THRUSH.—Light brown with a tinge of amber is the general colour of this bird on the upper plumage; but the wings are reddish, and the tail chestnut brown. The under parts are white, with a reddish tinge. The total length is 9 inches; tail $3\frac{3}{4}$.

The striated jay-thrush is reported to be of common occurrence about Darjeeling, frequenting the densest thickets in pairs, and feeding on fruit and insects, but principally on the latter.

THE ORIOLES.

The following has been selected for consideration.

Family—*Oriolidæ.*
Genus—*Oriolus.* *O. indicus.* Black-naped Oriole.
O. kundoo. Syke's Oriole.

BLACK-NAPED ORIOLE.—This bird is bright yellow, with a greenish tinge on the back and wing coverts. A black horse-shoe mark extends from the base of the bill through the eyes to the nape. The tail is black; the two central feathers are barely tipped with yellow, but all the rest broadly. The wings are black, the secondaries broadly margined with yellow, and the tertiaries have the whole of the outer web of the same colour suffused with a tinge of green. The female is greener above, but otherwise resembles the male.

The total length of the bird is 10 inches, of which the tail takes up 3½. In both sexes the bill is pinky red, and the legs and feet lead colour. It is met with throughout India, but is not very abundant anywhere.

SYKE'S ORIOLE.—In this species the head and neck are deep black, and the rest of the plumage is rich yellow. It is found in Southern India and Ceylon.

THE DRONGO.

Family—*Dicruridæ.*
Genus—*Chibia.* *C. hottentotta.*

This family has representatives in India and the Indian Islands, but we can only notice one of them.

INDIAN DRONGO.—Though an eminently "nice" bird, this Hottentot among birds is not an attractive-looking one, in spite of its long erectile crest and flowing racket-shaped tail, for it is black, but gorgeous in purple reflections on the neck and breast, and deep glossy bronze green on the wings and tail. The abdomen, bill, and legs, and feet are coal black. Only the two outer tail feathers are prolonged and racket-shaped. The others measure about 5 inches, and the whole bird (not including the long tail feathers) about 12 or 13.

It is essentially an arboreal creature, and would perish from hunger rather than demean itself by picking up an insect from the ground.

The eggs, which are white, with purple spots, and of an elongated form, are generally two in number. The song of the drongo is much esteemed; but it has harsh notes, too, one resembling the creaking of a rusty wheel.

THE WEAVER BIRDS.

This is a very extensive group, but has few typical representatives in India, their principal habitat being in Southern Africa; some of the other genera are better known, namely, the ESTRELDÆ and MUNIÆ.

Family—*Ploceidæ*.

Genus—1.	*Estrelda.*	*E. amandava.*	Avadavat.
		E. formosa.	Green Avadavat.
2.	*Munia.*	*M. punctularia.*	Nutmeg Bird.
		M. topela.	Topela Finch.
		M. malacca.	Black-headed Finch.
		M. cucullata.	Bronze-winged Finch.

	M. rubro-nigra.	Chestnut - bellied Finch.
	M. striata.	Striated Finch.
	M. acuticauda.	Sharp-tailed Finch.
	M. malabarica.	Indian Silverbill.
3. *Ploceus.*	*P. manyar.*	Manyar Weaver Bird.
	P. bengalensis.	Bengal Weaver Bird

AVADAVAT.—The male, in his full summer plumage, is more or less crimson in colour, darker on the throat, breast, cheeks, and upper tail coverts. The tail is black, and the flanks and sides covered with numerous small round white spots. The bill is vermilion, and the eyes crimson.

The female is olive brown above, with a reddish tinge on the rump, and grey underneath. After breeding, the males become like her, and so remain until the pairing season returns.

This little bird is found throughout India, but is of rarer occurrence in the south. It frequents gardens in large numbers, and more especially sugar-cane plantations and long grass. It makes a big nest of grass in a bush, or among reeds, and lays from six to eight small white eggs of a rounded form.

The avadavat measures about 4 inches in length, of which the tail takes up $1\frac{3}{8}$. It has a pretty little song, and feeds on small seeds, such as millet, bearing confinement well.

GREEN WAXBILL, or GREEN AVADAVAT.—The upper plumage is light olive green; the quills and tail dusky, tinged, as to the former, with brown; the under surface is pale yellow, with broad transverse dashes of dark grey on the flanks and sides of the abdomen; the bill is red, and the legs and feet brown. In total length it measures about 4 inches, of which the tail occupies $1\frac{3}{8}$.

The green avadavat is found in Central India, keeping to the woods, where it assembles in considerable numbers, except during the actual season for breeding, when it separates into pairs.

The nest and eggs resemble those of a common avadavat.

NUTMEG BIRD.—On the upper surface the colour of the plumage is brown, deeper on the head and neck, and inclining to whitish yellow on the rump; the throat, breast,

FIG. 46. *The Bronze-Winged Mannikin.*

and flanks are white, covered with numerous zigzag bars of black; the bill and legs are lead colour. In total length this little bird measures $4\frac{1}{2}$ inches, $1\frac{1}{2}$ of which go to the tail.

It is of common occurrence in Northern India, but of local distribution. The nest, which is very large, and usually built in thorny bushes, contains five or six eggs.

A curious feature in the natural history of this little bird is its habit of singing in dumb show, that is, for many human ears, for to judge by the attention paid to the performer by his companions the harmony must be audible to them.

Malacca Finch.—The head and neck are silvery grey; the under tail coverts are black; and all the rest of the plumage is rich cinnamon brown, brightest on the upper tail coverts. Length, 4½ inches; tail, 1½.

The nest is placed among reeds, is of large size, covered, and contains four or five white eggs.

Chestnut-Bellied Finch.—This bird has the head, neck, and upper part of the breast deep velvety black; and all the rest of the plumage bright cinnamon brown, passing to maroon on the upper tail coverts. In size, habits, and nidification, it is like the last.

Striated Finch.—The general colour of this little bird is brownish black, the quills of each feather forming a line of a lighter shade of the same colour, an arrangement that gives the bird the striated appearance from which its name is derived. Its white, fawn, and parti-coloured cage-bred descendants are known by the name of Bengalee, and are very generally bred in aviaries, where they nest as freely as canaries, and, like the latter, are at times but indifferent feeders; however, a good pair once secured, they will go on rearing brood after brood for years at all seasons. The statement made by a recent writer that only one, or, at the most, two young are hatched at a time is merely the result of inexperience, for they are very prolific when rationally treated; but all that person's statements must be taken *cum grano*, and a very big grain, too, for he has a characteristic habit of jumping to conclusions from insufficient data, and the worst of it is that he sticks to first impressions, even when disproved by subsequent ascertained facts, which is decidedly unwise.

Manyar Weaver Bird.—The headquarters of these

curious birds is in Africa, but this and the following species occur in India in considerable numbers; but, nevertheless, are often confounded with their African connections.

The manyar weaver has the crown of the head of an intensely yellow colour; the lores, cheeks, ear coverts, chin, throat, and breast are brownish black; the back, wings, and tail brown, the feathers of the back being marked with a mesial dark line; the primaries and the tail feathers are edged with yellow, and the upper tail coverts are reddish: the bill is black, and the length of the bird $5\frac{7}{10}$ inches, of which the tail takes up $1\frac{3}{4}$. The female has the head brown, streaked with black; the bill is pale horn-colour.

The nest of the manyar weaver is built among reeds, near their summit, and contains two or three eggs.

Bengal Weaver.—The crown is golden yellow; the back dusky brown; rump greyish brown, and the throat white; below it extends a broad brown pectoral band; bill pearly white. In the female the head is dull greyish brown. In length this weaver measures $5\frac{1}{4}$ inches; the tail, $1\frac{3}{4}$.

It is found in Lower Bengal, and builds in low bushes; the nest is not pensile, and is made of grass; many birds build in company, and it is thought they are polygamous.

THE FINCHES.

These birds curiously enough, are blended in an extraordinary manner with a variety of others, among which are a number of buntings, which is certainly confusing; but the whole subject of bird nomenclature is full of difficulties, and calls loudly for rearrangement on a "natural" basis, such a readjustment in "natural orders" as was effected by De Candolle for the plants; but who is to undertake the task?

The following have been selected for consideration :—

Family—*Fringillidæ.*

Genus		Species	Common name
1.	*Chrysomitris.*	*C. spinoides.*	Indian Siskin.
2.	*Emberiza.*	*E. luteola.*	Red-headed Bunting.
3.	*Melopus.*	*M. melanicterus.*	Crested Black Bunting.

INDIAN SISKIN.—In the male the forehead, occiput, and nape are yellow, and the remaining upper parts olive brown; the wings are black, with a yellow spot on the coverts, and a pale yellow band on the primaries; the tail is dusky in the centre, but the side feathers are yellow. The female is duller in appearance, her yellow parts not being as bright as in the male, and the black has a brownish tinge. The length of the Indian siskin is 5½ inches, of which the tail measures 2. It is found throughout the Himalayas.

RED-HEADED BUNTING.—The head, neck, and breast are bright deep chestnut brown; the back and scapulars yellow, with dark brown stripes; the rump and upper tail coverts are yellow; the primaries and the tail brown; the under parts below the breast are rich yellow. Its full length is 7 inches, of which the tail takes up 3.

The red-headed bunting is locally distributed throughout India during the cold weather only. It breeds in Afghanistan, and has a very sweet and melodious song, which causes it the loss of its liberty very often, when it does very well, providing a sufficiency of insects be added to its diet of seed.

CRESTED BLACK BUNTING.—The whole body, with the crest, is deep glossy black; the wings and tail are dark cinnamon, with dusky tips; the tail coverts at the base are black. The length is $6\frac{1}{2}$ inches, of which the tail measures $2\frac{3}{4}$.

The female is dusky brown above, with light olivaceous brown edging, and a much smaller crest. It frequents the Himalayas, and has an agreeable chirping song.

THE STARLINGS.

This group has numerous representatives in India, some of which are classified as follows.

Family—*Sturnidæ*.

Genus—1.	*Sturnopastor.*	*S. contra.*	Pied Mynah.
2.	*Acridotheres.*	*A. gingianianus.*	Indian Mynah.
		A. tristis.	Common Mynah.
		A. fuscus.	Brown Mynah.
3.	*Sturnia.*	*S. malabarica.*	Malabar Mynah.
4.	*Pastor.*	*P. roseus.*	Rose-coloured Pastor.
		P. blythi.	Blyth's Pastor.
5.	*Gracula.*	*G. intermedia.*	Larger Hill Mynah.
		G. religiosa.	Small Hill Mynah.

PIED MYNAH.—The head, neck, and upper breast glossy black; ear coverts white, a colour that extends in a narrow line on each side of the face to the nape; the back, wings, and tail are black, with a faint gloss; the upper tail coverts are white, and there is an oblique bar of the same on the wing. Underneath, from the breast backwards, the plumage is white, tinged with ashen red; the under tail coverts are white; the bill is red at the base, and has a yellow tip; the legs are yellow, and the eyes brown, but the orbits and the nude skin round them are yellow. In length it measures 9 inches, $2\frac{3}{4}$ of which belong to the tail.

The black of the adult is replaced by brown in the young.

In Bengal the pied mynah is known by the name of ablaka. It is a familiar bird, associating with its fellows in flocks, and when tame is extremely imitative.

The nest is large, and made with sticks, grass, etc., on trees at an elevation of 8 or 9 feet from the ground. The eggs are three or four in number, of a clear greenish blue.

INDIAN, or BANK MYNAH.—The head, short occipital crest, lores, ear coverts, and nape are glossy black, and the rest of the plumage dull cinereous black, fading on the under surface to grey; there is a red spot about, the centre of the wings, which are otherwise black. The tail is black, tipped with rusty black: the bill is red, with a yellow tip, and the nude skin on the face has a reddish tinge. The total length is $8\frac{1}{2}$ inches, $3\frac{1}{4}$ of which belong to the tail.

It is found in Bengal, more especially in the Gangetic district, where it burrows into the banks of rivers for the purpose of nidification; the eggs are as many as seven or eight, of a greenish blue colour. It feeds on fruit and insects of all kinds.

COMMON MYNAH.—The head, which is ornamented with an occipital crest, the neck and breast are deep glossy black, and the remaining parts are snuff brown, which is deepest on the back and wing coverts. The primaries are black, and have white spots at their base; the black tail is tipped with white, and the other under parts are white. The bill and the orbits are yellow, as are also the legs; the eyes are reddish brown. Total length, 10 inches, of which the tail occupies 3½.

It is found throughout India, preferring towns and villages to the open country; it is gregarious, and feeds on grain, fruit, and insects.

The common mynah is possessed of a great variety of notes, and breeds mostly under the eaves of houses. It is frequently domesticated, and learns to speak and repeat a great number of domestic sounds.

It is sacred to the god Ram Deo, and has been introduced to Mauritius, where it is now quite naturalised.

Brown Mynah.—In this bird the head, small frontal crest, and ear coverts are deep glossy black; the rest of the upper plumage is brownish black, with a vinous tinge; the primaries are black, with a white spot at the base, and the black tail feathers have each a white tip; the abdomen is reddish grey, and the under tail coverts are white; the bill is orange, and the legs yellow. The total length is 9 inches, of which the tail occupies 3.

It is found on hills and in jungles throughout India; and in the south it has grey eyes, but in the north they are yellow.

Its habits, food, and nidification are the same as the last and preceding species.

Malabar Mynah.—This small bird, which is also known by the name of grey-headed pagoda starling, has the bill yellow, with a tinge of blue at the base; the head and long feathers of the upper part of the neck, as well as the wings and the terminal half of the tail, are grey; the flights are bluish, and the neck and breast vinous brown; the legs and feet are very light grey. Its total length is about 6 inches, 2½ of which belong to the tail.

These rather pretty birds are easily kept, and will

breed in confinement; their natural diet consists for the most part of insects, but in the house they will partake of and thrive on a mixture of German paste, hard-boiled egg, crushed biscuit, and dried ants' eggs; if a few fresh insects can be added now and then, so much the better. They nest in holes of trees, or buildings, like most of the starling tribe.

Rose-Coloured Pastor.—This bird Morris includes among "British Birds" on the strength of an individual or two shot in England. The bill and long erectile crest are jet black; the throat, upper part of the breast, and the wings and tail are bluish and brownish black, and the rest of the plumage is a pale rose colour. The size is about that of the English starling, namely, 8½ inches, 2½ or 3 of which belong to the tail.

It devours vast quantities of insects of the grasshopper and locust tribes, and must be of immense value from an agricultural point of view. It is found throughout India, and derives its name of pastor from its habit of accompanying cattle in the field to feed on the insects disturbed by their feet.

Blyth's, or White-Headed Pastor.—The head, long crest, neck and breast are silvery white, and the back and scapulars grey: the belly and tail coverts rufous, and the outer webs of the primaries and tertiaries, as well as the coverts, grey; the bill is blue at the base, green in the centre, and yellow at the tip; the eyes are greyish white, and the total length of the bird 8½ inches, 3 of which belong to the tail.

It is found in Malabar in small companies among the dense forests of that region, where it feeds on fruit, rarely descending to the ground, but passing its life among the branches of the trees, in the hollow boughs of which it makes its nest.

SMALLER HILL MYNAH.—This bird, which Jerdon says is not held sacred like his larger relative, of which more anon, is black, with a white bar on the wings, but rich velvety black, with glossy green and purple reflections; the bill, legs, and feet, orbits, patches on the sides, and collar-like appendages of bare skin, are all bright orange yellow.

It is met with from Travancore to northern latitude 16° or 17°, breeding in holes of trees or of buildings, and is often caged on account of its imitative powers, which, however, are not as great as those of its relative, the

LARGER HILL MYNAH, which resembles it exactly in all but size, the latter bird measuring nearly a foot in length, and the former about 10 inches. It inhabits the lower ranges of the Himalayas, and is held in much esteem by the natives, as specially consecrated to some of their divinities.

THE CROWS.

These birds are represented in all parts of the world, and form a very distinct group or natural order. They are well represented in India, as the following selection will show:—

Family—*Corvidæ*.

Genus			
Genus—1.	*Corvus.*	*C. culminatus.*	Large-billed Crow.
		C. splendens.	Indian Crow.
2.	*Pica.*	*P. bootanensis.*	Himalayan Magpie.
3.	*Urocissa.*	*U. occipitalis.*	Occipital Blue Pie.
		U. flavirostris.	Yellow-billed Blue Pie.
4.	*Cissa.*	*C. venatoria.*	Hunting Crow.
5.	*Dendrocitta.*	*D. vagabunda.*	Wandering Tree Pie.

LARGE-BILLED CROW.—This bird is also called the Indian corby, and is glossy black above, dull black beneath, has a rounded tail, a raised bill with prominent culmen and a strongly curved tip; the bill, as well as the legs and feet, are black. Its total length is 21 inches, of which the tail takes up 7½.

It is the carrion crow of India, breeds from April to June on high, isolated trees, laying three or four eggs of a dull green colour, spotted with brown. It is very destructive to small animals, and domestic fowls and pigeons.

INDIAN CROW.—The scientific name of this bird would lead anyone unacquainted with its appearance to expect something in the bird of paradise line; and anyone forming such an opinion of it would be disappointed, for it is wholly black, shot with purple and steel blue reflections, after the manner of our own crows, but more glossy and brilliant. It measures from 15 to 18 inches in length, of which the tail occupies from 6¾ to 7.

This crow is widely distributed, and is found from the foot of the Himalayas to Ceylon; it is not strictly gregarious, but is rather of social habits, hunting in company for its food, which is extremely varied. The breeding season is from April to July.

OCCIPITAL BLUE PIE.—The head, neck, and breast are deep black; a long, occipital white band extends from the back of the neck down the whole length of it, gradually shading into blue; some of the feathers on the crown are tipped with white; the mouth and scapulars are cobalt blue; and the upper tail coverts are the same, but tipped with black; the wings are of a rich cobalt blue shade, but the quills are black, and the inner webs are all tipped with white; the tail is blue, and the two central feathers have white tips; all the others have a black, followed by a white, spot at their free extremities; the breast is white, with a purple tinge; the bill is coral, the legs reddish orange, and the eyes red. In length the occipital blue pie measures 26 inches, 17 to 18 of which belong to the tail.

It inhabits the lower ranges of the Himalayas, nesting in high trees, and down to a height of from 8 to 10 feet above the ground. The eggs number from three to five, are of a dull greenish grey with brown spots.

It is terrestrial in habit, seeking food on the ground, and bears confinement well.

Yellow-Billed Blue Pie.—The head, neck, and breast are black; there is a narrow white occipital band; the upper plumage is purple, shading to blue on the upper tail coverts; the bill is yellow. It inhabits the same localities as the last, and feeds chiefly on insects. It lays from three to five greenish fawn-coloured eggs, lightly blotched with brown.

Hunting Crow.—This magnificent specimen of the crow family is brilliant green, of the shade called chrysoprase, which fades gradually to a bluish greenish yellow on the head, the long feathers of which are capable of being raised into the form of a crest; black lines proceed from the lores, passing through the eyes to the nape; the wing coverts and primaries are dark red, fading to rusty brown; the secondaries are tipped with pale bluish green, and broadly edged with black; the central tail feathers have white tips, and the others are black and white; the bill and the legs are coral red.

This bird, which is frequently tamed and trained to hunt small birds, feeds naturally on insects for the most part. It is very shrike-like in its habits, and is mostly found in the South-East Himalayas.

Wandering Pie.—In this species the head, neck, and breast are of a dull sooty-brown colour, which is deepest on the forehead, chin, and throat; the scapulars are black, and the tail ashen grey; the bill is black. The total length is about 16 inches, 10 of which belong to the tail. It is found all over India; feeds on fruit, insects, young birds, and eggs, bats, and other small animals.

It makes a large nest of sticks in lofty trees, and lays from three to five eggs of a greenish fawn colour.

Like the last species it bears confinement very well, and becomes very tame and tricky.

THE LARKS.

These birds are represented in India by several species bearing more or less resemblance to our own well-known skylark, and from among them the following selection has been made:—

Family—*Alaudidæ.*

Genus		Species	Common name
1.	*Alauda.*	*A. gulgula.*	Indian Skylark.
		A. cristata.	Crested Lark.
2.	*Mirafra.*	*M. affinis.*	Madras Bush Lark.

Indian Skylark.—This bird bears considerable resemblance, both in habits and appearance, to its English congener; it is dark brown above, with a reddish margin to each feather, the forehead, chin, and throat being darker than the other parts. The under parts are white, with a tinge of red, and grey spots; there is a narrow pale eye-streak, and a moderately long erectile crest. The total length is 6½ inches, of which 2¼ belong to the tail.

Though generally like the English skylark, the species under consideration is ruddier, and those that are found in the hills are brighter in colour than others that frequent the plains.

It is found throughout India, and breeds from March to June on the ground, under cover of a tuft of long grass or a stone.

The eggs vary in number from three to five; the ground colour is greyish white, with many brown spots, streaks, and lines.

This lark, like its English namesake, soars when singing, and is in great request as a delicacy for the table, enormous numbers being captured for that purpose, so that in some quarters it has become visibly scarce within the last few years.

CRESTED LARK.—This bird has a wide habitat, and extends into Central and Western Europe. It is of a pale earthy-brown colour, redder above than below, with dark mesial lines to the feathers; the lower parts are whitish, with a few pale brown streaks on the breast; the bill is yellow. In total length it measures $7\frac{1}{4}$ inches, $2\frac{3}{4}$ of which belong to the tail.

It is of common occurrence in the Deccan, but is not known in Bengal or in the Himalayas; it generally frequents sandy plains, and rises when singing, but not to such an elevation or for so long a time as the last.

The nest is made on the ground, and contains four or five eggs of a yellowish white colour, with small greyish yellow spots scattered over the surface.

It is frequently caged on account of its song, and has considerable imitative power.

MADRAS BUSH LARK.—The plumage in the case of this species is dusky brown above, with reddish edging; the ear coverts are pale rufous brown, tipped with a darker shade of the same; the under parts are greyish white, with large oval white spots on the breast. In full length it measures about 6 inches, the tail taking up $1\frac{3}{4}$.

It is of common occurrence on the Malabar coast, Carnatic

Mysore, etc. Of familiar, bold disposition, frequenting gardens and cultivated ground, it may be seen perching on trees and shrubs, but nevertheless makes its nest on the ground.

The eggs are four or five in number, of a greenish grey colour.

The song of the bush lark is very agreeable, and is uttered for the most part during its short flights from one shrub or bush to another. It is often caged, and does well, if provided with a sufficiency of insect food.

THE PITTAS.

A very distinctive group, found for the most part in the islands of the Indian Ocean; but there is a continental example.

Family—*Pittidæ*.
Genus—*Pitta*. *P. bengalensis*. Bengal Pitta.

BENGAL PITTA, or YELLOW-BREASTED GROUND THRUSH, as it is also called.—The head is olive brown, with a median black stripe extending from the base of the upper mandible to the back of the neck, where it meets with another black line that passes over the ears; a white line about the eye on either side extends to the nape, but the two do not quite meet in the centre; the back, rump, scapulars, and wing coverts are dull bluish green, and the long upper tail coverts are pale blue; on the shoulder is an azure patch; the tail is black, tipped with dull blue; the chin, throat, and the sides of the neck are white; the rest of the lower parts are isabelline, except the middle abdomen, vent, and under tail coverts, which are scarlet. The length of this bird is 7 inches, 1$\frac{7}{10}$ of which belong to the tail.

It is found throughout India, affecting forest lands in preference to any other. Its wing power is feeble.

It is a shy and solitary species, nearly always met with singly, except during the actual pairing season.

It feeds almost entirely on the ground, where it finds an abundance of those insects on which, for the most part, it subsists.

Some of the insular pittas are very gorgeously attired, but they are very seldom seen in confinement, for which their habits and disposition seem to unfit them.

THE HORNBILLS.

Family—*Bucerotidæ*.

Genus		Species	Common name
1.	*Buceros.*	*B. rhinoceros.*	Rhinoceros Hornbill.
2.	*Dichoceros.*	*D. bicornis.*	Concave-casqued Hornbill.
3.	*Anthracoceros.*	*A. coronatus.*	Crowned Hornbill.
		A. malabaricus.	Indian Pied Hornbill.

These extraordinary birds, whose heads seem to be even more enormously over-weighted than the toucans, are, nevertheless, quite equal to bearing the burden that is laid upon them, and are even remarkable for the jollity, not to say levity, of their disposition. Of the several species resident in India, those selected for consideration have lived in the menagerie of the London Zoological Society.

RHINOCEROS, or GREAT HORNBILL.—Found in Malabar and the Malay Peninsula. A large bird, measuring 4 feet in length, 17 inches of which belong to the tail. It takes between two and three years to reach its full growth, and is consequently a long-lived bird. When alone—and it is rarely found in more than pairs—it is a quiet, silent creature; but when two or more are gathered together, they can, and often do, make an awful noise.

It breeds in holes of trees, and while the female is sitting on her two white eggs, the male plasters up the hole with mud, leaving but a small aperture through which she can only just poke the end of her bill in order to be fed, a duty he discharges very assiduously.

The head, base of the bill, back, wings, and belly are black; the neck ends of the upper tail coverts, tail, thighs, vent, and wing spot are white; a broad black band crosses the terminal third of the tail; the broad casque is red above, passing into yellow, the tip is red, and the lower mandible is whitish yellow.

CONCAVE-CASQUED HORNBILL.—This is a smaller bird than the last, measuring but 22 inches in total length, 8 of which belong to the tail. It is found in all parts of India, generally in pairs, and in some parts its flesh is partaken of as an adjuvant by parturient women. The plumage is grey, darker above; the tail is black towards the end, but the extreme tip is white.

CROWNED, or MALABAR PIED HORNBILL.—Found in the jungles of Southern India, where it lives mainly on fruit, breeding in holes of trees, which it plasters up with mud while the female is sitting.

The general colour is black, but the breast, tips of the primaries, and secondaries, and the three outside tail feathers on each side are white; the base of both mandibles is black, and the hinder margin of the casque also, in the male; the whole bill is very large and much compressed laterally. In length it measures about 3 feet, of which the tail takes up 14 inches.

THE BARBETS.

The following have been selected as representative of the group.

Family—*Capitonidæ*.
Genus—*Megalæma*. *M. asiatica*. Blue-cheeked Barbet.
M. virens. Great Barbet.
M. hodgsoni. Hodgson's Barbet.

BLUE-CHEEKED BARBET.—This bird is known to the natives of the parts it frequents by the name of "bussunt bairi," or "old woman of the spring." It is an extremely noisy creature, lives entirely on fruit, and usually has two broods each season.

Above, the colour is green, with a faint coppery gloss on the back; the under parts are paler, and have more of a grassy tint; the forehead, occiput, and a spot on each side of the fore-neck crimson; a black band crosses the crown and forms an upper eye-mark; the cheeks, ear coverts, moustache, throat, and front of neck, including a narrow, inferior eye-mark, are verditer blue; the bill is greenish yellow at the base, and black at the tip. The total length of the bird is 9½ inches, 3 of which are taken up by the tail. It is found in Lower Bengal, where it breeds in holes it excavates in trees.

The GREAT BARBET is found in the Himalayas, and is distinguished by its loud and plaintive notes. It measures 13 inches in total length, 3 of which belong to the tail.

HODGSON'S BARBET is another Himalayan species, green above, paler on flanks and belly; the vent and under tail coverts are yellow; the head, neck, throat, breast, and upper abdomen are whitish; the bill orange horn. It measures 10½ inches in full length, of which the tail takes up 3.

THE CUCKOOS.

Family—*Cuculidæ*.

Genus—1. *Eudynamis*. *E. orientalis*. Black Cuckoo.
2. *Centropus*. *C. rufipennis*. Indian Coucal.

Black Cuckoo, or Koel.—This bird is found all over Indian and in Ceylon. It frequents gardens and groves, feeds on fruit, and is not at all shy. When taking wing it emits a series of harsh cries, audible at a considerable distance, something after the fashion of the European jay, and, during the breeding season, it may be heard all through the night. The female deposits an egg in the nest of the common crow, by whom it is hatched and the young reared. The egg is pale olive green, with many dark red spots. The general colour of the bird itself is rich glossy greenish black; the bill is pale green, and the inside of the mouth red; the eyes are crimson, and the legs slaty blue. Length, 15½ inches; tail, 7½.

Indian, or Common Coucal.—This bird is frequently termed crow-pheasant in India, where it frequents timbered as well as cultivated grounds, feeding on insects, reptiles, and terrestrial molluscs. It builds a large domed nest of twigs, and lays from two to five eggs, oval in shape, and of a pure white colour, on which it sits like most other birds, so that it seems to be out of place among the parasite cuckoos. The breeding season lasts from January to July.

The head, neck, lower back, upper tail coverts, and all the under parts are purplish black, but the tail has a green gloss, and the upper back and the wings are deep rufous bay; the bill is black, the eyes crimson, and the legs black. Length, 19 inches; tail, 10.

The young are very different in appearance, being barred throughont with black and rufous on the upper surface, and dusky white beneath.

THE PARROTS.

A numerous group. The following have been selected:—

Family—*Palæornithidæ.*

Genus	Species	Name
1. *Palæornis.*	*P. Alexandri.*	Alexandrine Parrakeet.
	P. torquatus.	Ring-necked Parrakeet.
	P. cyanocephalus.	Blossom-headed Parrakeet.
	P. rosa.	Rosy Parrakeet.
	P. fasciatus.	Banded Parrakeet.
	P. columboides.	Malabar Parrakeet.
2. *Loriculus.*	*L. asiaticus.*	Ceylonese Hanging Parrakeet.
	L. galgulus.	Blue-crowned Hanging Parrakeet.
3. *Lorius.*	*L. domicella.*	Purple-capped Lory.

ALEXANDRINE PARRAKEET.—The name bestowed on this bird, under the supposition that it was brought to Europe in the first instance by the followers of Alexander the Great, is probably a misnomer, as in all likelihood, being so much generally distributed, it was the following species, and not the one under consideration, that was first seen in ancient Greece. However, the name has been bestowed, and there is nothing more to be said about it.

General colour, grass green. On the sides and back of the neck there is a band of rosy red, followed by one of a black colour, that broadens under the bill into a beard-like patch. On the top of each wing is a large dull red spot which serves to differentiate this bird from all its congeners. The bill is dark purplish red.

The female is all green, and has no band or ring on the neck. All the young resemble her, but the males are a couple of years, at least, before they assume the marks distinctive of their sex.

The four white round eggs are deposited in the hollow bough or trunk of a tree, and are hatched in about seventeen days. The breeding season is in December, and January to March.

Ring-Necked Parrakeet.—This bird, the green parrot of India, is little more than half the size of the preceding. It is green all over, and the male has a red and black band on the neck, but no moustache. The female lacks the band or ring, and is all green. The bill is dull coral red, and a variety found in Africa has the upper mandible black.

The ring-necked parrakeet nests in holes of trees, walls, and buildings. The eggs are white, rather round, and always four in number. Like the last, it is readily domesticated, and, when hand-reared from the nest, becomes very tame, and learns to speak more or less distinctly.

When acclimatised, that is, after having been turned out in May, these birds are quite hardy, and will winter safely out of doors in England, and breed, if suitable accommodation is provided for them, in a well-appointed aviary.

The food for both species is grain and seeds of all kinds. They do not drink much, but should have water for bathing.

BLOSSOM-HEADED PARRAKEET.—This pretty little species

FIG. 47.—*Purple-Capped Lory.*

is also known in England as the plum-headed parrakeet. It is found throughout India, but is less common than the preceding. In the male the head is a deep reddish purple or plum-colour; the upper mandible is red, and the lower black, and from its base starts a thick black line, tapering as it goes to meet its fellow from the opposite at the middle of the nape. There is a small red wing spot, and the tail is blue, tipped with pale blue and white. The female has a lavender grey head.

The male is between two and three years old before he puts on the distinctive mark of his sex, from which it may be inferred that the species is a long-lived one. It is as hardy as the preceding, and breeds freely in confinement. Like the species already mentioned, it lays four small round white eggs, which are hatched in about seventeen days.

Rosy Parrakeet.—The only difference between this and the species immediately preceding it is that this one has a brighter-coloured, rosier cap than the other, with little or none of the purple sub-tint that distinguishes the blossom-head. It is also a trifle smaller than the latter.

Banded Parrakeet.—Top of head and cheeks bluish yellowish grey; forehead and lores, and a deep moustache or neck band, black; nape grass green; large yellowish green wing spot; neck and breast pale rosy red; belly and remaining under parts bluish yellowish green; upper mandible red; lower black.

Malabar Parrakeet.—Narrow frontlet grey; lores, eye-streak, and cheek sea-green; head and back ashen grey; throat and ring black, then a ring of bluish green; on the upper part of the neck a bluish green shield; lower part of back green; rump and upper tail coverts bluish green; a black spot of small extent on the lesser wing coverts: the long central pair of the tail feathers dark blue, ashen grey on the under surface; vent and under tail coverts yellowish green; upper mandible dusky red; lower brownish red. The female is not different.

Ceylonese Hanging Parrakeet.—This little bird, whose form approximates it to the love-birds, from which it is widely differentiated by its habits, is a native of Ceylon, and about the size of a common sparrow, or

$5\frac{3}{4}$ inches in total length, of which the tail occupies about 2 inches. The general colour of the plumage is green, darker above, lighter on the under surface; the forehead and crown reddish purple; rump and upper tail coverts deep brick red.

BLUE-CROWNED HANGING PARRAKEET.—Both this species and the last should be called dwarf or pigmy parrots, and the name parrakeet be reserved for the species that possess long narrow, and for the most part pointed, tails. The general colour is grass green, with a bright blue spot on the crown of the head, a triangular deep orange mark on the upper part of the back, a scarlet spot on the breast, and a similar one on the rump and tail, the bill blackish, eyes dark brown, and the strong feet and legs flesh colour. The female has no red mark on the breast.

Notwithstanding the fact that their natural diet consists of the pollen and nectar of the flowers of the trees among which these birds pass their lives, clambering about with their heads hanging down, they soon become accustomed to a diet of rice and milk and sugar, and will live for a long time in health in a cage or aviary, providing their filthy habits do not bring about a shortening, by violence, of their existence.

THE OWLS.

Family—*Asionidæ.*

Genus—1. *Syrnium.*	*S. indranee.*	Indranee Owl.
2. *Bubo.*	*B. bengalensis.*	Bengal Eagle Owl.
	B. coromandus.	Coromandel Eagle Owl.
3. *Ketupa.*	*K. ceylonensis.*	Ceylon Fish Owl.
4. *Athene.*	*A. brama.*	Spotted Owl.

INDRANEE OWL.—This bird, also known as the brown wood owl, is found in all the southern parts of India; it is strictly nocturnal in its habits, and makes the night hideous with its doleful cries. It varies a good deal in size, measuring from 19 to 21 inches in full length, the larger birds being the females. The general colour above is brown, which is darkest on the head and neck; the greater wing coverts, scapulars, and tertiaries are banded with white; the rump and upper tail coverts are marked with rufous brown and white.

CEYLON FISH OWL.—This handsome owl is much less strictly nocturnal than the last, is of a rich tawny brown colour, variously marked and spotted with several shades of the same colour.

It frequents the banks of rivers, and feeds almost exclusively on fish, which it catches in its powerful feet; it flies swiftly and strongly, and breeds in February and March.

THE FALCONS.

Family—*Falconidæ*.

Genus			
Genus—1.	*Pernis.*	*P. ptilorhyncha.*	Crested Honey Buzzard.
2.	*Haliaster.*	*H. indus.*	Brahminy Kite.
3.	*Haliaetus.*	*H. leucoryphus.*	Mace's Sea Eagle.
4.	*Spizaetus.*	*S. ceylonensis.*	Ceylon Eagle Hawk.
		S. caligatus.	Malayan Eagle Hawk.
5.	*Spilornis.*	*S. cheela.*	Cheela Eagle.
6.	*Falco.*	*F. jugger.*	Jugger Falcon.
7.	*Milvus.*	*M. govinda.*	Indian Kite.

8. *Baza.*	*B. lophotes.*	Crested Black Kite.
9. *Vultur.*	*V. calvus.*	Pondicherry Vulture.
10. *Gyps.*	*G. bengalensis.*	Bengal Vulture.
11. *Neophron.*	*N. percnopterus.*	Egyptian Vulture.

CRESTED HONEY BUZZARD.—This bird is found all over India where there are forests; it feeds on honey, and supplements that with the insects that produce it, as well as with small birds, their eggs and young. The lores are thickly feathered, as well as the legs and feet, a provision of Nature that must serve to almost completely protect the despoiler from the attacks of the infuriated insects, whose labours of months it overthrows, so to speak, in a moment.

As the name implies, this buzzard's head is ornamented with a crest, which varies in degree of development with almost every individual. It flies strongly, but not very rapidly, in a straight line, and nests in trees, laying two or three white eggs speckled with numerous greyish red spots. The general colour of the plumage is brown; and, as usually happens among birds of prey, the female is considerably larger than the male, the total length of the latter being 23 inches, while that of the female is 25. The tail measures respectively 9 and 11 inches.

BRAHMINY KITE.—This bird also is found throughout India, in the neighbourhood of lakes, ponds, and cultivated ground; in Calcutta it fairly swarms in the neighbourhood of the shipping, where it acts the part of scavenger in the most approved manner.

It nests in trees during the months of February and March, making a nest of sticks among the branches, or taking possession of one already constructed by a crow.

The eggs are usually two in number, of a greyish white colour with rusty brown spots.

The head, neck, body below, as far as the middle of the abdomen, white, with long narrow streaks of dark brown: the rest of the plumage is bright reddish chocolate, darkest on the interscapulars and back; the primaries are black.

Total length, 21 inches, of which the tail takes up 6½.

MACE'S SEA EAGLE.—This species is pretty generally distributed throughout India, but chiefly on the coast and up the course of the large rivers, where it feeds principally on water snakes, but also catches fish, for which it does not dive, but of which it often robs fishing birds, such as the osprey, gulls, etc.; it also eats rats, crabs, and, in fact, anything it can catch and swallow. The breeding season extends from December to February.

CEYLON EAGLE HAWK.—This bird is of a deep brown colour on the upper surface of the body, especially on the interscapulars and the crown of the head, in which latter situation the feathers are almost black.

PONDICHERRY VULTURE.—This species is found in the south-eastern parts of India principally, but not in great numbers; it is rare for more than two of them to be seen in company. The general colour of the plumage is blackish brown; the bare parts of the head and neck have a fleshy tint, and a tuft of soft downy white feathers spring from the centre of the breast over the region of the crop.

In total length, the Pondicherry vulture measures about 3 feet; its powers of flight are considerable, the large broad wings reaching, when folded, nearly to the end of the tail.

EGYPTIAN VULTURE.—This bird properly forms part of the African avifauna, but as it also penetrates into our Indian Empire, as well as occasionally into Europe, it may be described in the present place.

It is almost white, in fact, quite so, with the exception of the quills of the wings or primaries, which are dusky brown. The bill, face, and legs are yellow, but in the immature subject the plumage is chocolate brown; the feathers of the neck and shoulders are tipped with grey, and the bill and feet are dull brownish yellow.

The full adult plumage is not attained until the bird is about three years old.

It is a powerful and graceful flyer, soaring at a considerable altitude without any apparent exertion for hours together.

The nest is made on a rocky ledge, and the eggs, two or three in number, are greyish white.

THE PELICANS.

Family—*Pelecanidæ.*
Genus—*Pelecanus.* *P. mitratus.*

Mitred Pelican.—There is no very marked difference between this bird and the other members of the family to which it belongs, as they all bear an unmistakable likeness to each other, the points of difference being only those of size (in which they do not vary much) and of colour, which is white, with various minor spots and marks of grey or black.

THE DARTERS.

Family—*Plotidæ.*
Genus—*Plotus.* *P. melanogaster.*

Indian Darter, or Snake Bird.—This curious creature,

whose long, thin, mobile neck and small pointed head give it an extremely snake-like appearance when seen protruded above the surface of the water, is found all over India wherever there is a pond of any extent. It swims low, and dives expertly, remaining for a long time beneath the surface, and when obliged to rise for air, the nostrils only are thrust above the water.

Its food consists chiefly of fish, of which it consumes an enormous quantity, as the digestion is extremely rapid. After feeding, it flies to the bough of some neighbouring tree to sleep off its meal, but the siesta is but of short duration, and the darter is quickly in the water again in quest of more prey.

The forehead, nape, and neck are brown, with a paler edging, which gives to these parts a mottled appearance; the median line is the darkest portion of each feather; the cheeks, chin, and throat are white.

The female is lighter in colour, but otherwise resembles her mate.

The snake bird nests in trees, making a huge pile of sticks, in which it deposits its three or four bluish eggs.

The total length of the adult bird is 32 inches, of which the tail occupies 9.

The scapular feathers are long and pointed, and are looked on as a badge of royalty by the Khasias, and esteemed for decorative purposes by all.

There are several other kinds of these birds, but the above is the only one for which we can find room.

THE STORKS.

Family—*Ciconidæ.*

Genus—

1. *Leptoptilus.*	*L. argala.*	Indian Adjutant.
2. *Pseudotantalus.*	*P. leucocephalus.*	Indian Tantalus.

ADJUTANT.—This well-known bird is common in Northern India, where it is migratory, arriving in April or May, and departing again in September and October; but a few unmated or barren individuals remain in their usual haunts all the year round. They are very familiar and fearless, and are of common occurrence in the streets of Calcutta, where it feeds on the offal of all kinds thrown from the houses in the native quarter of the city. It also kills snakes and rats, and generally comports itself like a vulture, to which bird its almost bare neck and head give it somewhat of a resemblance.

The head, neck, and gular pouch are bare, with a few short, reddish yellow hairs scattered over them. At the point where the neck joins the breast, there is a ruff of pure white downy feathers; the upper plumage is grey, and the lower almost white. The large bill is of a dull pale green colour.

The gular pouch has no connection with the gullet, but is probably connected in some way with the bird's respiratory system. It increases in size with the age of the individual, and is larger in the male than in the female.

In full length, the adjutant measures about 5 feet. The wings reach almost to the end of the tail, and the bird has great power of flight, frequently soaring at a considerable elevation for a long time together without apparent effort.

It breeds among trees and on cliffs, and lays two white eggs.

The feathers known by the name of "marabou" are the under tail coverts of the adjutant.

INDIAN TANTALUS.—Common all over India. This species frequents rivers, tanks, ponds, and water generally; it feeds on fish, and nests on high trees. The eggs are large, white, and usually four in number.

Like the preceding, this bird becomes very tame and fearless.

It is also named the pelican ibis, and is white in colour, with the quills and tail of a rich glossy green; the tertiaries are tinged with rose, have a dark band near the end, and white tips; the lesser and median wing coverts are glossy green, with white borders; the greater wing coverts are white. The bill is deep yellow, with a green tip.

The total length of the tantalus is 42 inches, 7 of which belong to the tail.

THE DUCKS.

Family—*Anatidæ.*

Genus—	1. *Anser.*	*A. indicus.*	Bar-headed Goose.
	2. *Dendrocygna.*	*D. javanica.*	Indian Tree Duck.
		D. major.	Larger Tree Duck.
	3. *Sarcidiornis.*	*S. melanonota.*	Black-backed Goose.
	4. *Anas.*	*A. pœcilorhynchus.*	Spotted-billed Duck.
	5. *Rhodonessa.*	*R. caryophyllacea.*	Pink-headed Duck.
	6. *Fuligula*	*F. rufina.*	Red-crested Pochard.

Bar-Headed Goose.—This goose appears to be peculiar to India, where it is found in immense flocks, grazing on the banks of rivers. It is migratory in its movements, arriving south in October, and again departing towards the north in March.

The head is white, with two blackish bars on the occiput and nape; the back of the neck is brown, its sides white; the rest of the upper plumage is ashen grey, edged with white and tinged with pale reddish brown; the chin and throat are white, with a cinereous shade; the breast white; the abdomen and flanks cinnamon brown; the bill is yellow, the eyes brown, and the legs orange. The total length is 27 inches.

Indian Tree Duck.—This species abounds throughout India, assembling in large flocks during the winter season; the flight is laboured, and while on the wing it gives utterance to a loud sibilant call that can be heard at a considerable distance.

It nests on the ground, concealing its eggs among grass; they are white, and from six to eight in number.

The head and occiput are dull brown; the face, ears, and neck pale whity brown; the back and scapulars dark, almost black, each feather with a broad brown edge; the rump is glossy black; the upper tail coverts chestnut, and the tail brown, with a paler border. The lesser and median wing coverts are fine maroon red. The under parts, various; chin and throat white; neck light brown, gradually getting darker to dark brown, and then changing to yellow; the rest of the under parts dark rusty red, except vent and under tail coverts, which are light grey. The bill is black, the eyes brown, with yellow orbits, and the legs and feet lead colour. The total length is 18 inches, 2 of which are in the tail.

Larger Tree Duck.—This bird rather resembles the

last, but is larger, 21 inches in full length, 2½ of which are in the tail.

The head and neck are chestnut, which is darker on the top of the head, whence a dark line extends down the back of the neck; the chin, throat, and front of the neck are paler, and on the centre of the neck is a small patch of white hackled feathers. The upper part of the back and the scapulars are deep brown, with chestnut edges; bill, lead colour.

Black-Backed Goose.—This species is common in Central and Western India, but rare in Lower Bengal. It frequents grassy tanks, and similar situations, also paddy fields, where it does a good deal of harm. During the rains it wanders about from place to place, and breeds among long grass in July and August, laying from six to eight white eggs.

It is a simple, unwary creature, and is not much esteemed for the table.

Spotted-Billed Duck.—This bird is found in wooded districts throughout India, also in Ceylon, Burmah, etc, nesting on the ground among long grass; the eggs are greenish white, and vary in number from eight to ten. It flies slowly, and is loath to take wing, a circumstance that is not unregarded by the fowler, for the spotted-billed is one of the very best birds of its kind for the table.

The top of the head and the neck are dark sepia brown, with a paler edging; a dark brown line ending in a point passes through the eye, and forms a supercilium above it. The face and neck are dingy red, with small brown streaks; underneath it is dingy white, but the vent and under tail coverts are deep blackish brown. The bill is black, with a large bright red spot at the base, and a yellow tip.

The total length is 24 inches, 4 of which belong to the tail.

PINK-HEADED DUCK.—This bird is chiefly found in Bengal, frequenting sheltered tanks and jheels; it breeds at the close of the hot season, quacks much after the fashion of the domestic duck, and displays a rosy tint under the wings when flying; its total length is 24 inches, of which the short tail takes up 4½. Head and upper parts pale rose pink; develops a small rosy crest during the breeding season.

RED-CRESTED POCHARD.—This duck has been already described under the heading of British birds, which see.

THE PIGEONS.

Family—*Carpophagidæ.*

Genus			
Genus—1.	*Carpophaga.*	*C. ænea.*	Bronze Fruit Pigeon.
2.	*Ptilopus.*	*P. jamboo.*	Jamboo Fruit Pigeon.
3.	*Erythrœnas.*	*E. pulcherrima.*	Red-crowned Pigeon.
4.	*Treron.*	*T. bicincta.*	Double-banded Pigeon.
		T. viridis.	Parrot Fruit Pigeon.
		T. phœnicoptera.	Purple-shouldered Pigeon.
		T. sphenura.	Wedge-tailed Pigeon.

We utterly fail to see the necessity or even the advisability of separating the pigeons that live on fruit from those whose principal diet consists of grain; but it has been thought otherwise by some authorities, and there for the present we leave the matter, in the hope of some day having an opportunity of reverting to it in a more satisfactory manner.

Sub-Family—*Columbidæ.*

Genus		Species	Common name
1.	*Geopelia.*	*G. striata.*	Barred Dove.
2.	*Turtur.*	*T. suratensis.*	Spotted Turtle-dove.
		T. meena.	Eastern Turtle-dove.
		T. picturatus.	Mauritian Turtle-dove.
		T. chinensis.	Chinese Turtle-dove.
		T humilis.	Dwarf Turtle-dove.
		T. aldabranus.	Aldabran Turtle-dove.
3.	*Chalcophaps.*	*C. indica.*	Green-winged Dove.
4.	*Calænas.*	*C. nicobarica.*	Nicobar Pigeon.

Barred, or Zebra Dove.—This little dove is found throughout the south of India, as well as in the Malaccan Peninsula, and the regions beyond to China; it is, perhaps, the most frequently imported of all the small foreign doves, and, where kept under favourable conditions as to temperature and space, breeds freely in confinement, the difficulty being to secure a veritable pair, as the sexes are almost exactly alike in outward appearance.

The forehead and throat are ashen grey, with a bluish tinge; the back and wings dark brown; the under wing coverts reddish brown, with fine black pencillings; the breast reddish; the abdomen and hinder parts whitish grey; the whole plumage, with the exception of the forehead, throat, tail, and under side of the wings, is streaked with black lines, finer on the under and wider on the upper surface of the body, so that every feather is marked or barred.

The voice of this little dove is a pretty and melodious

Fig. 48.—*Zebra Doves.*

coo, and in Java and parts of India it is caged on account of its "song." It is a very peaceful and retiring inmate of the mixed aviary, and yet the males at times have battles among themselves, when they manage to damage each other somewhat severely.

GREEN-WINGED DOVE.—This remarkably handsome pigeon is too big for an ordinary aviary, being about the

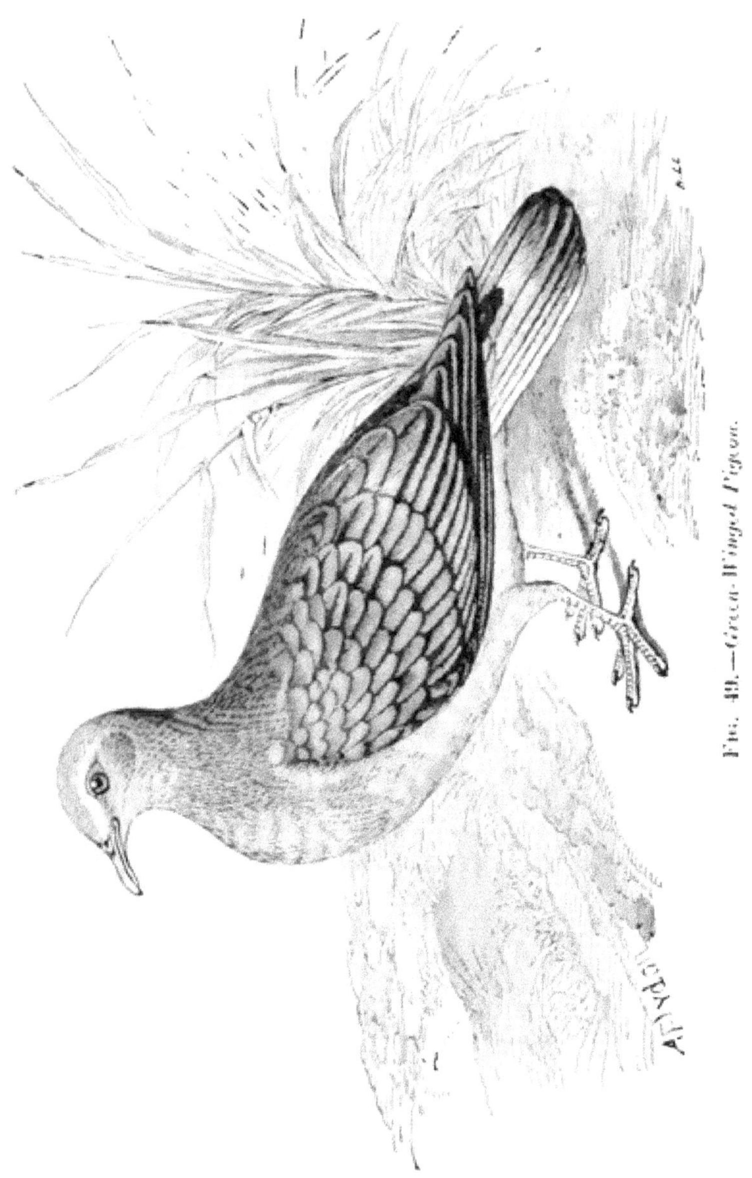

FIG. 49.—Green-Winged Pigeon.

size of the common blue rock pigeon; it is, however, very hardy and peaceful, and soon gets perfectly tame.

The general colour is brownish red, with green and gold metallic glossy reflections; the forehead is white, and there is a patch of the same colour on the shoulders; the bill is dark red, and the legs and feet coral red.

The female is much smaller than the male, but otherwise resembles him, except that her metallic colouring is not so vivid; the young resemble their mother at first, but the young males soon appear larger than the females.

These birds do not appear to mind the severest winter more than do our native pigeons; they breed freely, that is, two or three times in the season, laying two rather round white eggs on an apology for a nest, consisting of a few twigs carelessly collected together on any convenient ledge or shelf.

Any kind of small corn makes suitable feeding for them, but a little of Spratt's Patent Crissel is useful as a change, and they must have salt and gravel at their disposal, as well as some green food.

Nicobar Pigeon.—This fine pigeon is most resplendently attired, the long pointed feathers of the neck and flanks glistening with the brightest of metallic tints, among which green and gold predominate; the tail is short, square, and pure white. It is fairly hardy, but on account of its rarity is dear, and, consequently, it has not been fully proved as regards its powers of resistance to cold.

It should be fed and treated as recommended for the last species. Length about 14 inches; body plump.

GROUSE.

Family—*Pteroclidæ.*

Genus—*Pterocles.* *P. fasciatus.* Banded Sand Grouse.

Banded Sand Grouse.—This grouse is found throughout India, but not abundantly anywhere. It frequents bushy and rocky hills, where it lives in pairs. The eggs are cylindrical in conformation, and of a dark green colour, with black spots.

The general appearance of the bird is a bright fulvous yellow; the back, scapulars, and tail banded or barred with deep brown; a narrow white band marks the forehead; this is followed by a broad black one, which is succeeded by another narrow band of white, and after that is another black line, widening behind the eye and ending in a white spot; the occiput and the nape are marked with black streaks; the quills are brownish black, with narrow paler edges; the median and great wing coverts and some secondaries are broadly banded with deep black, and have white edges. A triple band separates the fulvous breast from the abdomen, the first maroon, the second cream, and the third unspotted chocolate brown, which last is the colour of the remaining parts where each feather is tipped with white. The bill is red, orbital skin lemon yellow, eyes dark brown. The total length is 10 inches, of which the tail measures 4. The weight is about 7 or 8 ounces.

THE PHEASANTS.

Family—*Phasianidæ.*

Genus—

1. *Galloperdix.*	*G. lunulata.*	Hardwick's Spur Fowl.
	G. spadicea.	Rufous Spur Fowl.
	G. ceylonensis.	Ceylon Spur Fowl.

2. *Francolinus.*	*F. vulgaris.*	Black Francolin.
	F. pictus.	Painted Francolin.
	F. ponticerianus.	Grey Francolin.
	F. gularis.	Wood Francolin.
3. *Arboricola.*	*A. torqueola.*	Hill Francolin.
4. *Rhizothera.*	*R. longirostris.*	Long-billed Francolin.
5. *Perdix.*	*P. hodgsoniæ.*	Hodgson's Partridge.
6. *Coturnix.*	*C. coromandelica.*	Rain Quail.
7. *Perdicula.*	*P. cambaiensis.*	Cambian Quail.
	P. asiatica.	Asiatic Quail.
8. *Rallilus.*	*R. cristatus.*	Crowned Partridge.
9. *Caccabis.*	*C. chukar.*	Chukar Partridge.
10. *Tetraogallus.*	*T. himalayensis.*	Snow Partridge.
11. *Phasianus.*	*P. wallachii.*	Cheer Pheasant.
12. *Lophophorus.*	*L. impeyanus.*	Himalayan Monaul.
13. *Pucrasia.*	*P. microlopha.*	Indian Pucras.
14. *Euplocamus.*	*E. horsfieldi.*	Purple Kaleege.
	E. albo-cristatus.	White Crested Kaleege.
15. *Gallus.*	*G. bankivus.*	Bankiva Jungle Fowl.
	G. sonnerati.	Sonnerat's Jungle Fowl.
	G. stanleyi.	Ceylon Jungle Fowl.
16. *Ceriornis.*	*C. satyra.*	Horned Tragopan.
	C. melanocephala.	Black-headed Tragopan.
17. *Pavo.*	*P. cristatus.*	Common Peafowl.
18. *Polyplectron.*	*P. chinquis.*	Peacock Pheasant.

HARDWICK'S SPUR FOWL.—This species is found in rocky jungles in Southern India. The male has the head, face, and neck variegated in black and white, the feathers being black, with each a white streak and triangular spot; the head is black; the back, neck, and wings are rich chestnut, with white spots on the sides of the neck, back, shoulders, and wing coverts; the primaries are brown; the tail dark sepia brown, showing a green gloss in old birds: the throat and front of neck are variegated with black and white, changing on the breast to ochrous buff, with small triangular black marks, which disappear on the abdomen; the flanks, thighs, and tail coverts are chestnut. The total length is 13 inches, 5 of which belong to the tail.

The female is smaller than the male.

HIMALAYAN MONAUL.—This magnificent bird, which rivals the humming-birds in the gorgeousness of its attire, is found at a great elevation on the Himalayan mountains, to which region it would appear to be confined.

The head and throat the most brilliant glossy golden green; the crest feathers are shafted for two-thirds of their length, the remaining part falling backwards in spatula-shaped expansion. The lower part of the neck and the back are purple, with green and red metallic gloss, the feathers having pointed ends something like the hackles of the domestic cock. A broad band of white crosses the lower part of the back, and the tail is brown, with alternate bands of a darker shade. The remainder of the plumage is dark steel blue.

The female is brown, with a white throat; she is smaller than the male.

The monaul is quite hardy, and breeds in confinement.

BANKIVA JUNGLE FOWL.—This bird is supposed to be the original of some, at least, varieties of domestic poultry, and, sooth to say, it bears a strong likeness to the old-fashioned type of English game-fowl.

Comb and wattles scarlet; the hackles of the neck and

lower part of back orange red; upper part of back deep blackish blue; shoulders ruddy chestnut; secondaries and great wing coverts steel blue, quills black, edged with reddish yellow. The tail long and arched, black, with a green gloss; breast and under parts black.

The female bears a general resemblance to the domestic game hen of the old, rather short-legged type, and looking at her, even more than at her mate, it is impossible not to see that she is the remote ancestress of some of our domesticated breeds.

SONNERAT'S JUNGLE FOWL.—This distinct species is found in the wooded districts of India. It is of smaller size than the domesticated fowl, but is very plucky and courageous, for which reason it is often used in its native country as a prize-fighter.

The formation of the hackles is different from the last; the webs of these and of the upper tail coverts are grey, but the shafts are orange, and dilate at the centre and tip into flat horny plates of a rich orange tint; the tips are rounded and not lanceolate. The back and lower portions of the body are dark grey; the tail is long, arched, and shining with changing colours, purple, gold, and green.

The female is smaller, brown, and destitute of comb or wattles.

Wood facetiously observes that a young cock with a sharp attack of whooping-cough, will, when attempting to crow, give a good idea of the voice of Sonnerat's jungle fowl.

HORNED TRAGOPAN.—This bird is remarkable for the loose pendant skin that proceeds from the base of the lower mandible, and can be inflated at the will of the owner; there are also two appendages of cornuted form that proceed from behind the eyes, and usually hang down the cheeks, but are susceptible of being inflated and raised, when they present the appearance of veritable horns.

It is found in the Himalayas, as well as in Thibet and Nepaul.

The bare skin round the eyes, the wattles and horns are deep blue, and the crest, chin, and back of the neck black; the upper breast, neck and shoulders, are cinnamon brown, shaded with purple and carmine, each feather having a rounded white tip; these spots become larger as they near the hinder parts, and are most conspicuous on the flanks: the tail coverts are yellowish brown, also spotted with white, and are so large as almost to hide the tail, which is rounded and rather short.

In size the horned tragopan almost equals an ordinary Minorca hen.

COMMON PEAFOWL.—Although for a long time acclimatised in England, this magnificent bird has its native home in India, where it occurs in great numbers in suitable, that is wooded, localities, for although they feed on the ground, these fine birds invariably roost in trees, and at as great a height as possible.

The hen lays from ten to fifteen eggs, and the breeding season extends in India from November to March.

The train of the male is popularly called his tail, but consists of the upper tail coverts enormously prolonged and terminated by a racket-like expansion usually called the eye. The real tail feathers are only seven or eight inches long, and of a greyish brown colour; they serve to support the train when the bird elevates the latter.

The female is much smaller, is of an ashy brown colour, and almost destitute of train.

The food of the peacock consists of grain, insects, snails, and the succulent shoots of various plants.

PEACOCK PHEASANT.—The term polyplectron applied

to this bird, signifies many-spurred, and is justified by the fact of its having two or more spurs on each leg. It is found in several parts of India, as well as in the Moluccas, and even, it is said, in the Soudan.

The head is surmounted by a crest, the points of which have a slight forward inclination, and, together with the head, neck, and breast, is of a very deep glossy violet blue colour; over the eye there is a white streak, pointed where it arises in front, close to the base of the upper mandible, and broadening towards the side of the back part of the head; there is another white spot below and a little to the back of the eye, and yet another, somewhat indistinct, about the middle of the side of the neck. The back is brown, with a number of wavy lines of a paler shade of the same colour, and the wing coverts and secondaries are bright sky blue, tipped with black. The brown tail is covered with numerous little yellowish white spots, and at the free extremity of each feather is a shining green spot of an oval shape, around which extends a narrow wavy black line, and beyond that a broader one of yellowish brown. Near the end of the feather is a black mark, and the extremity is fawn.

In total length, the polyplectron measures about 20 inches.

It is capable of domestication, appears to be as hardy as the ordinary pheasant, and has in many aviaries bred quite freely, while the young are not more difficult to rear than young pheasants, and less so than peafowl.

THE RAILS.

Family—*Rallidæ*.

Genus—1. *Porphyrio.*	*P. poliocephalus.*	Grey-headed Porphyrio.
2. *Gallinula.*	*G. phœnicura.*	White-breasted Gallinule.

Grey-Headed Porphyrio.—This bird is found all over India and in Ceylon. It is of social habits, and frequents tanks, jheels, the banks of rivers, etc., in large numbers.

The nest is made close to the water, of rushes, grasses, etc., and contains six or eight buff-coloured eggs, with numerous red spots.

The head, space round the eyes, lores, cheeks, back of head, and nape are purple grey, passing on the sides of the neck to pure purple at the back of the neck. The back, upper tail coverts, and wing coverts are pale blue; the quills are dark blue, with dusky webs; the tail feathers are black, edged with dull blue. Underneath, the lower half of the cheeks, chin, and throat are pale sky blue, more or less tinged with purple grey, passing into pure blue on the lower part of the neck and the breast; the abdomen, sides and vent are deep purple, the under tail coverts white, the lower wing coverts pale blue, the bill red, with a deeper red spot near the base of both mandibles; the casque cherry red, eyes brick red, and the legs pale brick red.

The grey-headed porphyrio measures 18½ inches in extreme length, of which 4 are comprised in the tail.

White-Breasted Gallinule, or Water Hen.—The upper plumage is black, with green reflections, especially on the wing coverts. The chin, throat, and breast are white; the lower abdomen and under tail coverts are deep chestnut;

the bill is greenish orange, deeper on the ridge; the eyes are blood red, and the legs green. The total length is 12¾ inches, bill 1½, and tarsus 2½.

It makes a nest of rushes by the waterside, and lays six or eight large eggs of a browny cream colour, spotted with brownish red.

THE BUSTARDS.

Family—*Otidæ.*
Genus—*Syphcotides.* *S. bengalensis.*

The BENGAL FLORIKEN inhabits Lower Bengal, and resembles the turkey in the manner of its courtship. The females lay from two to four eggs, each of a dull olive colour, spotted with grey, and take great pains to conceal them from observation. The food consists mainly of insects, and the birds are, nevertheless, highly esteemed for the table.

The male, in full dress, has the head, which is then fully crested, the neck, breast, and lower parts, including the thighs, of a deep glossy black, the long plumes of the breast forming a tuft together with those of the neck. The back, scapulars, and tertiaries, rump, and upper tail coverts are rich olivaceous buff, closely and minutely mottled with zigzag black marks, and a black line down the centre of each feather; the shoulders, wing coverts, and quills have white tips, and the shafts and outer edges of the three first primaries are black; the tail is black, minutely mottled with buff, and has a broad white tip. The bill is dusky above and yellow beneath; the eyes are brown, legs dingy yellow, knees and toes livid blue.

The total length is 26 inches, 7 of which belong to the tail.

The female has only a moderately-sized crest, and her

whole plumage is pale fulvous, with black and white marks. Her eyes are dull yellow. . She is rather the larger, measuring 27 inches in full length.

THE CRANES.

Family—*Gruidæ.*		
Genus—*Grus.*	*G. antigone.*	Sarus Crane.
	G. leucogeranos.	White Crane.

Externally the CRANES seem to be allied to the bustards, but their internal anatomy is more akin to that of the plovers; they are of large size, have long necks and legs, and feed on grain, plus insects, frogs, and fish; the head is either crested or altogether devoid of feathers; their figure is elegant, and their movements are graceful; they fly with outstretched neck, and have a loud trumpeting call; they are mostly of migratory habits, and gregarious. The nest is placed on the ground, and the young are able to run about almost from the egg.

SARUS CRANE.—This crane is found throughout the greater part of India, as well as in Burmah. It consorts in pairs, and the female lays two pale bluish green eggs, with a few red spots on them. It is a bold and fearless bird, and has bred in captivity.

The head and neck are naked, and covered for three or four inches down the latter by numerous crimson papillæ and a few black hairs, which accumulate into a broad ring on the neck, and form a kind of mane down the nape: the ear coverts are white, and below them the neck is whitish grey, which gradually passes into pale blue, which is the colour of the rest of the plumage; the quills and the inner webs of the tail feathers are dusky slate. In the breeding season these birds assume a white collar below the crimson papillæ, which become much more vivid. In old birds the scapulars and tertiaries hang over the tail, which they exceed in length; the bill is pale sea-green, with a brown tip; the eyes are orange red; and the legs and feet pale rose.

The total length of the sarus crane is 52 inches, 9½ of which belong to the tail, and 13 to the tarsus. The weight of the adult bird is about 18 pounds.

White Crane.—In this species the whole plumage is white, but the quills are black; the tertiaries are long; the bill and the bare face, as well as the legs, are red.

The total length of the adult bird is about 4 feet; it is a winter visitor to Northern India, and has its summer residence in the northern parts of Asia and in Japan.

THE PLOVERS.

Family—*Charadriidæ*.
Genus—*Sarciophorus*. *S. bilobus.*

Yellow-Wattled Peewit.—This species is found in the greater part of India, and also in Ceylon. It is rare in forest-clad and rainy districts, but is abundant where the ground is drier; it lives on beetles, white ants, worms, etc. It nests on the ground, and lays four eggs of a reddish stone-colour, spotted with brownish purple.

The head and nape are black, and the rest of the plumage, including the wing coverts, tertiaries, chin, throat, and upper part of the breast, are a pale ashen brown; a white streak proceeds from behind each eye, and meeting, make a black band all round the head; the primaries are black; the secondaries are white at the base, then brownish black for the greater part of their remaining length, the white increasing towards the end, which is white. The greater wing coverts combine to form a not very conspicuous wing band; the upper tail coverts are white, and the tail the same, with a broad black subterminal band. Beneath, from the middle breast, the plumage is white posteriorly; the bill is yellow at the base, and has a black tip; the lappet is pale yellow; eyes silvery grey; and the legs yellow.

The length of an adult bird is about 12 inches, 3¼ of which are included in the tail.

PART III.

THE BIRDS OF AFRICA.

THE avifauna of the Dark Continent, even of those parts of it which are comprised within the limits of the British Empire, is one comprising so many families, genera, and species, of all sorts and conditions of birds, that it is absolutely impossible to review them all in the limits at our disposal, so that a selection will have to be made, as comprehensive a one as possible, but not by any means exhaustive.

Thirty of the first will be considered in reasonable detail, eighty-nine of the second, and one hundred and fifty-nine of the last,—a selection, it is hoped, that will give a good, general idea of the birds of Africa included within the borders of Queen Victoria's dominions, but not necessarily confined to them.

THE WEAVERS.

This group receives its name from perhaps the most remarkable of the many types included in it, not the most brilliant in point of colouring, indeed, though some of them are sufficiently noticeable in that respect, but on account of the extraordinary development of the nest-building instinct, which is scarcely equalled, and certainly not surpassed, in any other bird.

Family—*Ploceidæ.*

Genus—

1.	*Estrelda.*	*E. cinerea.*	Common Waxbill.
		E. rubriventris.	Red-bellied Waxbill.
		E. dufresni.	Dufresne's Waxbill.
		E. melpoda.	Orange-cheeked Waxbill.
		E. phœnicotis.	Crimson-eared Waxbill.
		E. cœrulescens.	Cinereous Waxbill.
		E. subflava.	Zebra Waxbill.
2.	*Spermestes.*	*S. cucullata.*	Hooded Finch.
		S. fringilloides.	Pied Grass Finch.
3.	*Pytelia.*	*P. melba.*	Crimson-faced Waxbill.
		P. citerior.	Western Melba Waxbill.
		P. phœnicoptera.	Crimson-winged Waxbill.
		P. wieneri.	Wiener's Waxbill.
4.	*Amadina.*	*A. fasciata.*	Ribbon Finch.
		A. erythrocephala.	Red-headed Finch.
		A. bicolor.	Cape Palmas Finch.
5.	*Munia.*	*M. cantans.*	African Silverbill.
6.	*Vidua.*	*V. paradisea.*	Paradise Whydah Bird.
		V. principalis.	Pin-tailed Whydah Bird.
		V. ardens.	Red-chested Whydah Bird.
7.	*Chera.*	*C. progne.*	Long-tailed Weaver Bird.
8.	*Hypochera.*	*H. nitens.*	Shining Weaver Bird.
		H. splendens.	Resplendent Weaver Bird.
9.	*Coliopasser.*	*C. macrurus.*	Yellow-backed Whydah.
10.	*Urobrachya.*	*U. albonotata.*	White-winged Whydah.

	U. axillarus.	Red-shouldered Whydah.
11. *Euplectes.*	*E. oryx.*	Grenadier Weaver.
	E. flammiceps.	Crimson-crowned Weaver.
	E. afer.	Black-bellied Weaver.
	E. nigriventris.	Black-chested Weaver.
	E. capensis.	Yellow-shouldered Weaver.
12. *Foudia.*	*F. erythrops.*	Red-faced Weaver.
13. *Pyrenestes.*	*P. albifrons.*	White-fronted Weaver.
14. *Spermospiza.*	*S. hæmatina.*	Blue-beaked Weaver.
15. *Quelea.*	*Q. sanguinirostris.*	Red-billed Weaver.
	Q. russi.	Russ's Weaver.
16. *Hyphantornis.*	*H. textor.*	Rufous-marked Weaver.
	H. capensis.	Olive Weaver.
	H. castaneofusca.	Chestnut-backed Weaver.

Common Waxbill.—The pretty little creature is about the size of a European wren, but of slimmer build; its general colour is grey, darker above, lighter underneath: there is a rosy flush on the lower breast, deepening towards the vent; the tail and flight feathers are black, with a metallic gloss. The male and female are almost alike, but the latter has a little less of the rosy-red tinting.

The nest is a large affair compared with the size of its architect. It is made of hay, and is lined with a few small feathers; the five or six eggs are white.

The food consists principally of white millet.

It has bred in confinement.

Red-Bellied Waxbill.—This bird, also called, somewhat absurdly, the pheasant finch, and, more appropriately,

St. Helena waxbill, is not unlike the last, but is large, and its plumage all throughout is crossed with dark undulating lines, which give it a waved appearance. The tail is long, and perpetually in motion. Food, habits, etc., the same as the last.

The female is the smaller of the two, and has much less red on the lower parts. Breeds pretty freely in confinement, but the young are not very often fully reared, probably on account of something missing in the food.

DUFRESNE'S WAXBILL.—So called after a French naturalist of that name. It is a sprightly little bird, about the size of the common waxbill. It has a black face, with whitish throat and back part of neck; the rest of the plumage greenish grey except the back, which is almost black. As in the case of the two preceding species, the bill is bright red, but the lower mandible here is darker than the upper.

The female is of much duller appearance, her face being greenish grey.

ORANGE-CHEEKED WAXBILL.—This is a common species of a dull greenish colour, darker above than below; a patch of orange red marks the cheeks; the rump is reddish, and the tail blackish brown; the hinder lower parts are whitish grey; bill red. Female indistinguishable.

This species also breeds pretty freely in confinement.

CRIMSON-EARED WAXBILL.—This bird is, perhaps, better known by the name of "cordon-bleu." It is very pretty, and though long reputed delicate, is perfectly hardy. The face, breast, sides, and rump bright sky blue. The male, however, has a patch of deep crimson on each cheek, the female being known by its absence; the bill is bright red.

This little bird, which is much the same size as the others, breeds freely in confinement, but the young are very seldom fully reared. The nest and eggs are like those of the common waxbill; food the same.

CINEREOUS WAXBILL.—Is also known as the lavender finch, a title that aptly describes its prevailing colour; but the rump and tail are dark red; the bill is of the same colour. Both sexes are alike.

FIG. 50.—*The St. Helena, or Red-Bellied Waxbill.*

It has bred in confinement, and the young, like those of the other waxbills, have the beak of a dull black colour when they leave the nest.

They are confirmed feather eaters, so that a pair will

pluck each other perfectly bare. Add ants' eggs to their diet of white millet.

Zebra Waxbill.—The smallest of all these little birds, it is no bigger than a golden-crested wren. The general colour is greenish grey; the breast of the male is orange, and that of the female pale yellowish grey; the bill is red; the sides are marked by many faint undulating grey lines.

It breeds freely in confinement; the eggs, of course, being very minute. Bass records the case of one of these miniature birds that laid more than 70 eggs in one season.

Hooded Finch.—Better known by the name of bronze-winged mannikin. This little bird is a general favourite with amateurs, and deservedly so, for it is pretty, hardy, and a free breeder in confinement. It is brownish black above, and white on the under surface; on the lesser wing coverts are some glossy spots of a bronzed green colour, whence its name, that of hooded finch being derived from the blackish brown of its head.

Pied Grass Finch, or magpie mannikin, is about the same size as an English goldfinch, but it has a much stouter beak, which is of a dark, leaden blue colour; the head and neck are bluish black, and the under parts white, except a small chestnut-coloured spot about the middle of the flank on either side; the wing coverts have a brown shade.

Male and female alike.

This species also breeds freely in the aviary.

Food—white millet and canary seed.

Crimson-Faced Waxbill.—Upper parts olivaceous greenish yellow; tail brownish black, with central pair of a deep red colour; rump the same; forehead, face, and back of neck dull crimson red; breast orange, with wavy white lines; other under parts white; bill coral red; eyes red.

Crimson-Winged Waxbill.—This bird is a little smaller

than a goldfinch, and very handsome. The head and back are a soft grey; under parts rather darker, and crossed by

FIG. 51.—*The Ribbon Finch.*

undulating bars, as in that of the last; but the wings and tail are bright red; the bill is black. The female is similar, but her colours are not so brilliant.

They have bred in confinement, and, like all the preceding, are fed with white millet and a little canary seed.

WIENER'S WAXBILL.—Wings and greater part of the plumage deep orange, shaded with olivaceous green; under parts greyish olive, with yellow undulations; head and face crimson.

RIBBON FINCH.—At one time this bird was very generally known by the objectionable name of cut-throat, which is being superseded by the more euphonious and equally descriptive appellation we bestowed upon it when describing the bird in "The Amateur's Aviary" some years ago.

The general colour is fawn, with numerous darker spots all over. In the male a red band extends across the throat from ear to ear, which is always wanting in the female.

These birds breed freely, generally nesting in a cocoa-nut husk, and but rarely make a domed nest like those already mentioned. The eggs are four or five in number, and quite white. The young are very often thrown out by the parents when a few days old.

It is desirable to add ants' eggs, fresh, if possible, to their diet of white millet and canary seed.

CAPE PALMAS FINCH.—This bird is very generally known as the two-coloured mannikin. The upper parts are black, and the lower white; both sexes are alike. It lacks the brown shading that distinguishes the hooded finch, which it resembles in regard to size.

The Cape Palmas finch also breeds in confinement.

AFRICAN SILVERBILL.—There is but little difference between this bird and its Indian namesake; the former is a little darker, that is all, but is as desirable a cage bird as the other, being hardy, frugal, and ready to breed in cage and aviary, beside possessing one of the sweetest voices among foreign, as opposed to British, birds. Upper plumage fawn colour, wings and tail darker, and the lower

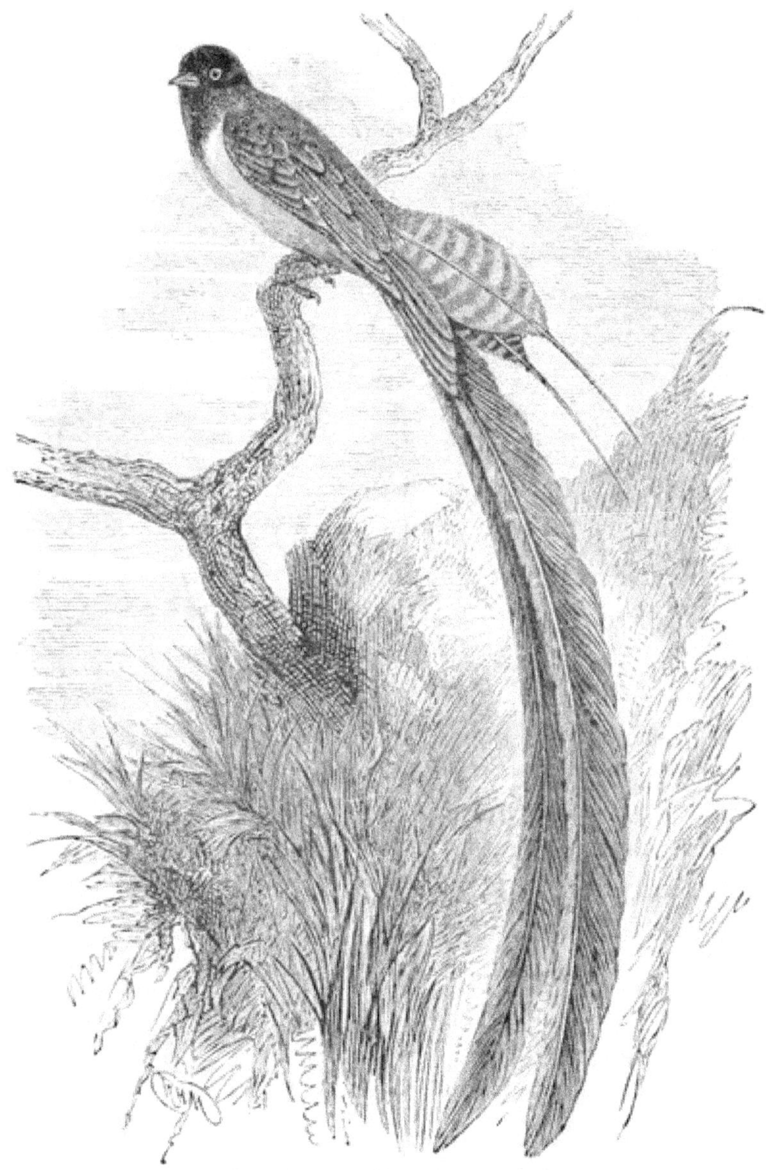

FIG. 52.—*The Paradise Whydah.*

parts greyish white; the thick beak is bluish grey. Male and female are much alike.

The nest is made in a bush or small box or covered basket. The eggs are white, from three to five in number, and the young are reared quite easily on seed, white millet and canary.

PARADISE WHYDAH BIRD.—The male when in full colour has the bill a very dark lead colour, the head and chin black; then comes a broad collar or band of a golden shade of brown, which merges into the same shade on the throat and breast, getting lighter towards the vent; the back, wings, and curiously-developed long arched tail are black, the legs and feet greyish flesh-colour.

Out of the breeding season he is not unlike a house moulted redpoll, which the female always resembles. The elongated tail feathers vary in length from 12 to as much as 14 inches, getting longer at each successive moult. A hair-like prolongation of the shaft of the second longest of the tail feathers gives the bird the name of shaft-tailed whydah, by which it is also known.

Although of frequent occurrence in British South African, as well as Western African territories, not much appears to be known about the habits of this bird in its wild state. In the house it eats white millet, canary seed, and ants' eggs, but has not hitherto been known to breed.

PIN-TAILED WHYDAH BIRD.—This is a smaller bird than the last, being about the size of a redpoll, while the paradise whydah is as big as a linnet, that is, without counting the long tail. When in full plumage the pin-tail is black on the head, back, and wings, which last have a white mark on them; the under parts are white, and the bill red. The central pair of tail feathers are about 8 inches in length, but are not broader than the short ones, which are of the ordinary size. The female is grey, with darker centres to the feathers on the back, head, and neck, and when out of colour the male resembles her. Some of these birds have four long feathers on the tail, and others only two. In the aviary this little bird is apt to be quarrelsome.

Feeding and treatment as the last.

RED-CHESTED WHYDAH BIRD.—In his nuptial dress this bird is jetty black, with a metallic gloss all over the body, except a broad collar, of a deep red colour, on the lower part of the front of the neck. It is rarely imported into England, but appears to require the same treatment as the two preceding species. It is found in South and Eastern Africa.

LONG-TAILED WEAVER BIRD.—The largest of all the family, this grand bird is indifferently known as whydah and weaver. It is about the size of a starling, and in configuration and colouring bears a strange resemblance to the paradise whydah, for whose "big brother" it might readily pass; but there is no doubt that the two species are quite distinct.

SHINING WEAVER BIRD.—This bird is jetty black, with metallic blue reflections, and a white bill. The female resembles a hen sparrow, than which it is a little smaller. It is found in South and Eastern Africa. The tail is short.

Food same as the preceding.

YELLOW-BACKED WHYDAH BIRD.—The general colour of this bird is black, except the wing coverts, which are yellow; the bill and legs and feet are dark lead colour. The size of the bird is that of a well-grown sparrow; the tail is about as long as the body, or a little longer. The female has a reddish brown bill.

GRENADIER WEAVER.—This bird is also known as the oryx and the oryx bishop; in colour the bill is yellowish horn; the head and face black, which is also the colour of the lower breast and belly; the wings are brown, and the rest of the plumage rich orange red, with a yellow or golden tinge; the legs and feet are flesh-colour. The tail is very short, and is dark brown, with orange edges. The female is like a hen sparrow in size and appearance, and the male resembles her when he is out of colour.

CRIMSON-CROWNED WEAVER.—In the breeding season the head of the male is a bright red colour verging on crimson; the rest of the body is brownish, with dark centres to every feather; the legs and feet are flesh-colour.

BLACK-BELLIED WEAVER.—This species has a large greyish flesh-coloured bill, black face, throat, lower breast and belly, a brownish back and wings, and the top of the head, nape, neck, and upper breast scarlet.

There are many other different kinds of weaver birds in Africa and its geographical dependencies; but even the most curtailed description of them would occupy more space than can be spared. They are all fairly hardy, but cannot stand much frost, and should not be exposed to it. They feed on white millet and canary seed, and most of the males are indefatigable nest-builders, but not so the females, which rarely breed in confinement.

THE FINCHES.

This group is numerously represented in Africa, the original home of the domesticated canary and its offshoots, but we can only glance at a few of the more familiar species.

Family—*Fringillidæ*.

Genus—1. *Passer*.	*P. luteus*.	Yellow Sparrow.
	P. simplex.	Grey-headed Sparrow.
	P. alario.	Alario Finch.
	P. diffusus.	Black-breasted Sparrow.

2. *Petronia.*	*P. petronella.*	Yellow-throated Rock Sparrow.
3. *Crithagra.*	*C. butyracea.*	St. Helena Seed-Eater.
	C. sulphurata.	Sulphury Seed-Eater.
	C. chrysopyga.	Yellow-rumped Seed-Eater.
	C. musica.	Singing Finch.
	C. albogularis.	White-throated Seed Eater.
4. *Serinus.*	*S. canicollis.*	Wild Canary.
5. *Fringillaria.*	*F. capensis.*	Cape Bunting.

Grey-Headed Sparrow.—This bird is also known by the name of Swainson's finch. Its head and neck are greyish brown; shoulders and back chestnut brown; wings and rump red brown, with darker undulations; lower parts greyish white; under tail coverts pure white. About the size of an ordinary English sparrow.

The female is paler, but otherwise like the male.

Alario Finch.—As this bird has frequently bred mules with the canary, it is clearly not a sparrow, and should not be called one, as it often is. Head, throat, and upper breast black; back, wing coverts, and tail brown; neck, and sides of breast white; under parts brownish white; eyes black; bill horn grey. Size that of a siskin.

The female has no black, but is brownish, with a yellow tinge.

Food same as a canary, which the alario much resembles in its habits; it sings prettily, and soon becomes reconciled to confinement.

Black-Breasted Sparrow.—Brown above, and greyish white below, except the throat and upper part of the breast, which are black. This is a true sparrow, and resembles its typical English namesake in size and appearance.

ST. HELENA SEED-EATER.—This bird is also known by the name of green singing finch. It is greenish grey above and golden yellow below; a grey streak passes across the eye to the back of the head, and a black one below it from the base of the lower mandible; the rump is yellow; the legs, feet, and bill are yellowish grey. In size it about equals a redpoll.

The female is not as brightly tinted as the male.

The green singing finch breeds freely in confinement, both with a mate of its own kind and with a canary, in which case the mules resemble the father, but are larger, and show but little trace of their maternal descent.

It has a sweet song, and is somewhat quarrelsome in a mixed aviary.

Food similar to the canary.

It is a native of Eastern Africa, but has been naturalised at St. Helena.

SULPHURY SEED-EATER.—Very much like the last, from which it is chiefly distinguished by the paler tint of its yellow rump and breast.

YELLOW-RUMPED, or HARTLAUB'S SEED-EATER.—Upper parts greenish yellow, wing coverts something darker, with small blackish brown spots and greenish lines; head and face grey; rest of plumage yellow. Female like the male, but paler. Size and shape of the siskin.

It breeds freely in captivity, both with a mate of its own species and with other finches.

Food and treatment the same as the preceding.

SINGING FINCH.—This rather insignificant-looking little bird is about the size of a redpoll, of a grey colour above and white on the lower surface. It possesses considerable faculty for song, and is reported to have bred mules with the canary.

Male and female are alike.

The principal food is white millet, to which millet in the ear and canary seed may be added.

White-Throated Seed-Eater.—This bird has been referred to as the "wild canary," but it is more than doubtful

Fig. 53.—*Green Singing Finch.*

if it really represents the original of our domesticated breeds.

THE STARLINGS.

This group is well represented in Africa; among its members are the following:—

Family—*Sturnidæ*.

Genus—

1. *Lamprocolius*.	*L. auratus*.	Purple-headed Glossy Starling.
	L. rufiventris.	Rufous-vented Glossy Starling.
2. *Lamprotornis*.	*L. æneus*.	Long-tailed Glossy Starling.

PURPLE-HEADED GLOSSY STARLING.—This splendid bird is about the same size as its English namesake, and is perhaps the most brilliant in colouring of all its relatives. The head and lower part of the body are purple, with a violet blue tinge, which is deeper on the throat; the wings and back are green, with a metallic gloss, and the short tail purple. The head is remarkably flat; and the eye, being large and of a bright yellow hue, gives the bird a very peculiar appearance.

In confinement, this bird should be fed like its European relative; it is easily kept, and has bred in more than one aviary.

The female is like her mate, but has less of the bright metallic gloss that adds such lustre to his plumage.

RUFOUS-VENTED GLOSSY STARLING.—This species is of a dark purplish green all over, except on the lower part of the body, where the purple deepens into a deep rufous in a strong light.

Male and female are much alike, but the latter is less brilliant in appearance.

The treatment should be the same as for the last, which it resembles as regards size and habits. It has bred more than once in confinement.

LONG-TAILED GLOSSY STARLING.—This magnificent bird which, by the brilliance of its colouring, reminds the spectator of the trogons, is almost as big as a magpie, which it somewhat resembles in form and appearance, except that it displays no white upon its person, but is altogether of a purple and blue colour, except the head, which is deep black, and the tail, which has purple and red and blue metallic reflections.

The female is precisely similar to the male, and does not differ from him even in size, so that it is impossible to determine the sex of a given specimen, even by comparison.

The food of this species, in its wild state, consists of fruit and insects. In confinement it will eat anything that is offered to it, and thrive if kept fairly warm and has plenty of room to turn about in.

THE CROWS.

The Crow family is not as numerously represented in Africa as it is in India, or even in Europe. The best-known is the following:—

Family—*Corvidæ.*
Genus—*Ptilostomus.* *P. senegalensis.*

PIAPEC, or SENEGAL CROW.—When the fact is mentioned that it is a crow pure and simple, there is absolutely nothing left to say about it, so that it may be summarily dismissed.

THE LARKS.

These popular birds are found in every part of the world, and are not unrepresented in Africa.

Family—*Alaudidæ.*
Genus—

1. *Alauda.*	*A. crassirostris.*	Thick-billed Lark.
2. *Phyrrhulauda.*	*P. verticalis.*	White-headed Bullfinch Lark.

THICK-BILLED LARK.—This species is sufficiently characterised by mentioning its bill.

WHITE-HEADED BULLFINCH LARK is distinguished by its large white head, and rather compact form. Neither of the above can be mentioned in the same breath with their European congener, as far as their musical abilities are concerned.

THE HORNBILLS.

These curious creatures, with which we have already made acquaintance in India, have their headquarters in Africa, where numerous species are found, from among which we select the following for description:—

Family—*Bucerotidæ.*

Genus—

1. *Bucorvus.*	*B. abyssinicus.*	Ground Hornbill.
2. *Ceratogymna.*	*C. elata.*	Elate Hornbill.
3. *Sphagolobus.*	*S. atratus.*	Black Hornbill.
4. *Psycanistes.*	*P. subcylindricus*	Sub-cylindrical Hornbill.
5. *Toccus.*	*T. melanoleucus.*	Black and White Hornbill.

ABYSSINIAN GROUND HORNBILL.—Although more common in Northern Africa, this extraordinary bird is found as far south as Mozambique and Zanzibar.

The colouring is as follows: General tint dusky black, changing to whitish grey on the under parts; the head and neck feathers are elongated and loose; the tail is whitish grey, crossed by a broad black band at its lower third; the huge bill is yellowish grey, with a red mark at the base of the upper mandible; the lower mandible is dark horn-black, while the helmet is black and white. The bill measures 10 inches in length; at first it is comparatively small, but it increases in size every year, and in old birds assumes preposterous proportions; it is, however, light and porous in structure, and does not seem to inconvenience its owner in the least; when flying it strikes the mandibles together, and so makes a considerable noise.

THE HOOPOE.

Family—*Upupidæ.*
Genus—*Upupa. U. epops.*

Hoopoe.—Notwithstanding the fact that an occasional straggler finds its way to our shores, to be there incontinently shot, this bird cannot be rightly considered a British species. Its home is in Egypt, where it is sufficiently common, though it extends into Syria, Asia Minor, and even into Greece.

It is a graceful, if not a pretty, bird, but the popular pictures of it convey a false impression of its appearance, for it does not habitually wear its crest displayed fan-wise, but rather furled like an umbrella out of use, and it is only when alarmed or excited that it expands the characteristic ornament.

Male and female are almost alike, and may be kept for a time in confinement, but with every care it is difficult to tide them over one of our winters.

Natural diet—insects of all kinds.

THE CUCKOOS.

Family—*Cuculidæ.*
Genus—*Centropus. C. senegalensis.*

Senegal Coucal.—So little is known of this bird and its habits that it may be dismissed with the simple intimation that it is found in most parts of Africa.

THE PLANT CUTTERS.

Family—*Musophagidæ*.

Genus—

1. *Musophaga.*	*M. violacea.*	Violet Plantain Eater.
2. *Schizorhis.*	*S. africana.*	Variegated Touracou.
3. *Corythaix.*	*C. buffoni.*	Buffon's Touracou.
	C. albocristata.	White-crested Touracou.
	C. persis.	Senegal Touracou.
	C. macrorhyncha.	Great-billed Touracou.
	C. erythrolophus.	Red-crested Touracou.
	C. porphyreolophus.	Purple-crested Touracou.

Violet Plantain Eater.—These birds are about the size of the European jay, and their plumage is gorgeous, with glancing tints of green, purple, and violet. They are natives of the Gold Coast and adjacent parts, where they live among the trees.

The beak is large, and the base of the upper mandible spreads broadly back to the crown; it is yellow below, but the cephalic part is crimson, which is also the colour of the head feathers next adjoining it. There is a patch of carmine on the wings, which are tipped with violet.

The food consists entirely of fruit.

Variegated Touracou.—This bird is also called the blue plantain eater, its general colour being blue, marked with azure, but the handsome upright crest is black; the legs and feet are very strong, and suitable for living among the branches of trees, on the fruit of which, as well as on the insects that frequent them, it is accustomed to feed.

WHITE-CRESTED TOURACOU.—Tolerably well known, because more easily kept alive in confinement than the preceding. This bird is of a delicate olive green above,

FIG. 54.—The Hoopoe

except the crest, which is of a lighter shade, and tipped with white; the wings have a purple tinge. In size it about equals the European jackdaw. It is a wary bird, keeping to the trees, among which it finds its food, and along the branches of which it runs swiftly, leaping lightly from bough to bough.

THE PARROTS.

Family—*Psittacidæ*.

Genus—

1. *Palæornis*.	*P. docilis*.	Rose-ringed Parrakeet.
2. *Agapornis*.	*A. pullaria*.	Red-faced Lovebird.
	A. roseicollis.	Rosy-faced Lovebird.
3. *Coracopsis*.	*C. barklyi*.	Praslin Parrot.
4. *Psittacus*.	*P. erithacus*.	Grey Parrot.
	P. timneh.	Timneh Parrot.
5. *Pæocephalus*.	*P. fuscicollis*.	Brown-necked Parrot.
	P. robustus.	Levaillant's Parrot.
	P. gulielmi.	Jardine's Parrot.
	P. senegalus.	Senegal Parrot.
	P. fuscicapillus.	Brown-headed Parrot.
	P. meyeri.	Meyer's Parrot.
	P. ruppelli.	Rüppell's Parrot.

Rose-Ringed Parrakeet.—This parrakeet differs from the Indian ring-neck only in being a little smaller, in having a fainter pink-coloured band on the nape of the neck, and in having the bill of a dusky red, or almost black, colour. It should be fed and treated like its Asiatic congener, and is equally docile and companionable, but does not learn to talk very much.

Red-Faced Lovebird.—These well-known little birds are about the size of a plump cock sparrow, but have, of course, the big head, strong-hooked bill, and short, strong legs, common to their race. The general colour is vivid grass green, with a yellowish tinge on the hinder parts below, and a red line on the face. The young have little of the characteristic ruddy orange colour, and were long taken to be females. The sexes are differentiated by the

FIG. 55.—*The Grey Parrot.*

colour of the under wing coverts, which are black in the male and green in the female. They are rather impatient of cold, but will live for years in the house on canary seed and millet.

Rosy, or Peach-Faced Lovebird.—This species is a little larger than the last, to which it bears a general resemblance, but the mask is of a pinky red, and the white bill has a greenish shade on the upper mandible; the tail, as in the case of the last, is marked with alternate bands of red, black and yellow; the rump is bluish.

Both this species and the last line their nest-holes with fragments of bark, which they carry in fixed between the long upper tail coverts.

The rosy-faced lovebird breeds freely in confinement, and should be fed and treated like the last.

Praslin Parrot.—This little brownish black parrot bears a strong resemblance, except as regards size, to the Vasa parrots of Madagascar; it has a whitish beak, and a rather long, broad tail. It is found, but sparsely, in Zanzibar.

Grey Parrot.—This familiar bird is too well known to need description; it inhabits all the Gold Coast, and is plentiful in and around Lagos. Unfortunately, most of those imported into Europe die from septic fever, to which they appear to be very liable.

Timneh Parrot.—This bird would appear to be a local variety merely of the last, from which it differs chiefly in its darker colour, both of body, feathers, and tail, the last being of a dull reddish brown colour. It comes from the hinterland of the Gold Coast, but is seldom imported.

Brown-Necked Parrot.—This parrot bears a good deal of resemblance to the Senegal parrot, but is larger and has a bigger bill. Head black, neck brownish black, and the remainder of the plumage olivaceous green, darker above than below. It inhabits the country from Senegambia, to the Gaboon, and is seldom imported.

LEVAILLANT'S PARROT.—The general colour of this species is olivaceous green, but the forehead and cheeks appear to be red, for, although the feathers are really grey, each of them has a broad margin of bright red that overlaps the next.

It is found in the extreme south of Africa, but is seldom imported into Europe.

JARDINE'S PARROT is rather a pretty bird, less than a grey but larger than the Senegal, to which it bears a strong likeness, in form if not in colour: this is green of several shades; the head has a good deal of red on it, and the back and shoulder feathers have green margins on a dark ground. The sexes are alike.

SENEGAL PARROT.—This parrot has the head and neck of a rusty blackish brown colour, the throat and breast yellowish orange, and the rest of the plumage green. The female is greyer on the head and rather smaller. It has bred freely in confinement, but can scarcely be called an accomplished talker, though individuals sometimes will learn to repeat a few words with tolerable distinctness.

BROWN-HEADED PARROT.—This bird is not unlike the last, but is smaller and has a browner head. It is found on the Eastern African coast and may only be a local variation of the last.

MEYER'S PARROT.—Head, neck and upper parts brownish olive; wing coverts bright blue; primaries brown, with green spots; under parts bright green, every feather faintly tipped with blue. Inhabits Eastern Africa.

RUPPELL'S PARROT.— Is very like the last, but is darker, and the blue on the wing is shaded with green; it is found on the west coast from Senegambia to Damaraland.

THE OWLS.

Represented in Africa by species and genera, are among the handsomest and most useful to man of the feathered tribes that inhabit the Continent.

Family—*Strigidæ.*

Genus—1.	*Strix.*	*S. capensis.*	Cape Grass Owl.
2.	*Asio.*	*A. capensis.*	Cape Eared Owl.
3.	*Syrnium.*	*S. woodfordi.*	Woodford's Owl.
4.	*Bubo.*	*B. capensis.*	Cape Eagle Owl.
		B. maculosus.	Spotted Eagle Owl.
		B. cinerescens.	Grey Eagle Owl.
		B. lacteus.	Milky Eagle Owl.
		B. poensis.	Fraser's Eagle Owl.
5.	*Scops.*	*S. leucotis.*	White-eared Scops Owl.

THE FALCONS.

Abundant everywhere, and especially well represented in British Africa :—

Family—*Falconidæ.*

Genus—1.	*Buteo.*	*B. jacal.*	Jackal Buzzard.
		B. auguralis.	Augural Buzzard
2.	*Helotarsus.*	*H. ecaudatus.*	Bateleur Eagle.
3.	*Aquila.*	*A. verreauxi.*	Vulturine Eagle.
4.	*Lophoaetus.*	*L. occipitalis.*	Black-crested Eagle.

5. *Melierax.*	*M. musicus.*	Chanting Hawk.
	M. monogrammicus.	One-streaked Hawk.
6. *Falco.*	*F. biarmicus.*	Bearded Falcon.
	F. concolor.	Ash-coloured Falcon.
7. *Milvus.*	*M. egyptius.*	Egyptian Kite.
	M. migrans.	Black Kite.
8. *Neophron.*	*N. percnopterus.*	Egyptian Vulture.
	N. pileatus.	Pileated Vulture.
9. *Gypohierax.*	*G. angolensis.*	Angolan Vulture.

Ash-Coloured Falcon.—This bird bears a remarkable resemblance to the hawk known by the name of Montagu's harrier, which is a British species, also met with in India and other parts of Asia; if it is the same, it has a very wide habitat, which is no more than might be expected from a creature endowed with such wonderful powers of flight. It is a slim, elegantly-shaped bird, and extraordinarily active and daring.

Egyptian Kite.—This well-known species is rather a handsome one. It is greyish brown on the upper parts of the body, but the head and neck are marked with long stripes of black and white; underneath it is reddish brown, each feather marked down the centre with a line of deeper colour than the outer portion; the tail is crossed by several bands, and is slightly forked. It is not quite 2 feet in length, the female being the larger.

Black Kite.—This is merely a darker variety of the preceding, and, like it, inhabits all the northern parts of Africa, including Egypt.

EGYPTIAN VULTURE.—This bird is also found in many parts of Southern Europe. The general colour of the adult is white, but the quills of the wings, or primaries, are dark brown; the bare face, the bill, and the legs are yellow. Both sexes are alike in appearance. The young are of a chocolate brown shade, and do not assume the full adult plumage until they are three years old.

They are generally protected by law in all the places they frequent, and justly so, for they make excellent scavengers, that do not require either backsheesh or wages.

The next family on the list is rather an artificially formed one, and consists of one genus only, and one species.

THE SECRETARY VULTURE.

Family—*Serpentariidæ.*
Genus—*Serpentarius. S. reptilivorus.*

SECRETARY VULTURE.—The first name is derived from a tuft of long feathers that projects from the ear coverts to the back of the neck in a horizontal direction, like a pen stuck behind a clerk's ear; and the second from the vulturine appearance of the head and beak.

The general colour is bluish grey, but the crest feathers are black, as are those of the thighs and the primaries; the tail has a white tip.

A good deal of nonsense has been written about this bird's mode of killing the reptiles on which it chiefly feeds. It does not strike them with its wings, but tramples them with its strong feet, which, owing to the length of the shank, it can bring down on its victim with the force of a sledge-hammer, breaking the reptile's back at once; but the blows are repeated again and again until the last vestige of life is stamped out of the victim. The wings are kept tightly closed during the "combat," which is a very one-sided one from the first, and the bird never touches the

Fig. 56.—*The Pelicans.*

serpent with its bill until the creature is dead, when it is picked up and tossed into the air, deftly caught by the head, and swallowed whole. The writer, having repeatedly been a witness of the performance, has just described what he has seen, and not copied what he heard at second hand.

The secretary vulture makes a nest of sticks in a lofty tree, lays generally three round white eggs, and feeds its young with large insects, as well as with snakes and other reptiles.

THE PELICANS

Are represented in Africa, as in most parts of the globe. We select the following:—

Family—*Pelecanidæ.*
Genus—*Pelecanus.* *P. rufescens.*

Red-Backed Pelican.—There are few birds that bear a more striking resemblance to each other, some slight variations in size and colour alone serving to distinguish one "species" from another. The one under consideration has the back feathers of a ruddy tinge, otherwise it might very well pass, as regards size and shape, for any of the rest, which are too well known to need detailed description.

THE DARTERS.

Not numerous, and principally confined to America and Asia. However, they are not without a representative in British Africa.

Family—*Plotidæ.*
Genus—*Plotus.* *P. levaillanti.*

Levaillant's Darter.—This bird has the long, thin, or narrow, head and the extended neck, that so vividly recalls the snake to anyone who sees it for the first time swimming in a lagoon or creek, with its body submerged, and only the serpentine neck and head above the water, where it darts about in an undulating fashion with great swiftness in search of prey.

When alarmed, it draws its head and neck below the surface, only just exposing the nostrils to enable it to breathe. The darter can remain submerged for a very protracted period.

THE STORKS.

Family—*Ciconiidæ.*

Genus—

1. *Ciconia.*	*C. episcopus.*	White-necked Stork.
2. *Abdimia.*	*A. sphenorhyncha.*	White-billed Stork.
3. *Balæniceps.*		Shoebill.

SHOEBILL.—This is a very curious bird, at least it has a very strange bill, and is known by a number of names, in addition to the one here adopted, and among them figure whalebill, whalehead, and hook-billed boathead.

It is chiefly found in Egypt, in the swampy ground, where it exists, along the banks of the Nile, but chiefly in the Rhol district, according to Petherick, who met with it there.

Sometimes it is seen in pairs, and sometimes in flocks of a hundred or more, which means that during the breeding season the pairs prefer the absence of their companions to their presence near them, but that when released from the cares (and pleasures?) of family life, the social instinct brings them together again.

They breed during the rainy season, depositing their two

or three eggs on the ground, the young running about as soon as they leave the shell.

Their diet consists mainly of fish, but they will also eat offal and various reptiles and small mammals.

THE IBIS.

Family—*Plataleidæ.*
Genus—*Geronticus.* *G. calva.*

Bald-Headed Ibis.—This well-known bird is a visitor to Egypt, where it occurs in considerable numbers during the rainy season, departing when the gradual subsidence of the river deprives it of the food it collects in the shallow water, namely, frogs, shell-fish, and aquatic insects.

It is a curious fact that in feeding their offspring the old birds swallow, so to speak, the bill and head of the young, and then disgorge into the gaping mouth of the latter the food it had itself previously taken.

The colour is for the most part white, of a glossy kind, but some of the secondaries, which are much elongated, fall over the sides of the back, and are black and shining.

Another species, or variety, known as the Glossy Ibis, has the head, neck, and upper part of the back of a dark chocolate colour; the wing coverts are glossed with purple, the primaries with green, and the tail with purple. The under parts are chocolate brown; the naked space round the eyes is green, and so are the legs and feet.

The young birds are mottled irregularly.

THE PIGEONS.

Family—*Columbidæ*.

Genus—1. *Columba*.	*C. guinea*.	Triangular-spotted Pigeon.
	C. arquatrix.	Spotted Pigeon.
2. *Œna*.	*Œ. capensis*.	Cape Dove.
3. *Turtur*.	*T. senegalensis*.	Cambayan Turtle-Dove.
	T. vinaceus.	Vinaceous Turtle-Dove.
	T. semitorquatus.	Half-collared Turtle-Dove.
4. *Chalcopelia*.	*C. chalcospilos*.	Bronze-spotted Dove.
	C. afra.	Emerald Dove.
	C. puella.	Schlegel's Dove.
5. *Tympanistria*.	*T. bicolor*.	Tambourine Dove.

Triangular-Spotted Pigeon.—This is a fine bird, about as big as the European ring-dove. It is of a greyish blue colour, darker above than below, and has on the sides a number of small white patches of the shape from which it derives its English name. It is readily domesticated, and should form a desirable addition to the columbarium.

Cape Dove.—This pretty little species is about the size of the skylark, but its much longer tail makes it look bigger. The head and face of the adult male are black, hence the names of masked and harlequin dove by which it is also known. The female has no black, but is grey of several shades. They nest freely in confinement, but, unless the weather is very warm, will not rear the young out of doors, these dying as soon as the parents cease to brood them at night. The eggs are two in number.

They are fed on white millet, canary seed, and a little coarse oatmeal, but must have access to rock salt and grit, or sand of suitable size.

FIG. 57.—*Cape Doves.*

CAMBAYAN TURTLE-DOVE.—This bird is about half as big again as the common Barbary turtle, so often misnamed ring-dove, with which it will breed and produce hybrids. It is darker than the smaller bird, but otherwise resembles

Fig. 58.—*The Cambayan Dove.*

it. Feed as an ordinary pigeon. It is quite hardy, and winters out of doors without inconvenience.

Vinaceous Turtle-Dove.—This bird is much like the last, but has a vinous red shade on the breast.

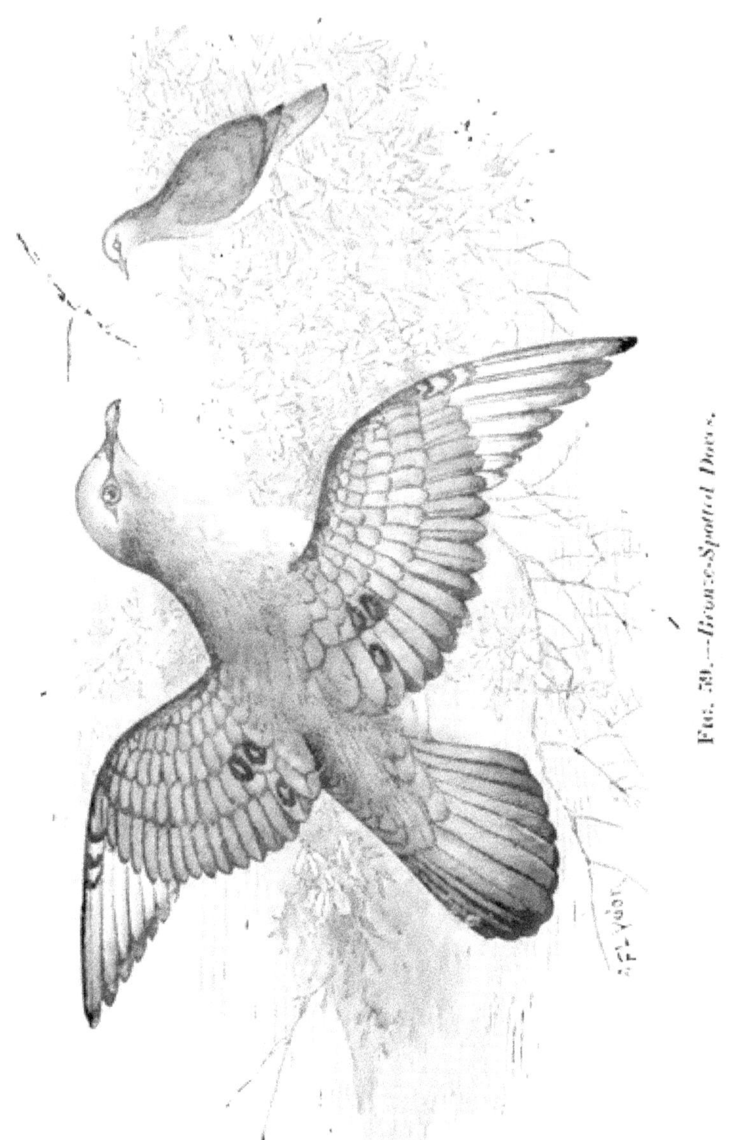

Fig. 39.—*Bronze-Spotted Doves.*

Bronze-Spotted Dove.—This little bird is about the size of a common quail, and is equally plump. Its colour is brown, darker above than below; on the shoulders are some bronze spots, with metallic reflections, whence the

FIG. 60.—*The Tambourine Doves.*

name. Male and female are alike. It is half hardy, and has bred in several aviaries.

Food—millet, canary seed, and dari.

TAMBOURINE DOVE.—This is a compact little bird, somewhat larger than the bronze-spotted dove. It is dark chocolate brown on the upper, and white on the lower side. The female is of a lighter brown, and has the under parts shaded with grey.

It is not hardy, and requires to be kept during the winter in a warmed aviary, where it will breed.

Food same as the bronze-spotted dove.

THE PHEASANTS.

Family—*Phasianidæ.*

Genus—1. *Francolinus.*	*F. rubricollis.*	Red-throated Francolin.
	F. bicalcaratus.	Double-spurred Francolin.
	F. afer.	South African Francolin.
	F. clappertoni.	Clapperton's Francolin.
	F. capensis.	Cape Francolin.
2. *Numidia.*	*N. meleagris.*	Guinea Fowl.
	N. randalli.	Randall's Guinea Fowl.
	N. cornuta.	Horned Guinea Fowl.
	N. cristata.	Crested Guinea Fowl.
	N. pucherani.	Pucheran's Guinea Fowl.
	N. vulturina.	Vulturine Guinea Fowl.

RED-THROATED FRANCOLIN.—This fine bird, which is

about the size of an ordinary fowl, has the chin and throat of a deep ruddy sanguine tint, and the upper part of the breast white, streaked with black. The female is reddish brown.

GUINEA FOWL.—This domesticated species is too well known to need description. Male and female are much alike, but the latter is somewhat smaller than her mate, and has less conspicuous comb and wattles.

THE HEMIPODES.

Nearly related to the quails. In Africa the family is represented among others by the Lepurana Hemipode.

Family—*Turnicidæ.*
Genus—*Turnix.* *T. lepurana.* Lepurana Hemipode.

THE RAILS.

Family—*Rallidæ.*

Genus—			
1.	*Hydrornia.*	*H. halleni.*	Allen's Porphyrio.
2.	*Gallinula.*	*G. nesiotis.*	Island Hen Gallinule.
3.	*Fulica.*	*F. cristata.*	Crested Coot.

ISLAND HEN GALLINULE.—This bird is found in the desolate island named Tristan d'Acunha, an isolated rock to the south of Africa. It maintains a small English community, and has this one indigenous land bird, which, however, departs from it in winter.

THE BUSTARDS.

Family—*Otidæ.*		
Genus—*Eupodotis.*	*E. kori.*	Burchell's Bustard.
	E. senegalensis.	Senegal Bustard.
	E. ruficollis.	Red-necked Bustard.
	E. denhami.	Denham's Bustard.

The bustards are a peculiar group intermediate between the poultry and crane families, to both of which they bear some resemblance in habits, etc. They resemble the European bustard already described.

THE CRANES.

Family—*Gruidæ.*			
Genus—1.	*Tetrapteryx.*	*T. paradisea.*	Stanley Crane.
2.	*Balearica.*	*B. pavonina.*	Balearic Crane.
		B. chrysopelagus.	Cape Crowned Crane.

Cape Crowned Crane.—This fine bird is found in Western and Northern Africa in marshy localities, where it feeds on reptiles, molluscs, and fish. The top of the head is decorated with a number of filamentary feathers of a golden yellow colour, fringed with delicate black barbules. The cheeks are bare, and the skin thereof scarlet. The general colour of the feathers is pale slate; but the quills of the wings and tail are black, and the elongated secondaries brown. This species thrives well in confinement.

THE PLOVERS.

Family—*Charadriidæ.*
Genus—*Hæmatopus.* *H. niger.* Black Oyster-Catcher.

This bird is very like its European namesake, but has less white about it than the latter. It feeds in a similar manner, frequents similar localities, and feeds on the same kind of food, which it displays equal ingenuity in securing. It is probably only a local variety.

THE SHEATHBILLS.

Family—*Chionididæ.*
Genus—*Chionis.* *C. minor.*

Black-Billed Sheathbill.—This remarkable bird has a snow-white plumage and a jetty black bill, which, as the name implies, has a sheath or hood of a horny consistence placed over the nostrils. The generic name, Chionis, is derived from the Greek word signifying snow. The black-billed chionis measures about 15 inches in total. Little or nothing is known of its habits in the wild state.

THE OCEANIC GULLS.

Family—*Procellariidæ.*
Genus—*Daption.* *D. capense.* Cape Pigeon.

Cape Pigeon.—There are a variety of birds, of which this is one, that follow in the wake of vessels in their route from England to Australia. They breed for the most part on the rocky peaks of Tristan d'Acunha, and on Kergulen's

Land, which is still further to the south, but is geographically considered to be part of Africa.

THE OSTRICH.

Family—*Struthionidæ.*
Genus—*Struthio.* *S. camelus.* Ostrich.

It is strange that most countries have a wingless bird peculiar to them. Thus Australia has its emu; New Guinea its cassowary; New Zealand its apteryx; America its rhea; and small islands, such as Mauritus and Bourbon, had their dodo and solitaire respectively; but Africa has its well-known OSTRICH, the monarch of them all, rivalling the extinct dinornis in point of size.

This fine bird is so well-known as the provider of the plumes that figure so largely in court ceremonies, as well as in the attire of ladies of all nationalities, that it may be summarily dismissed with the remark that the feathers are cut from the adult birds when they are still in their recent or finest condition, and are not plucked—an operation that is apt to cause the mutilated bird to die from inflammatory fever.

PART IV.

THE BIRDS OF AMERICA.

THE THRUSHES.

We commence with these as before:—

Family—*Turdidæ.*

Genus—

1. *Turdus.*	*T. falklandicus.*	Falkland Island Thrush.
2. *Sialia.*	*S. wilsonii.*	Common Blue Bird.

The Falkland Island Thrush.—Except that it is a native of these far-off, and to a great extent ice-bound, islands, there is nothing peculiarly characteristic about this bird, which is a thrush to all intents and purposes.

The Common Blue Bird.—It seems absurd to class this decided robin with the thrushes. In every respect, except a trifling difference in size and the azure blue of its back and wings, it is very like its familiar English congener, even to its habit of frequenting the neighbourhood of the abode of man.

The breast is dull reddish brown, and the rest of the plumage blue.

The female is like the male, but her colours are not so bright, and she is a trifle smaller.

The blue bird is a disappointing inmate of the aviary, in which it will live for years, if treated in accordance with the method already prescribed for other soft-billed birds, but it disappoints its guardian by its readiness to nest, and

FIG. 61.—*The Blue Jay.*

the unfailing desertion of its young ones when they are a few days old.

THE FINCHES.

Well represented in America, including Canada and the remaining portions of the British dominions. They may be summed up as follows :—

Family—*Fringillidæ.*

Genus—

1. *Phonipara.*	*P. olivacea.*	Olive Finch.
	P. bicolor.	Dusky Finch.
2. *Guiraca.*	*G. cærulea.*	Blue Grossbeak.
3. *Hedymeles.*	*H. ludovicianus.*	Rose-breasted Grossbeak.
4. *Zanotrichia.*	*Z. leucophrys.*	White-eyebrowed Finch.

Dusky Finch.—This bird, also known by the name of Jamaica finch, is a native of that island, and inconspicuous either as regards song or colouring. It does very well in confinement if treated like an ordinary canary, with which it will inter-breed and produce mules.

Blue Grossbeak.—As its name implies, this little bird is of a bright blue colour, of about the size of a canary; it occurs in British North America somewhat sparingly, and succeeds very well in confinement on the ordinary seed. The song is a pleasing little twitter. The female is brownish, with a shade, or suspicion rather, of blue here and there.

Rose-Breasted Grossbeak.—Dark, almost black above, and carmine on the breast; this is a very pretty bird. The female is greyish brown without any red; it will breed in confinement, and the young at first resemble their mother. A report that it has paired and produced mules with a canary requires confirmation. Food and treatment as the preceding.

WHITE-EYEBROWED FINCH.—This bird is also known and more correctly, as the white-crowned sparrow; it is very inconspicuous in appearance, and has no song to speak of. If desired as an inmate of the aviary, it should be fed and treated as the preceding.

THE STARLINGS.

The BLACK TROUPIAL belongs to this group.

Family—*Icteridæ.*
Genus—*Quiscalus.* *Q. lugubris.*

The colour is black, with a purple metallic gloss; the feet and legs are black, and the eyes yellow; the female is duller in her appearance. Food and treatment as recommended for the common starling.

THE TOUCANS.

Occurring in Southern America, and, among other places, in the British Colony of Demerara; these remarkable birds constitute the

Family—*Ramphastidæ.*
Genus—

Ramphastus.	*R. toco.*	Toco Toucan.
	R. erythrorhynchus.	Red-billed Toucan.
	R. dicolorus.	Green-billed Toucan.

They are all remarkable for the apparently disproportionate size of their bills, which almost rival those of the hornbills. They are sufficiently amusing by their quaint ways to induce some aviarists to give them a trial; but, as a rule, they do not live long in captivity.

The general colour of the plumage is black, diversified with red and yellow; the bills in some species are very gaudily tinted.

They must be kept warm, and fed on a mixture of fruit, vegetables, and insect and animal matters.

THE OWLS.

Family—*Asionidæ.*

Genus—

1. *Asio.*	*A. grammicus.*	Gosse's Eared Owl.
2. *Syrnium.*	*S. nebulosum.*	Barred Owl.
3. *Surnia.*	*S. funerea.*	American Hawk Owl.

Habits and mode of treatment in captivity—in which, by the by, no owl should ever be kept, as they are of so much use in their natural habitats—same as in the case of the members of the family already noticed.

THE HAWKS, OR FALCONS.

The British North American species are included in the

Family—*Falconidæ.*

Genus—

1. *Buteo.*	*B. borealis.*	Red-tailed Buzzard.
2. *Haliaetus.*	*H. leucocephalus.*	White-headed Sea Eagle.
3. *Hierofalco.*	*H. candicans.*	Greenland Falcon.
4. *Milvago.*	*M. australis.*	Forster's Kite.

Demands on our space preclude any detailed notice of the above.

THE DUCKS AND GEESE.

Family—*Anatidæ*.

Genus—

1. *Bernicla.*	*B. canadensis.*	Canada Goose.
	B. hutchinsi.	Hutchin's Goose.
	B. magellanica.	Upland Goose.
	B. rudiceps.	Ruddy-headed Goose.
	B. antarctica.	Kelp Goose.
2. *Tachyeres.*	*T. cinereus.*	Loggerhead Goose.

The CANADA GOOSE has been so long acclimatised in England that it is very generally known; it is a smaller bird than the common goose, and of a darker and more uniform colour; the cry is particularly loud and sonorous. According to Seebohm, the egg measures 3·65 inches in length and 2·3 inches in breadth, and is of a dull white colour.

THE PIGEONS.

Well represented in America, that is, in British America, as follows:—

Family—*Columbidæ*.

Genus—

1. *Columba.*	*C. leucocephala.*	White-crowned Pigeon.
	C. carribbea.	Ring-tailed Pigeon.
2. *Ectopistes.*	*E. migratorius.*	Passenger Pigeon.
3. *Zenaida.*	*Z. amabilis.*	Zenaida Dove.
	Z. martinica.	Martinican Dove.
	Z. leucoptera.	White-winged Dove.
4. *Leptoptila*	*L. jamaicensis.*	White-fronted Dove.
	L. rufaxilla.	Red Under-Winged Dove.
5. *Geotrygon.*	*G. sylvatica.*	Mountain Witch Dove.

PASSENGER PIGEON.—It has been pretty well established that the movements of this bird are rather due to the

FIG. 62.—*Scaly-Breasted Dove.*

necessity for finding food than from any real migratory

instinct, as their movements do not always take place at the same period of the year, and sometimes they remain for several years in the same locality without making any attempt to go away.

It has been rather absurdly placed among British birds by Morris on the strength of a few specimens shot in several places, but of course these were escaped from aviaries, in which, by the by, the passenger pigeon will breed. It only lays one egg at a time, and feeds on all kinds of grain and corn, as well as berries.

THE PARROTS.

The following occur in British America :—

Family—*Psittacidæ.*

Genus—

1. *Chrysotis.*	*C. levaillanti.*	Levaillant's Amazon.
2. *Bolborhynchus.*	*B. monachus.*	Monk Parrakeet.
3. *Conurus.*	*C. leucotis.*	White-eared Conure.

LEVAILLANT'S AMAZON is a handsome bird of considerable size, larger than the well-known Grey. Its general body colour is green, but the head and neck are primrose yellow; the bill is white, and the legs and feet grey. It is the next best imitator of human speech after the grey parrot, which it occasionally equals, or even surpasses, in linguistic capacity. It is met with in Demerara and the adjacent parts of South America, is fairly hardy, and lives for many years in confinement, eating grain of all kinds, and a little fruit. The sexes are much alike in appearance, but the male is the larger, and his head and neck of a brighter shade of yellow.

Several other kinds of amazons are found in Demerara

and in British Honduras, as well as in the West Indian Islands, but they have been so exhaustively considered elsewhere that we must not stay to attend to them any further in the present place.

The MONK, or QUAKER PARRAKEET is more common in Monte Video than elsewhere, but stragglers have been met

FIG. 63.—*Hawk-Headed Parrots.*

with in the hinterland of Demerara. It is remarkable for being the only member of the family that builds itself a nest of sticks among the branches of a tree. It is about the size of a turtle dove, green on the upper, and ashen grey on the lower, surface of the body. It has bred freely in numerous aviaries.

The WHITE-EARED CONURE is a well-known representative of a sub-family or genus of South American parrots, differentiated by their moderately long wedge-shaped tail. It occurs in the northern parts of South America, and is a pretty bird about the size of an English blackbird. The bill is black, the head and cheeks brown, the ear coverts white, the breast grey, the belly, vent, and under surface of the tail red, and the rest of the plumage green.

It is easily reconciled to captivity, and will breed in an aviary, but is quarrelsome and dangerous with other birds, epecially smaller parrakeets.

THE GROUSE.

The American members of this group now claim our attention.

Family—*Tetraonidæ.*

Genus—

1. *Tetrao.*	*T. cupido.*	Prairie Grouse.
	T. phasianellus.	Sharp-tailed Grouse.
2. *Odontophorus.*	*O. guianensis.*	Guiana Partridge.
3. *Meleagris.*	*M. gallo-pavo.*	Turkey.

The GROUSE are well known for their peculiar habits during the breeding season, when the males, which had consorted together in perfect harmony during the winter, separate in the spring, each bird taking a particular station, from which he drives every rival who ventures to approach, and there he struts and crows and displays his ruff and crest and elongated plumes for the delectation of the females that assemble to his call. When these have laid, the males forsake them, and, after remaining solitary for a while, again unite with their fellows till the following season.

The TURKEY.—There is no doubt that this well-known bird had its origin in North America, where it is yet to be met with in a wild state. It is an example of perfect reclamation, for it has long been fully domesticated, and is one of the most useful birds we have. The size and quality of the flesh have been much improved, but no marked varieties, as in the case of the common fowl, have as yet been obtained.

THE CURASSOWS.

A peculiar group of birds peculiar to the northern parts of South America, where many of them are fairly common in the unreclaimed parts of British Guiana.

Family—*Cracidæ.*

Genus			
Genus—1.	*Crax.*	*C. alector.*	Crested Curassow.
2.	*Mitua.*	*M. tuberosa.*	Razor-billed Curassow.
		M. tomentosa.	Lesser Razor-billed Curassow.
3.	*Penelope.*	*P. marail.*	Marail Guan.
4.	*Pipile.*	*P. cumanensis.*	Piping Guan.
5.	*Ortalis.*	*O. motmot.*	Little Guan.
		O. ruficauda.	Red-tailed Guan.

All attempts to reclaim these large and for the most part handsome birds have failed, for, unlike the turkey, peacock, and guinea-fowl, they do not breed in confinement, and rarely even deposit an egg, while they are not sufficiently hardy to admit of their being turned out of doors and made to shift for themselves like the pheasant.

There are several other species besides those enumerated above, but they are all alike in this respect that they refuse to be made to minister to the wants of human kind.

THE GULLS.

This group is not so numerously represented in British America as at home, but two genera and two species are found in it.

Family—*Laridæ.*

Genus—1. *Larus. L. dominicanus.* Falkland Island Gull.
2. *Anous. A. stolidus.* Noddy.

Both the FALKLAND ISLAND GULL and the NODDY are southern species, and although the latter extends across the whole of the Southern Pacific, it is more frequent towards the west than the east, and properly comes under consideration in our next and concluding section.

THE PENGUINS.

Several kinds of PENGUINS belonging to the

Family—*Sphenicidæ.*

Genus—1. *Aptenodytes. A. pennanti.* Falkland Island Penguin.
2. *Pygosceles. P. tæniatus.* Gentos Penguin.
3. *Spheniscus. S. megallanicus.* Jackass Penguin.
4. *Eudyptis. E. chrysocoma.* Rock Hopper Penguin.

are found in different parts of the British Empire, but as it is so extremely unlikely that anybody would want to keep any of them, it is not worth while occupying space with particulars of perhaps the most uninteresting of birds.

THE TANAGERS.

This is a fairly individualised group, which has been constituted a distinct

Family—*Tanagridæ.*
Genus—*Tanagra.* *T. sayaca.* Sayaca Tanager.

One genus may be briefly referred to. It is also called the grey tanager, and is found among other places in British Guiana. The general colour is ash-grey, with a bluish gloss on the head, neck, and upper parts generally; the wings and tail are black, with greenish blue bands or lines; the eyes are brown, and the legs and feet blackish. The female only differs in being a little duller in appearance. It is about the size of a European lark, and may be fed in the same way, with the addition of fruit.

THE LARKS

Are represented in America by the well-known Shore Lark, which is included among British birds by Morris and other writers, on the strength of a few specimens caught, or more frequently shot, in Britain nearly every winter.

Family—*Alaudidæ.*
Genus—*Otocorys.* *O. alpestris.* Shore Lark.

The generic name *Otocorys* bestowed on these birds

signifies "eared," and has been given to them on account of the tuft that projects from the front towards the back of the head, bearing some resemblance to a pen stuck behind each ear of a city man of business.

It is a native of Northern America, where it is migratory, that is, in the winter it directs its flight to the south, and returns in the spring to its native haunts.

It is easily kept in confinement if treated as recommended for the European lark, than which it is rather smaller, although resembling it in a general way.

PART V.

THE BIRDS OF AUSTRALIA.

THE birds of Australia are so many and various that to describe them all would be to make a book about four times the size assigned to the present volume, and then but a scanty notice only of each would be practicable, so that a rigid selection only can be made of one or two of the most prominent members of each family or group.

THE ORIOLES.

Family—*Oriolidæ.*
Genus—*Sericulus.* *S. melinus.* Regent Bird.

The REGENT BIRD is a magnificent creature, whose gorgeous plumage of rich velvety black, shot with a variety of brilliant tints, make it a sight not soon to be forgotten. It is rare, and of local occurrence, about the size of a magpie, but rather approaching the woodpeckers in habits and configuration.

The natural food is insects, centipedes, and creatures of that kind, with which its native "bush" abounds, and it can only be preserved for a short time in confinement.

THE WOOD SWALLOWS.

Family—*Artamidæ.*
Genus—*Artamus.* *A. superciliosus.* White-eyebrowed Tree Swallow.

Among the prettiest and commonest inhabitants of sparsely-wooded districts, these birds may be seen in groups or flocks of from ten to twenty, flying swifty to and fro under the trees during all the hours of daylight in pursuit of flies and other winged insects, and when tired, resting in rows on the lower horizontal branches beneath which they had been disporting themselves. As bitter foes of the ubiquitous mosquito, they should be encouraged and protected in every way.

The nest is a neat cup-like structure, made of strips of barks and lichens. It is always placed resting against the trunk of a tree, generally a small one. The eggs are only two, of a white colour and of elliptical shape.

The writer has seen them caged, but they are as much out of place in such a situation as one of our martins. These captives fed mainly on flies that were attracted into the cage by means of a piece of meat hung to the perch on which the prisoners sat.

THE ZOSTEROPS, OR WHITE EYES.

These are very peculiar-looking birds on account of the white circle of corrugated skin that surrounds the eyes, giving the appearance of spectacles or "goggles," whence the name spectacle birds by which they are also known. They are olive green above, and white below, and about the size of a blackcap. They can be caged, and live for a considerable time in captivity, eating ants' eggs and similar things, and fruit.

The zosterops is a native of New Zealand, and belongs to the

Family—*Nectariniidæ.*

Genus—*Zosterops.* *Z. lateralis.* Lateral White Eye.
Z. dorsalis. Grey-backed White Eye.

THE FINCHES.

The following is an enumeration of the genera and species more usually imported :—

Family—*Ploceidæ*.

Genus—		
1. *Estrelda*.	*E. ruficauda*.	Red-tailed Finch.
	E. phaeton.	Crimson Finch.
	E. bichenovi.	Bicheno's Finch.
	E. temporalis.	Australian Waxbill.
	E. bella.	Beautiful Finch.
2. *Amadina*.	*A. modesta*.	Modest Grass Finch.
	A. castanotis.	Chestnut-eared, or Zebra Finch.
	A. lathami.	Side-spotted Finch, or Diamond Sparrow.
	A. gouldiæ.	Black-faced Gouldian Finch.
	A. mirabilis.	Red-faced Gouldian Finch.
3. *Paephila*.	*P. cincta*.	Parson Finch.
4. *Donacola*.	*D. castaneothorax*.	Chestnut-breasted Finch.

Diamond Sparrow.—These lively birds are well known as inmates of the cage and aviary in Britain, and are about the size of a plump redpoll. Grey above, and white beneath ; the sides are black, spotted with numerous white spots ; a black band crosses the breast, and the rump is red.

The sexes are alike. The food in confinement, in which these birds do well, is millet and canary seed. The nest is made of grass, and placed in a low bush ; it is domed, and lined with feathers. The white eggs are four in number.

Zebra Finch, or Sparrow.—A smaller bird than the

preceding, of an ashen grey colour above, and white beneath; there is a red spot on the face, and the sides and tail coverts are spotted with black and white; there is a moustache or two black lines diverging from the corners of the carmine red bill. The female is all grey.

Food and treatment like the preceding. It is a native of

FIG. 64.—*The Parson Finch.*

New South Wales, but the diamond sparrow is found also in Victoria in the Murray district.

GOULDIAN, or PAINTED FINCHES.—They are well known, and more frequently met with than they were a few years ago. There are two principal varieties or species—it is not yet satisfactorily determined in which relation they stand to each other—the red-faced and the black-faced. They are almost the size of the diamond sparrow, and are coloured in almost all the tints of the rainbow, but have, nevertheless, a decidedly neat and trim appearance.

They will breed freely in confinement if kept at a suitable temperature, that is, from 60 to 90 degrees; but if exposed for any length of time to anything lower than the

Fig. 65.—*The Chestnut-Breasted Finch.*

former, they quickly get out of health, and lose their neat appearance, and, if the low temperature continues, die.

They are very frugal feeders, white millet being their chief diet; a little canary seed may be added, but they do not care about it much. The nest is a huge affair made of grass, and the eggs, from three to five in number, are white; incubation lasts about seventeen days, and in five or six weeks the young come out of the nest fully fledged, but grey and insignificant-looking creatures with dusky bills.

Unless they have plenty of room in which to exercise, the females are apt to become egg bound, and die before their unfortunate predicament is discovered.

Advice that was recently given respecting them by an "expert" that they were not to be allowed seed, but fed entirely on fruit, quickly resulted in the death of the unfortunate bird subjected to the experiment. The same "authority" also stated that the painted finches were indifferent to cold! which, seeing that they are found chiefly in North Australia, would be decidedly singular if it were correct; but it is not, as amateurs have found to their cost, for owing to their living in single pairs, and not in flocks, they are not imported in large numbers, and the price, although lower than it was, remains high, say, fifty shillings a couple.

The Parson Finch is another member of the family that is very well known to amateurs in England, although less frequently in the market than it used to be. It is rather smaller than the diamond sparrow. Its general colour is brown, with the head and neck bluish grey; a black band crosses the throat, and another passes behind the thighs: the under tail coverts are white, and the tail bluish black.

It breeds freely in English aviaries, but the young rapidly deteriorate in size and colour, as well as in stamina, so that an aviary-bred parson finch of the fourth generation is still a desideratum, and likely to remain so, unless the bird can be kept under conditions more nearly resembling those that obtain in its native country than is usually the case. Price, about twenty to twenty-five shillings a pair. Food and treatment like the preceding.

Most of the foregoing birds are more nearly related by their habits to the sparrows than to the finches, properly so called.

THE HONEY-EATERS.

The Honey-eaters, or nectivorous birds are a fairly numerous group found in Australia, New Guinea, New Zealand, and some of the islands in the Pacific. The best known of them is the Poë, or Parson Bird of New Zealand, where it used to be found in abundance, but now is much reduced in numbers.

It is a large bird, about the size of a jackdaw, but with a longer and slimmer build. It is in much request for its song and great imitative powers. It requires good management to keep it alive in confinement, but, by a judicious mixture of insect with vegetable matters and honey, this can be done; though even under the most favourable circumstances, the poë will often be unreasonable enough to have a fit and die, the result, probably, of digestive trouble. From the disinclination it evinces to go on the ground, it is probable that in its native islands it catches its insect prey on the wing, or, at least, among the branches of the trees it frequents.

Family—*Meliphagidæ.*

Genus—

1. *Prosthemadura.*	*P. novæ zelandiæ.*	Poë.
2. *Anthornis.*	*A. melanura.*	Black-tailed Flower Bird.
3. *Xanthomyza.*	*X. phrygia.*	Warty-faced Honey-Eater.
4. *Entomyza.*	*E. cyanotis.*	Blue-faced Honey Eater.

THE BOWER-BIRDS.

There are few Australian birds better known by repute than these, of which several species are met with. They are easily kept in confinement, and are extremely interesting and handsome. They are about the size of the jackdaw.

Their principal characteristic is building bowers, or playing runs of considerable extent, the entrances to which they decorate with any glittering object they find lying about, and, failing such, with shells, bits of glass, bone, and with feathers.

They are classed and divided as follows:—

Family—*Ptilonorhynchidæ.*

Genus—

1. *Ptilonorhynchus.*	*P. violaceus.*	Silky Bower Bird.
	P. smithi.	Cat Bird.
2. *Chalamydodera.*	*C. maculata.*	Spotted Bower Bird.

THE BIRDS OF PARADISE.

These gorgeous creatures are well known, and, with one or two minor exceptions, are found in the comparatively unknown island of New Guinea; perhaps it would be better to say were found, for owing to the request for their marvellous plumes for the decoration (?) of feminine headgear, they have become much more scarce than they were, if some of them have not been altogether exterminated.

At one time they were classed with the crows, but recently they have been divided from them, and placed by themselves.

Family—*Paradiseidæ.*

Genus—

1. *Paradisea.*	*P. minor.*	Lesser Bird of Paradise.
	P. rubra.	Red Bird of Paradise.
2. *Ptilorhis.*	*P paradisea.*	Rifle Bird.
3. *Seleucides.*	*S. nigricans.*	Twelve-wired Bird of Paradise.
4. *Manucodia.*	*M. chalybeia.*	Green Manucode.

Some of the above-named species, which do not nearly exhaust the list of the beautiful birds of paradise, have lived for a considerable time in the parrot house in the Zoological Society's Gardens in Regent's Park, London, where they were fed as stated for the starling.

Common, or Emerald Bird of Paradise.—Perhaps the best known of these magnificent creatures. It is as large as a jay, and of a delicate chocolate brown colour, but the face and throat are rich metallic green; the scapular feathers are long and filamentous, and the bird has the power of spreading them out round its body in a kind of cloud. These beautiful plumes are cream colour.

The female is devoid of this exuberance of feathering, and might be called plain-looking, but for the golden green and yellow of the head and neck which she wears in common with her partner.

Red Bird of Paradise.—About the size of a thrush, also possesses a great quantity of sub-alar feathering that quite conceals the tail, from among the quills of which project two long filamentous feathers that are more than twice the length of the bird itself. These are black, but the rest of the long feathers are red.

Golden Bird of Paradise.—Another splendid creature, with a plumage of velvety black, changing into metallic green of the most brilliant tint. The throat is emerald green, and shines like burnished brass. The immensely long tail consists of twelve feathers in graduated pairs, the

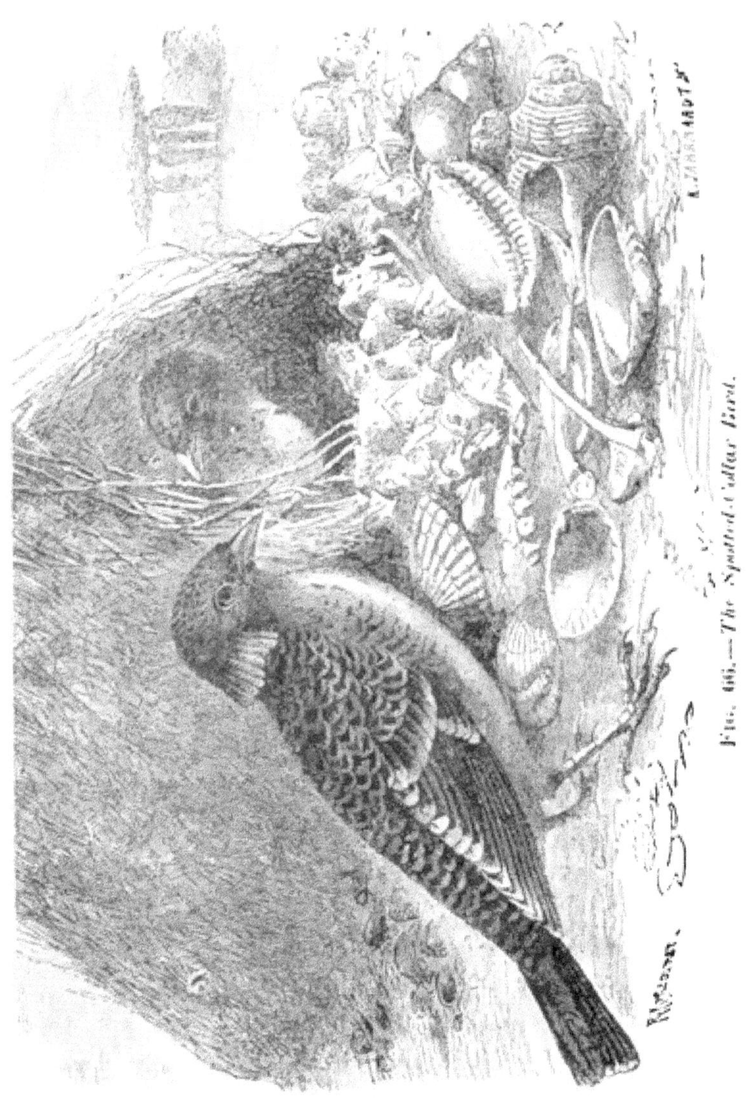

Fig. 66.—The Spotted Cellar Bird.

last of which are more than three times the length of the bird.

Those beautiful creatures, however, fairly beggar description, and require to be seen in order to be appreciated as they deserve. It is to be regretted that the request for

FIG. 67.—*The Bird of Paradise.*

their plumage for feminine hat decoration is slowly but surely leading on to their extermination.

THE CROWS.

These birds are well represented in Australia, where the more prominent members are to be found, though some species inhabit New Guinea, and rival the birds of paradise in the brilliancy of their colouring.

Family—*Corvidæ.*

Genus—

1. *Corvus.* *C. australis.* Australian Crow.

2. *Corcorax.*	*C. melanorhamphus.*	White-winged Chough.
3. *Heteralocha.*	*H. gouldi.*	Huia Bird.
4. *Strepera.*	*S. graculina.*	Pied Crow Shrike.
	S. fugilinosa.	Sooty Crow Shrike.
	S. arguta.	Hill Crow Shrike.
5. *Gymnorhina.*	*G. leuconota.*	White-backed Piping Crow.
	G. organica.	Tasmanian Piping Crow.
	G. tibicen.	Black-backed Piping Crow.
6. *Barita.*	*B. destructor.*	Long-billed Butcher Crow.

PIPING CROW.—One of the "common objects" of the Australian bush, and a very delightful one, for his cheery notes always announce the vicinity of water, a treasure that is only rightly appreciated by those who have wandered in weary search of it for many long hours under a burning sun. The general colour is black and white; the bill has a bluish tinge, and is decidedly corvine in appearance. Male and female are very much alike, and their food consists of insects of all kinds, and small reptiles, of which they consume an enormous quantity.

The magpie, as the bird is called by the colonists, is readily tamed, learns to talk very well, and to pipe tunes in a surprisingly correct manner; it will live on ordinary house scraps for years, and become so tame that it may be accustomed to go out and return at a given signal.

PIED CROW SHRIKE.—Very like the magpie in general appearance, but has less white on its plumage, which s black, with metallic reflections on the head and breast; the long broad tail is crossed at its upper part by a wide band of white, and is tipped with a narrow one at its free extremity; there is also a white patch on the centre of each wing; the bill is black, and the eye a clear yellow.

TASMANIAN PIPING CROW.—Does not differ greatly from its relatives on the mainland, except in point of size, for it is much larger than the Australian magpie, nearly equalling in dimensions the common English rook. It is a very hardy bird, and will live for a number of years in confinement, affording its owner or guardian a good deal of cheap amusement by its curious artful-simple ways.

When a tame crow is surrounded and attacked by a number of wild ones, it throws itself on its back, and fights with bill and claws; but when it finds this mode of self-defence insufficient, it will suddenly jump up and begin to swear at its assailants in the most "colonial" fashion, a ruse that always has the effect of immediately dispersing its foes.

THE MENURA.

The MENURA, or LYRE BIRD of South-Eastern Australia is perhaps one of the most remarkable of the many strange birds that are to be met with in the great island-continent, for although about the size of a farm-yard pullet, it is really a wren, and has a tail like the musical instrument used by the Greek poetess Sappho, which tail consists of two broad feathers, that have an outward curve at their free extremities; they are barbed heavily on their inner aspect, and more slightly on the outer one, and from between them spring twelve or fourteen light, graceful plumes, almost like in construction to those of the emerald bird of paradise, but that they are of stiffer habit, and do not droop gracefully like those of the latter bird but stand up and represent the strings of the lyre.

The menura is a ground-loving bird, and has very strong legs and feet. The nest is large, domed, and placed on the ground, under the shelter of some overhanging bush; only one egg appears to be laid, and the young one grows slowly, but it is able to run swiftly long before it can fly.

The food consists of insects, such as beetles, centipedes, scorpions, and also snails.

It somewhat resembles the bower-bird in its habit of making "play-grounds," in and on which it is in the habit of spending a good deal of its time; but it is exceedingly wary, and can rarely be discovered when engaged in its amusement.

It has a sweet song of its own, and, in addition, possesses great imitative powers. So far it has been found impossible to preserve it for any length of time in captivity.

Family—*Menuridæ.*

Genus—*Menura.*	*M. superba.*	Lyre Bird.
	M. alberti.	Prince Albert's Lyre Bird.

This last differs from *Superba* in having a less developed tail.

THE NIGHTJARS.

The MOREPORK, or PODARGUS, is another very singular bird of pretty frequent occurrence in all parts of Australia; it is, in fact, a kind of goatsucker, and, like that bird, nocturnal in its habits. No sound is more familiar to the bushman than its weird cry, which is supposed to resemble the syllables, "more pork," to which it owes its most familiar name, though it is also known as the cuckoo.

Its food consists chiefly of cicadas, and beetles, which it captures when asleep among the bushes, and not on the wing, like its European congener, from which it also differs by its habit of sitting across the branch and not along it, as the latter does.

The eggs are white, two in number, and are laid in a hollow in a decayed branch or trunk, without any attempt being made at nest construction. It is about the same size as the English bird, to which it bears a general resemblance.

Family—*Podargidæ*.
Genus—*Podargus*. *P. cuvieri*. Cuvier's Podargus.

THE KINGFISHERS.

Almost everyone has heard of the strange bird known in the Australian Colonies by the name of LAUGHING JACKASS, and more scientifically, DACELO. It belongs to the Kingfishers, and is usually classed as follows:—

Family—*Alcedinæ*.

Genus—*Dacelo*.	*D. gigantica*.	Laughing Kingfisher.
	D. cervina.	Buff Laughing Kingfisher.

The latter is the representative of the family in the northern and the former in the southern parts of Australia, where few travellers through the bush have failed to be startled when first at or before day-break they listened to its powerful voice and weird cachinnation, which some writers have likened to the laugh of an idiot, and others to the braying of a donkey; the fact being that it is something between both and unlike either, a note entirely *sui-generis* and inimitable, at least on paper.

The bird is short-legged, big-billed, and thickset; its plumage is grey, diversified by hints of green and buff on

FIG. 68.—*The Laughing Jackass.*

the wings, and blue on the head, which is covered with thick, rather long feathers, which it can erect into a very tolerable crest at will. It is found in the driest and most arid places, as well as in the vicinity of lagoons and creeks, and preys on reptiles chiefly, snakes, lizards, and so forth, as well as insects of a larger growth, the gigantic centipede, that makes dead timber a horror in the bush, centipedes and coleoptera of various kinds, as well as cicadas that murder sleep, and mantides that mock the praying friar, for they only pray to prey on the unwary creatures smaller than themselves that venture within their reach.

A useful bird is the dacelo, and protected by law—at least, if it is not it ought to be, in consequence of the number of deadly reptiles it destroys. The writer once found a lizard in the crop of a dacelo that was as long as the bird itself, and it will kill and swallow a snake twice at least its own length, and repeat the operation in an hour.

THE STRUTHIDEA.

Family—*Craterapodidæ.*
Genus—*Struthidea.* *S. cinerea.* Grey Struthidea.

These birds are sometimes spoken of as oven-birds, but are quite different from the members of the *Dendrocolaptidæ* family, of which the RED OVEN-BIRD (*Furnarius rufus*) is a typical example; but as it is found in South America (Buenos Ayres), it is outside the scope of the present work.

The Grey Struthidea, however, is a native of Australia, and is sufficiently (or was) plentiful in the park-like country round Lake Burrumbeet in the colony of Victoria, where it affixes its curious oven-like nest to the horizontal branches of the dwarf gum-trees or the banksias that, with várious mimosas, form the sylva of that picturesque region.

They are not very attractive-looking birds, for the colour, as the name indicates, is not a brilliant one, and they have no voice to speak of—at least, not a musical one—to compensate for their lack of brilliant attire. The wings are short and round, but the rather long tail, broad and rounded at the free extremity, is their most remarkable feature, and a fairly good example of perpetual motion.

In confinement they are fed on the usual "insectivorous birds' food," dry crumbled biscuit and seed. Raw and cooked meat is mixed with the first, as well as a little preserved yolk of egg.

THE CUCKOOS.

Wherever they are found, the Cuckoos are a mysterious race, and Australia, New Zealand, and New Guinea have each their own members of the

Family—*Cuculidæ.*

Genus—

1. *Eudynamis.*	*E. taitensis.*	Long-tailed Cuckoo.
2. *Centropus.*	*C. phasianus.*	Pheasant Coucal.

Long-Tailed Cuckoo.—A native of New Zealand and a true parasite, laying an egg here and there in the nest of some other bird, such as the grey warbler, which is not more than quarter of its size. It is a handsome and rather peculiar-looking creature. The long tail is brown, barred with black, and the wings are the same, but marbled, in addition with white and yellowish brown; the breast and under parts are creamy white, with long black spots, the thin end of which is directed upwards; the iris is yellow, and the strong legs and feet of a yellowish grey colour.

The sexes are alike in outward appearance, but the young are more spotted than their elders.

PHEASANT COUCAL.—A native of New South Wales, and of local occurrence there, keeping for the most part to low-lying places. It has the configuration of the cuckoo, but makes a nest, and incubates its own three or four greyish white, round eggs.

It is of a brownish grey colour, and the tail is tipped with white; unlike the *Eudynamis*, it is a ground-loving bird, and makes a large domed nest of sticks under some convenient bush.

THE PARROTS.

Australia, with its dependencies, is decidedly the land of parrots, and to more than glance at some of the more prominent species that are there to be met with is absolutely out of the question in the space at our disposal. Indeed, for the same reason, we cannot even enumerate them all.

They have been much divided by writers, and the London Zoological Society, in their list, have made three distinct families of them, while the great German ornithologist, Dr. Carl Russ, has classed them all together, under the general name of *Psittacidæ*. We have, however, adopted the "Zoo" classification modified as follows:—

Family—*Psittacidæ*.
Sub-family—*Cacatuinæ*.
Genus—

1. *Cacatua*.	*C. galerita*.	Great Lemon-crested Cockatoo.
	C. triton.	Triton Cockatoo.
	C. leadbeateri.	Leadbeater's Cockatoo.
	C. sanguinea.	Blood-stained Cockatoo.
	C. gymnopis.	Bare-eyed Cockatoo.
	C. roseicapilla.	Roseate Cockatoo.

2. *Licmetis.*	*L. tenuirostris.*	Slender-billedCockatoo.
	L. pastinator.	Western Billed Cockatoo.
3. *Callocephalon.*	*C. galeatum.*	Ganga Cockatoo.
4. *Calyptorhynchus.*	*C. banksii.*	Banksion Cockatoo.
	C. funereus.	Funereal Cockatoo.
	C. naso.	Western Black Cockatoo.
5. *Microglossa.*	*M. aterrima.*	Goliath Aratoo.

Sub-family—*Stringopinæ.*

Genus—

1. *Stringops.*	*S. habroptilus.*	Night Parrot.
2. *Pezoporus.*	*P. formosus.*	Green Ground Parrakeet.

Sub-family—*Palæornithinæ.*

Genus—

Trichoglossus.	*T. novæ hollandiæ.*	Swainson's Lorikeet.
	T. coccinus.	Musky Lorikeet.
	T. chlorolepidotus.	Scaly-breasted Lorikeet.

Sub-family—*Electinæ.*

Genus—

1. *Eclectus.*	*E. pectoralis.*	Red-sided Eclectus.
2. *Polytelis.*	*P. barrabandi.*	Barraband's Parrakeet.
	P. melanura.	Black-tailed Parrakeet.
3. *Aprosmictus.*	*A. erythropterus.*	Red-winged Parrakeet.
	A. scapulatus.	King Parrakeet.
4. *Euphema.*	*E. pulchella.*	Turquoisine Parrakeet.
	E. elegans.	Elegant Parrakeet.
	E. chrysostoma.	Blue-banded Parrakeet.
	E. splendida.	Splendid Parrakeet.

	E. chrysogaster.	Orange-bellied Parrakeet.
	E. bourkii.	Bourke's Parrakeet.
5. *Melospittacus.*	*M. undulatus.*	Budgerigar.

Sub-family—*Psittacinæ.*

Genus—		
1. *Platycercus.*	*P. pennanti.*	Pennant's Parrakeet.
	P. adelaidæ.	Adelaide Parrakeet.
	P. flaveolus.	Yellow-rumped Parrakeet.
	P. icterotis.	Stanley Parrakeet.
	P. eximius.	Rosella Parrakeet.
	P. pallidiceps.	Pale-headed Parrakeet.
	P. pileatus.	Pileated Parrakeet.
	P. flaviventris.	Yellow-bellied Parrakeet.
	P. barnardi.	Barnard's Parrakeet.
	P. semitorquatus.	Yellow-collared Parrakeet.
	P. zonarius.	Bauer's Parrakeet.
2. *Calopsitta.*	*C. novæ hollandiæ.*	Cockatiel.
3. *Cyanorhamphus.*	*C novæ zelandiæ.*	New Zealand Parrakeet.
	C. alpinus.	Alpine Parrakeet.
	C. auriceps.	Golden-headed Parrakeet.
4. *Psephotus.*	*P. hæmatogaster.*	Blue Bonnet Parrakeet.
	P. hæmatonotus.	Blood-rumped Parrakeet.
	P. multicolor.	Many-coloured Parrakeet.
	P. pulcherrimus.	Beautiful, or Paradise Parrakeet.

5. *Lathamus.*	*L. discolor.*	Swift Parrakeet.
6. *Pyrrhulopsis.*	*P. tabuensis.*	Feejee Parrakeet.
	P. personata.	Masked Parrakeet.
7. *Nestor.*	*N. hypopolius.*	Ka-Ka Parrot.
	N. notabilis.	Mountain Ka-Ka Parrot.

A tolerably long list, but by no means an exhaustive one. As the first is the GREAT LEMON-CRESTED COCKATOO, so common in many parts of Australia and Tasmania, we feel bound to give it a few words of welcome, for it is really a grand creature, and a great ornament to its native country, whether seen flying at a great elevation above the head of the spectator, or covering a hillside, as with the aid of its powerful bill it digs out the roots, bulbs, and ground-nuts, upon which it feeds, or fed before the white man invaded its happy hunting grounds; but since then its habits have somewhat changed, for, abandoning its former laborious method of providing for its living, it prefers the easier way of attacking the farmer's crop, to which, as may be readily imagined, it does no small harm, so that in some parts it has already been exterminated, and, in course of time, will assuredly be extinguished everywhere.

It is the size of an ordinary farm-yard fowl, only its long, broad wings and tail, and its bold, upstanding, primrose-coloured crest, give it a different and much more distinguished appearance; the delicate tint of the crest contrasts elegantly with the snow-white colour of the back and breast, but the underside of the tail and wings have a faint reflection of the sulphury hue so conspicious when the top-knot is expanded.

The TRITON COCKATOO from New Guinea bears a considerable resemblance to the last, as does also the BLUE-EYED COCKATOO, but can be distinguished from it by the large area of naked blue skin round the eye of the latter, and the triton has a more decided yellow tinge on the lower parts, as well as a stronger and blacker bill.

The Bare-Eyed Cockatoo is from Western Australia. It has a very short crest, and a triangular-shaped spot of

Fig. 69.—*Leadbeater's Cockatoo.*

bare skin round the eye; it is, perhaps, the best talker among the cockatoos, certainly among those that are found in Australia.

The Roseate Cockatoo has a rosy-white head and crest, a grey back, wings, and tail, and a bright rosy-red breast and under parts; it is very tricky and amusing, but makes a poor talker.

The SLENDER-BILLED COCKATOO is like the bare-eyed, but has a very long, projecting, curved upper mandible.

FIG. 70.—Scaly-Breasted Parrakeets.

The PASTINATOR is from Western Australia, and differs from the eastern species, or variety, in size, being considerably longer. It will learn to say a few words very distinctly, and to imitate ordinary domestic sounds.

The BLACK COCKATOOS are very different in their appearance from their white brethren, being, for the most part, dressed in deep mourning, except as regards the tail, which is barred on its under surface with red and yellow. The females are, for the most part, spotted with the same colour. These birds rather approach the macaws in configuration than they do the cockatoos, but are classed with the latter on account of the crest.

The GOLIATH ARATOO, or GREAT BLACK COCKATOO of New Guinea, is a very different-looking creature, the colour being rather dark leaden blue than black. It has a finely divided crest, that hangs down the nape, but can be erected at pleasure, an enormous black upper mandible, a comparatively small lower one, and a little round button in its mouth by way of a tongue, and a large patch of bare reddish skin on the face.

When eating, it fills the lower mandible with seed, which it afterwards picks up, grain by grain, with its tongue, cracks, and, swallowing the kernel, lets the husk fall to the ground. It appears to be devoid of the imitative faculty, but is not more difficult to keep than the other members of the family. In size it equals a good-sized fowl.

The GANGA COCKATOO occurs in Tasmania. It is a small grey bird, about the size of the African grey parrot, but has an upstanding crest, which, together with the head and upper part of the neck, is of a vividly red colour.

The STRINGOPS, or NIGHT, or OWL PARROT of New Zealand is (or was, for it has been reported extinct) a large bird, with such small wings that it could not fly, but burrowed under the roots of the trees, where it lay close during the daytime, and came out to feed at night.

The Australian GROUND PEZOPORUS resembles it in

colour, green, spotted with yellow, but is much smaller, and is capable of flight.

FIG. 71.—*Paradise Parrakeets.*

SWAINSON'S LORIKEET is perhaps better known by the name of BLUE MOUNTAIN LORY. It is a very gorgeous

FIG. 72.—*The Goliath Cockatoo.*

creature, with a red bill, blue head and face, orange red breast and sides, blue belly, and the remaining parts green. It is a honey feeder naturally, and subject to fits if fed on seed. Appropriately treated, it will live for a long time in confinement, and breed freely. The female is smaller, but otherwise like her mate. They are very savage when nesting, and are then dangerous companions for other birds. Rice boiled in milk, well sweetened with honey or cane sugar, will keep them in health for years, and they enjoy a few fresh ants' eggs and mealworms now and then.

The ECLECTUS is from New Guinea, and presents the curious anomaly of brilliant red and purple in the female, while the male is grass green, with a red patch on the side. There are several species. In confinement they eat the seeds of all kinds of fruit.

The POLYTELES are BARRABAND'S, also called GREEN LEEK, and the BLACK-TAILED PARRAKEET, or ROCK PEPLER. The former is green, with an orange red shield on the breast, and the latter is a mixture of black, dark olive brown, and yellow, with a black tail. Both are very subject to ophthalmia in confinement, and when attacked with it, generally die. They are not particularly interesting birds.

The RED-WINGED and the KING PARRAKEETS are larger sized birds, of a bright grass green; the former has a spot of vivid red on the wings, and the male of the latter species has the head, neck, and breast of a rich crimson tint; on the wing shoulder is a small patch of verditer blue green.

These birds must have as much variety as possible of food, for if confined to one sort, they will sulk, and often get so weak that they waste away, and die from sheer debility. Both species have frequently bred in confinement.

The next group, that of the GRASS PARRAKEETS, so

called because they feed, for the most part, on the seeds of the various grasses found in their native land, include some well-known and very desirable species, of which one

FIG. 73.—*The King Parrakeet.*

is the TURQUOISINE, which is about the size of a blackbird. It has a blue head and face, and yellowish under parts, with the remainder green. It feeds freely in the aviary, and feeds there on canary seed and millet. The ELEGANT is not unlike it, but has less blue and more yellow in its plumage. A cross has been obtained between the two species, which, strange to say, is considerably larger than the parents, to both of which it bears resemblance.

BOURKE'S PARRAKEET is a pretty little creature from Central Australia. Its colour is rich brown, but the breast is pink, and it has a blue line over the bill. It is very scarce, and appears to be delicate.

The well-known BUDGERIGAR, or UNDULATED GRASS PARRAKEET is the smallest member of the family met with in Australia. It is green, with a yellow cap and a blue tail, but the upper parts are marked with undulating dark grey lines, which mask the brilliant green, especially on the neck.

This little bird breeds very freely in confinement, but has developed a tiresome disease called "French Moult," in consequence of its having made its appearance first in some Continental aviaries, when the feathers either fall out and are not reproduced, or, in extreme cases, are never developed, so that the young leave the nest partially, or even entirely, bare, and unable to fly. The complaint, which is a manifestation of the scrofulous diathesis, is incurable, but may be prevented by not allowing premature breeding, by the introduction of new blood, imported if possible, and by plenty of space for exercise and fresh air.

The food should consist of canary seed and white millet, to which oats or coarse oatmeal should be added when there are young ones in the nest. The eggs are five or six in number, often laid on alternate days, and are white like those of every member of the family.

The male has the naked membrane round the nostrils, technically cere, of a bright blue colour, while in the female it is cream or brown; it is somewhat difficult to determine the sex of the young, as in their case the cere is more or less shaded with blue.

Imported birds nest from August to Christmas, and aviary bred ones, as a rule, from May to September.

The BROADTAILS (*Platycerci*) are a numerous group,

FIG. 74.—*The Rosella.*

and include some great favourites, *e.g.*, the ROSELLA, a many-coloured bird, about the size of a Barbary turtle-dove, and decked with pretty well every colour of the rainbow. The PALLICEPS resembles it, but is somewhat larger, and has a yellow, instead of a crimson, head, while the STANLEY PARRAKEET from Western Australia is smaller, but otherwise not unlike the rosehill, as the rosella parrakeet is also called.

The PILEATED BROADTAIL is from Western Australia, and is a very charming bird. Its crown, or cap, is ruby red; the face yellowish green; the breast lilac; the rump yellow, and the rest green, except the under surface of the tail, which is lavender, tipped with white.

The COCKATIEL is a well-known bird, from the northern parts of South Australia. Its general colour is grey, but the face is yellow, as likewise is the crest; and the ear coverts are brick red; the wing coverts white, and the under side of the tail black in the male. In the female it is barred and spotted with yellow. She has no yellow on her face.

The NEW ZEALAND PARRAKEET is green, with a bright red band above the upper mandible; the flights are blue. Sexes alike. AURICEPS is smaller, about the size of a song-thrush. It has a yellow frontlet instead of a red one. Both species are very gentle, quiet birds, and have bred in confinement, the former freely.

The BLUE BONNET, the MANY-COLOURED, and the BEAUTIFUL, or PARADISE PARRAKEETS are lovely creatures, but rather more delicate than many of their congeners, especially the last. However, with care they can be preserved for a good many years; but the least excitement is apt to give rise to a fatal fit. Canary seed and white millet, with a few oats now and then, are the best feeding for them.

The SWIFT PARRAKEET is from Tasmania, and is remarkable for the vivid red colour of the under wing coverts. It feeds partly on seed, but also extracts honey from the flowers of the gum trees in its native country.

The SHINING PARRAKEET, from the Feejee Islands, bears a striking resemblance to the king parrakeet, but is, if anything, a trifle smaller. It has the bill black, and lacks the wing mark that distinguishes the latter.

FIG. 73.—*The Cockatiel.*

The MASKED PARRAKEET is a large bird, with a long tail, also from Feejee. It is of a rich grass green colour, with a black head and face. It makes a nice cage bird, as it rarely screams, and gets very tame, but has not much imitative faculty.

The NESTORS, or NEW ZEALAND HAWK PARROTS, are very peculiar birds, about the size of a crow, and quite as active among the branches as the latter, for, instead of crawling about with the aid of the bill, like the rest of their congeners, they hop in a free and lively manner from bough to bough, or from perch to perch.

The oft-repeated fable of their killing sheep for the sake

Fig. 76.—*The Nestor Parrot.*

of eating the kidney fat dies hard, but has received no reliable confirmation. In all probability the Kea was confounded with a hawk, which it somewhat resembles. It is found about the snow line of the New Zealand Alps, and is consequently quite hardy, yet in the "Zoo" it is placed in the parrot house, where the temperature is usually 80 or 90 degrees Fahrenheit. A bit of meat, raw, is ostentatiously hung up in its cage, but is never touched by the bird, which seems to live chiefly on maize.

A very similar species was found in an island, known by the name of Philip Island, that lies between Australia and New Zealand, but it is now believed to be extinct, as the kea and ka-ka parrots certainly soon will be.

New Guinea contains some of the most remarkable examples of the great parrot race to be met with anywhere, namely, pigmies fashioned after the true parrot type, but some of them so small as to be less than 2 inches in length, or smaller than a European wren. Several of them are figured in Gould's "Birds of New Guinea," and are certainly miniature parrots, and the prettiest feathered gems it is possible to imagine.

Needless to say, none of these tiny creatures have so far been imported, and, as they are believed to subsist wholly on the nectar of flowers, it is doubtful if they will ever be seen alive in England.

THE OWLS

Are represented in Australasia by the following, among others.

Family—*Strigidæ.*

Genus—

1. *Strix.*	*S. delicatula.*	Australian Barn Owl.
	S. novæ hollandiæ.	Masked Barn Owl.

2. *Sceloglaux.*	*S. albifrons.*	White-faced Owl.
3. *Spiloglaux.*	*S. novæ zelandiæ.*	New Zealand Owl.
4. *Ninox.*	*N. boobook.*	Boobook Owl.
	N. novæ zelandiæ.	New Zealand Owl.

The WHITE-FACED, or WHITE-FRONTED OWL of New Zealand is named somewhat incorrectly, for it has not got either a white face or a white front, but round its eyes, at some distance from them, is an indistinct ring of a creamy white colour, dotted with minute black specks. The general colour is tawny brown, strongly marked with black; the legs and toes are covered with minute hair-like feathers of a buff colour. The iris is hazel or dark brown, and not as large as usually happens in the family to which it belongs.

The New Zealand SPILOGLAUX is generally not unlike the last, but it lacks the ring round the eyes, and is darker, especially on the back, where are a number of tawny yellow spots. The eyes are yellow, and the bird is smaller than the preceding.

In both cases the sexes are alike, except that the females are larger than their mates.

The BOOBOOK OWL—so called from its cry—is generally known among the colonists as the cuckoo, and, as Mr. Wood observes, the fact of its calling in the night is noticed as an instance of the perversity of the Australian climate, which reverses the usual operations of Nature, and forces the cuckoo to take the place of the nightingale and pour forth its song at night.

THE HAWKS.

These birds have numerous representatives at our antipodes, and among them we enumerate the following, some of which we propose to consider in detail, regretting that want of space precludes the possibility of going regularly through a most interesting group.

Family—*Falconidæ.*
Genus—

Genus	Species	Name
1. *Circus.*	*C. gouldi.*	Gould's Harrier.
2. *Aquila.*	*A. audax.*	Wedge-tailed Eagle.
3. *Astur.*	*A approximans.*	Allied Gosshawk.
	A. novæ hollandiæ.	White Eagle.
4. *Hieracidea.*	*H. berigora.*	Berigora Hawk.
	H. novæ zelandiæ.	New Zealand Hawk.
5. *Tinnunculus.*	*T. conchroides.*	Nankeen Kestrel.
6. *Milvus.*	*M. isurus.*	Long-winged Kite.
7. *Elanus.*	*E. scriptus.*	Letter-winged Kite.
	E. melanopterus.	Black-winged Falcon.

Wedged-Tailed Eagle.—This noble-looking bird is more generally known in the Colonies by the name of eagle hawk. At one time it was numerous, but owing to its depredations among the flocks it is much less frequently met with than it was a few years ago. There is a well-known story of a fugitive from justice, who secreted himself on a rocky ledge where a pair of these birds had a nest, and by cutting the quills of the young ones' wings, was enabled to hide himself for nearly a year, for the young eagles being unable to fly, remained in their nest, and were assiduously fed by the parent birds, the fugitive sharing in the food that they brought to the nest. When spring set in, however, the old eagles, impelled by instinct, forsook their offspring, and when the man had killed and eaten them, he was forced by hunger to give himself up.

This bold and handsome bird is found in Van Diemen's Land and the islands in Bass's Straits, as well as on the mainland. In colour it is brown, with a blackish tinge, turning to reddish brown on the back of the neck.

The WHITE EAGLE occurs in the land of paradoxes that has given birth to black swans and nocturnal cuckoos—that goes without saying—but it is only in advanced age that the ferocious creature in question assumes the white garb of spotless innocency. In its youth and middle age it is grey on the upper surface and vested in white below. The female is nearly twice as big as her mate, and has reddish yellow eyes, while his are dark brown.

The BERIGORA HAWK is a native of Tasmania; it is mainly insectivorous in its habits, but also eats small animals and reptiles, as well as carrion. It occasionally picks up a stray chicken, and is consequently looked upon as an enemy by the colonists, but it is really their friend, and its ultimate destruction will tend to the increase of creatures a thousandfold more destructive than itself. The general colour of the adult bird is brown above, and white with a shade of cream on the lower surface of the body.

The nest is built among the topmost boughs of the tallest gum-trees, and the breeding season extends from September to December.

THE PELICANS.

This group has a representative in Australia, which does not differ to any material extent from those found elsewhere.

Family—*Pelecanidæ.*

Genus—*Pelecanus.* *P. conspicillatus.* Australian Pelican.

An allied species, known as the FRIGATE BIRD, is found in Tropical Australasia. It is endowed with far greater powers of flight than the pelicans, which it resembles in the possession of a large sub-mandibular pouch, but its bill is much smaller than that of the pelicans, and it also has a larger tail, which is rather milvian in appearance, being deeply forked. It is somewhat of a pirate, and prefers despoiling the large gulls of their prey to fishing on its own account.

The colour is deep black, glossed with the richest shade of metallic green ; the pouch is scarlet ; the wing expanse is about 8 feet, and the length of the bird from the point of the bill to the end of the tail is, or about, 3 feet. The body is comparatively small.

The female frigate bird is rather brown than black, and light brown streaked with white on the under surface.

Where such accommodation is available, the nest is built on a ledge of some precipitous rock, but failing this, on a tree, or even among low bushes on the seashore. There is only one egg, which is white, and has a rough shell.

THE HERONS.

The chief representative of these birds in our Australian colonies is known there by the name of the NANKEEN NIGHT HERON from its rich buff or light cinnamon colour, and its nocturnal habits. It is pretty well distributed throughout the Continent, but is more abundant in New South Wales than in Western Australia.

In its manner of flight and of feeding it resembles the true Herons, the head being retracted into the breast, and the long legs stretched out behind. It lives rather on reptiles, frogs, lizards, etc., than on fish, which, however, it sometimes captures in shallow lagoons during the heat of summer, when the water has evaporated to a great extent in the creeks.

The nest is built among the branches of tall trees. The eggs, generally three in number, are of a pale green colour.

The sexes are almost indistinguishable during life, but the young differ considerably from their parents. The head is ornamented by a tuft of feathers that droop nearly down to the shoulders when the bird stands upright.

Family—*Ardeidæ*.
Genus—*Nycticorax*. *N. caledonicus*. Nankeen Night Heron.

THE IBIS.

The Straw-Necked Ibis is a peculiar bird confined to Australia, and derives its name from a confused mass of long yellow narrow feathers that hang down from the front of its neck. The head and upper part of the neck are bare, and of a dingy black colour. The back and wings are bright green, with a metallic gloss, but the neck and lower parts are white. The sexes, when adult, are indistinguishable during life.

It is very deliberate in all its movements, and very shy and wary. It is very local in its distribution, and disappears from a given locality for several years, to be found only in another. Where does it go? inquires Gould, and can give no answer to his question, beyond a conjecture that there may be a fertile oasis in the centre of the island-continent, which is the natural habitat of the bird which only leaves it when some untoward atmospheric or climatic influence compels it to seek a refuge and food elsewhere.

Family—*Plataleidæ*.
Genus—*Corphibis*. *C. spinicollis*. Straw-necked Ibis.

THE DUCKS.

This group is very abundant in all the Australian colonies, where, among other members of the family *Anatidæ* it is represented by the following genera and species :—

Family—*Anatidæ*.
Genus—

1. *Anseranas*.	*A. melanoleuca*.	Black and White Goose.
2. *Cereopsis*.	*C. novæ hollandiæ*.	Cereopsis Goose.
3. *Bernicula*.	*B. jubata*.	Maned Goose.
4. *Cygnus*.	*C. atratus*.	Black Swan.
5. *Tadorna*.	*T. tadornoides*.	Australian Sheldrake.
	T. variegata.	Variegated Sheldrake.
6. *Anas*.	*A. superciliosa*.	Australian Wild Duck.
	A. castanea.	Chestnut-breasted Duck.
	A. gibberifrons.	Slender Duck.
7. *Biziura*.	*B. lobata*.	Musk Duck.
8. *Fuligula*.	*F. novæ zelandiæ*.	Blue Duck.
9. *Hymenolæmus*.	*H. malachorhynchus*.	Striped Duck.

CEREOPSIS, or CAPE BARRON GOOSE.—This bird is found in the south-east part of Australia, as well as on the islands in Bass's Straits. It is a fine bird, and receives its

FIG. 77.—*The Black Swan.*

first name from the large size of the cere or naked membrane surrounding the nostrils, and its second one from the place where it is found in most abundance. It is a grazing bird, and would be a valuable addition to domesticated poultry were it not for its quarrelsome disposition.

The colour is greyish brown, with lighter patches on the back, and with black on the wings; the head is very light grey; the short powerful bill is black, and the cere greenish buff. The legs are grey-pink, and the eyes red.

It breeds freely in England; the eggs are cream coloured.

The BLACK SWAN is a handsome bird, but not nearly as big as its white congeners, nor has it as long and graceful a neck; but it puffs out its wings much in the same manner when swimming. The general colour is black, but the feathers appear to have a grey edging, which is really due to the way in which they are curved at the free extremity. The bill is deep red, and the primaries white.

The eggs are green, seven or eight in number, and the young at first are covered with grey down.

The black swan breeds freely in England.

The BLUE DUCK is a native of New Zealand; the bill is dark green; the head and neck very dark blue, with a metallic gloss; the wings and back blue, with a bronzed tinge: the greater wing coverts have white tips, which form a line across nearly the middle of the wing; the lower breast, belly, and hinder parts are grey, with a reddish brown tinge at the sides; the feet are dark greenish grey.

The HYMENOLÆMUS DUCK has a dull yellow bill, and is all over of a dull leaden blue colour, except on the breast, on which occur a number of dotted lines of a dull chestnut brown. The legs and feet are dull yellow. It is a native of New Zealand.

THE PIGEONS.

The FRUIT PIGEONS, as might be supposed, are not very numerous in Australia, which contains no edible fruit, but there are a good many of them in New Guinea, and some other of the British possessions in the Pacific.

Family—*Carpophagidæ.*

Genus—

1. *Carpophaga.*	*C. luctuosa.*	White Fruit Pigeon.
2. *Lopholæmus*	*L. antarcticus.*	Double-crested Pigeon.
3. *Ptilopus.*	*P. superbus.*	Superb Fruit Pigeon.

The DOUBLE-CRESTED PIGEON is a remarkably fine bird that is found in South-Eastern Australia. Gould met with it in the basins of the Illawarra and Hunter Rivers. It is strictly arboreal and gregarious in habit, and not very brilliant as to colour, but is rendered sufficiently conspicuous by its curious double crest, the hinder part of which consists of feathers at least twice the length of those in front. Silvery grey is the colour of the crest and head and neck, with dark lines where the latter is merged in the breast; the rest of the plumage is dark slate grey, but the primaries and secondaries are black. A wide grey band crosses the middle of the tail, which also has a dark extremity. The iris is red, and the feet reddish purple.

The second division of the pigeon family is classified as follows:—

Sub-Family—*Columbidæ.*

Genus—

1. *Geopelia.*	*G. tranquilla.*	Peaceful Ground Dove.
	G. placida.	Placid Ground Dove.

	G. cuneata.	Graceful Ground Dove.
	G. humeralis.	Barred-shouldered Dove.
2. *Macropygia.*	*M. phasianella.*	Pheasant-tailed Pigeon.
3. *Ocyphaps.*	*O. lophota.*	Crested Dove.
4. *Chalchophaps.*	*C. chrysochlorus.*	Green-winged Dove.
5. *Phaps.*	*P. chalcoptera.*	Bronze-winged Pigeon.
	P. elegans.	Brush Bronze-winged Pigeon.
	P. histrionica.	Harlequin Bronze-winged Pigeon.
6. *Leucosarcia.*	*L. picata.*	Wonga-Wonga Pigeon.
7. *Goura.*	*G. coronata.*	Crowned Pigeon.

The PEACEFUL, PLACID, and GRACEFUL GROUND DOVES are all charming little birds, the last of which is better known to amateurs by the name of DIAMOND DOVE. They are easily kept in confinement if protected from cold; and, if the aviary is of sufficient size, will live pretty comfortably together, each couple taking up a position in it to which it will keep without unduly interfering with its neighbours; but if in the least crowded, they quickly belie their names, and it will become a case of the survival of the fittest in the shortest possible time.

For food, they should have millet and dari; hemp is bad for them, and canary seed, as a rule, they do not care about, while rape, and all that sort of thing, they do not touch; but if they have young, a little coarse oatmeal, or some of Robinson's patent groats, may be added to their bill of fare.

The nests consist of a few sticks or sprays of heather placed on any convenient shelf. It is a good plan to turn these beautiful little birds out in May, and take them indoors again towards the middle or end of September.

The CRESTED DOVE is a handsome and most graceful creature; it is about the size of a common Barbary dove, and has an upstanding pointed crest about 1½ inches long; it is grey and white, with a patch of metallic green on the wings. If treated as advised for the preceding, it is a very free breeder, but it cannot stand cold. By the expedient of transferring the eggs to a couple of Barbary doves, as many as eighteen or twenty young ones may be obtained from one pair in the season, without any visible deteriorating effect on the birds themselves; but they should be allowed to hatch and rear the last pair themselves.

The GREEN-WINGED PIGEON, or DOVE is the counterpart of its Indian namesake, but may be distinguished from it by being a little larger, and having more white over the eye.

The BRONZE-WINGED PIGEON is a much bigger bird than any of the preceding. It is not gregarious, each pair keeping together, but in certain localities it is sufficiently numerous. The front of the head is buff, the neck grey, the face plum colour, the upper parts of the body brown, and the wing coverts are distinguished by green spots, with a bronzed or metallic reflection; the breast is purple, with a tinge of brown. The legs and feet are bright red, and the eyes hazel.

In size it equals the largest of the domesticated breeds, has a broad back, and rather short legs.

It will breed freely in confinement if protected from extreme cold, and may be fed like the ordinary inmates of the dovecote.

The WONGA-WONGA PIGEON has long borne the reputation of being an excellent table bird. It is a little larger than the last, and requires the same treatment. The chin and forehead are white, and the lores black; the upper

FIG. 78.—*The Goura Pigeon.*

parts are slate grey, and the breast nearly black; a broad white band crosses the chest, and is prolonged up the sides of the neck nearly to the nape. The sides are white, but each feather has a broad spot of dark brown. The bill is red, with a black point, the legs and feet carmine, and the eyes reddish brown.

The Goura, or Crowned Pigeon is found in New Guinea and adjacent parts, and is the giant of the pigeon race, equalling a small turkey in size; the long, strong legs and bold upstanding crest of upright feathery plumes making it look larger even than it really is.

The general colour is leaden blue, but the wing coverts are dull purple and white; with the latter colour the tail is also tipped. These noble-looking birds are fairly hardy, but apt to lose their toes if exposed to frost or cold wet weather. If properly housed and fed (on any kind of poultry mixture) they will breed in confinement; but as only one egg is laid, the multiplication of the species proceeds at a slow rate. However, as they command a high price, the acquisition of a pair for £15 or £20 may well turn out to be a not unprofitable speculation.

Needless to say, they require a considerable range, but under cover, or they would quickly fly away, for, notwithstanding their size and weight, they have great powers of flight, as they also have of swallowing, for a large walnut will disappear down the gullet apparently without the least exertion on the part of the bird.

The Victoria Crowned Pigeon differs from the ordinary goura in having the ends of the crest feathers more divided; in all probability it is only a local variety of the former.

THE PHEASANTS.

The Quails form the only representatives of the pheasant family found in Australia, but they are fairly numerous, especially in cultivated districts, where they are often killed by striking violently against the wire fences when passing from one field to another.

Family—*Phasianidæ.*

Genus—1.	*Coturnix.*	*C. pectoralis.*	Pectoral Quail.
2.	*Synoicus.*	*S. australis.*	Australian Quail.
		S. diemenensis.	Tasmanian Quail.

THE HEMIPODES.

Nearly allied to the quails, two species belonging to the genus *Turnix* are found at our antipodes. As they are rarely if ever imported, it will be sufficient to name them.

Family—*Turnicidæ.*

Genus—*Turnix.*	*T. varia.*	Varied Hemipode.
	T. pyrrhothorax.	Red-chested Hemipode.

THE BRUSH TURKEYS

Form a very interesting group, thought at one time to be peculiar to Australia, but now known to occur in the New Guinea Archipelago. They are polygamous, and, instead of incubating their eggs, the females lay them in a heap of fermenting vegetable matter collected by the whole company, where they are hatched by the heat generated by the decomposing matters. But the birds, nevertheless, attend to the eggs, turning them, and placing them nearer to or further from the surface as occasion requires.

Family—*Megapodiidæ.*

Genus—1.	*Tallegallus.*	*T. lathami.*	Brush Turkey.
2.	*Leipoa.*	*L. ocellata.*	Mallee Hen.

The family name of these birds is derived from the great development of their feet, which enable them to grasp and throw up into heaps the various vegetable matters they require for their nest-heaps. The naked head and neck, as well as the singular flap that depends from the neck, give the brush or bush turkey a somewhat vulturine, rather than a turkeyish, appearance; but the *Leipoa*, or mallee hen, is dressed in a more becoming manner, for it has a small crest, and the plumage is prettily diversified with grey and white.

THE RAILS.

A very natural group, for all the members of it bear a considerable resemblance to each other, as well in form as in habits. Their headquarters are in New Zealand, which islands were at no distant date inhabited by allied species of very great size, in comparison with which their existing relatives are the merest pigmies.

Family—*Rallidæ*.

Genus—

Genus	Species	Common name
1. *Rallus.*	*R. pectoralis.*	Australian Rail.
2. *Rallina.*	*R. pœciloptera.*	Bar-winged Rail.
3. *Ocydromus.*	*O. australis.*	Weka Rail.
	O. earlei.	Earl's Rail.
	O. fuscus.	Black Wood Hen.
4. *Porphyrio.*	*P. melanotus.*	Black-backed Porphyrio.
5. *Tribonyx.*	*T. ventralis.*	Black-tailed Water-hen.
	T. mortieri.	Mortier's Waterhen.
6. *Gallinula.*	*G. tenebrosa.*	Sombre Gallinula.
7. *Fulica.*	*F. australis.*	Australian Coot.

All these birds are formed on pretty much the same plan, and have considerable power of movement both on the dry ground and in the water, running, swimming, and diving with great elegance and ease; but, as a rule, their flight is weak, and incapable of being prolonged for any extended period, the birds never taking to the wing as long as there is water to hide in, and a clear field across which to save themselves from an enemy by swift running.

They differ most in size and in the formation of the feet, the rails proper having divided toes like ordinary land birds, while the coots have a web-like projection round each of them, but, nevertheless, free, and not united as in the case of the ducks; while the gallinules and some of the others have their toes so enormously produced that the birds are able to run along the surface of the water on the leaves of the aquatic plants as readily as on dry land.

Some of them are rather brilliantly coloured, but the majority are dull of plumage, and all make their nests and lay their eggs in the immediate vicinity of water.

The food consists of aquatic insects, molluscs, and vegetable matters. If desired, they can all be kept in confinement if fed as nearly as possible in accordance with their natural habits: and many species, especially those from New Zealand, can be acclimatised with care, and will live and breed on any ornamental water where a little sequestered island has been thoughtfully provided for their accommodation.

THE BUSTARDS.

The AUSTRALIAN BUSTARD (*Eupodotis*) is the only representative of the family to which it belongs that is found in that dependency of the British Empire; it bears a considerable likeness to the bird that was once so common on

Salisbury Plain, and similar localities in England, but which, unfortunately, has long disappeared, and like its European congener, will, according to appearance, soon be as rare in its native haunts as the latter has become, for it is a conspicuous-looking bird, and, though capable of strong flight, rarely uses its wings, so that it falls an easy prey to man and dog.

Family—*Otidæ.*
Genus—*Eupodotis.* *E. australis.* Australian Bustard.

THE CURLEWS.

The AUSTRALIAN THICKNEE, or THICK KNEE, does not materially differ from its European namesake, and, probably, relative, so it will not be necessary to do more than name it.

Family—*Œdicnemidæ.*
Genus—*Œdicnemus.* *Œ. grallarius.*

THE PLOVERS

Call for no very extended remarks; the former is by no means unlike its British namesake, and the latter is remarkable chiefly for the small appendages that ornament, or disfigure, according to the taste of the beholder, the sides of its neck.

Family—*Charadriidæ.*
Genus—1. *Sarciophorus.* *S. pectoralis.* Black-breasted Peewit.
2. *Lobivanellus.* *L. lobatus.* Wattled Peewit.

SNIPE AND WOODCOCK.

There are, in various parts of Australia, birds that in a general way bear a great likeness to our English Woodcock and Snipe. There is also a WHIMBREL, or LITTLE WHIMBREL, to which the same remark applies.

Family—*Scolopacidæ*.
Genus—

1. *Scolopax.*	*S. australis.*	Australian Woodcock.
2. *Gallinago.*	*G. novæ hollandiæ.*	Australian Snipe.
	G. tasmanicuis.	Tasmanian Snipe.
3. *Numenius.*	*N. minutus.*	Little Whimbrel.

THE GULLS

Have some well-known representatives at our antipodes, several of which have bred freely in the Gardens of the London Zoological Society.

Family—*Laridæ.*
Genus—

Larus.	*L. novæ hollandiæ.*	Jameson's Gull.
	L. bulleri.	Buller's Gull.
	L. dominicanus.	Large Black and White Gull.

The two last are found in New Zealand, and the first in the south-eastern parts of Australia, and in Tasmania, or rather on the coasts of both countries.

BULLER'S GULL is a small bird, about 15 inches in length. The bill is black, and the head, neck, and lower parts white, faintly tinged with lead blue, deepening towards the under tail coverts: the wings are light slate blue; the outermost great wing coverts are white, and the outer primaries edged with black; the legs and feet are blackish brown: the eyes are blue grey, but the orbits are red.

The DOMINICAN GULL has a dull yellow bill, of which the tip of the lower mandible is red: the head, neck, under parts, and tail, are white, tinged with blue grey, which deepens to the latter part: and the wings are black; coverts and primaries boldly tipped with white; legs and feet dull blue grey. It is a rather large bird, measuring about 32 inches in length.

APTERYX.

We now come to a family or group of birds peculiar, as far as known, to the New Zealand group of birds, namely the APTERYXES, of which several species have been differentiated, while the remains of several colossal members have been discovered in different parts of the islands.

Family—*Apterygidæ*.

Genus—*Apteryx*.	*A. australis*.	Keewee.
	A. mantelli.	Mantell's Apteryx
	A. oweni.	Owen's Apteryx.
	A. hasti.	Haast's Apteryx.

In all these birds the wing is in a merely rudimentary condition, hence the name apteryx, which signifies wingless. They are all nocturnal in their habits, and feed principally on earth worms, which their long, strong and pointed bills enable them to capture with readiness in their burrows.

The plumage consists of a thick coating of hair-like feathers abundantly furnished with silky down at the base, and terminating in a filamentous point; the base of the bill is furnished with a number of strong bristle-like hairs, which, no doubt, play the part of feelers, like the so-called "whiskers" of the domestic cat, which predatory animal,

FIG. 79.—*The Apteryx.*

by the by, is guilty of the proximate, if not actual, extermination not only of the harmless wingless birds under consideration, but of the night parrot and other peculiar Australasian birds; for pussy has taken to the bush and runs wild in those parts, where she plays sad havoc with the unique aboriginal avifauna.

As the legs of this bird are set very far back, it has

rather an upright gait: but when it runs the head is set well back, the neck raised, and the body oscillates from side to side; but a high rate of speed is nevertheless attained.

The egg is relatively very large for the size of the bird, for it weighs some 15 or 16 ounces, while the bird itself turns the scale at about 4 pounds avoirdupois, or about four times the weight only of its egg.

The bill is long and slightly curved with a small hook at the tip, near to which the small nostrils are also placed, so that in all probability the apteryx is, at least partially, guided to its prey by the sense of smell.

It is about 2 feet in length, of a brownish grey colour, as befits a pilgrim of the night, on which a robe of gaudier colours would be altogether thrown away, for does not the proverb tell us that by night all cats are grey?

THE OSTRICHES.

The well-known rhyme: "If I were a cassowary on the plains of Timbuctoo, I would eat a missionary, gown, bands, and hymn-book, too," bristles with topographical and ornithological blunders, for the bird in question, the CASSOWARY, or PACIFIC OSTRICH, or MOORUK, as it is also called, is not an inhabitant of Africa, but is found in New Guinea, Northern Australia and its dependencies; and, moreover, there are several varieties, or species, of it, and it is not addicted to the use of animal food, but like the ostrich is graminivorous, or, at least to a certain extent, frugivorous.

Like the ostrich, the cassowary has wings that cannot be used for flight, but, unlike its relative from the Dark Continent, Nature has not decorated it with a number of showy plumes either in tail or wings, but more like the emu it is clad with an abundance of hair-like feathers, mostly of a deep blue-black colour.

Some of these birds have the head decorated with a kind of horny helmet or comb, and others have wattles

FIG. 80.—*The Cassowary.*

of various size, which are of different gaudy colours, blue, red, and yellow, while the loose skin that covers the neck is gorgeous with iridescent hues, that rival those of the rainbow in brilliance and variety.

The strong legs being placed as nearly as possible in the middle of the body, the back is pretty well horizontal, but the long neck can be extended upwards to a height of five feet or thereabouts.

The cassowaries have three toes, of which the inner one is armed with a formidable nail; needless to observe, these birds run with great swiftness, and but little is known of their habits in the wild state.

In confinement they are described as very active and somewhat noisy, while they must be extremely hardy, for some of them have survived for a long time in a place utterly unsuitable, as it is damp and sunless, and they are in the open air, practically—for they do not seem to use the miserable sheds provided for their accommodation—both day and night, and at all seasons of the year.

Like the ostrich, the cassowaries will swallow any object of available size that comes within their reach, whether digestible or not.

Family—*Casuariidæ*.

Genus—

1. *Casuarius*.	*C. australis*.	Australian Cassowary.
	C. beccari.	Beccari's Cassowary.
	C. uniappendiculatus.	One-wattled Cassowary.
	C. westermanni.	Westermann's Cassowary.
	C. picticollis.	Painted-necked Cassowary.
2. *Dromæus*.	*D. novæ hollandiæ*.	Emeu, or Emu.

The EMU, or EMEU, used at one time to be extremely common in all parts of Australia, but in the settled districts it has been practically exterminated by "Sunday shooters," who could not resist the temptation of "potting" game that was nearly as easy to shoot as the proverbial flying haystack, which some of the fraternity are nevertheless said to miss occasionally.

It is considerably like the cassowary in shape and habits, and is rarely correctly delineated, the back, as a rule, being made to slope far too much towards the tail, whereas it is carried horizontally. The neck is long, and the head very flat on the top; the large expressive eyes are deep hazel, and very soft and liquid; the bill is flattened, large and black, and the general colour of the hair-like plumage is dark grey.

The eggs of this species are of a deep green colour, and are deeply pitted all over with small round depressions; when mounted in silver they make very pretty cups and ornaments, which will, no doubt, be valuable by and by when the bird that provides them has been improved off the face of the earth, as it has every prospect of being before long.

The task of incubation is performed, at least in confinement, by the male alone, who collects the eggs that the female drop about anywhere, sits on them with exemplary patience, and takes sole charge of the porcupine-looking young ones as soon as they chip the shell; whether these birds act in the same manner in the wild state is uncertain.

We have now come to the end of our allotted task, perhaps somewhat abruptly, certainly with more expedition than we had intended when we began, but circumstances alter cases, it is well-known, and we have had to bow to necessity. However, we trust that the various details given, especially in the earlier portions of the work, will prove of interest to readers interested in maintaining the unity of the British Empire—an Empire that, composed as it is of a great variety of heterogeneous parts, is, in the opinion of many, capable of being welded together into one homogeneous mass, able to look a united universe in the face, and boldly hold its own against all comers.

THE END.

INDEX.

A

Abdimia sphenorhyncha, 261
Accentor modularis, 3
Accipiter nisus, 90
Acridotheres fuscus, 187
,, *gingininanus*, 187
,, *tristis*, 187
Acrocephalus streperus, 3
Adjutant, 211
Ægitialis hiaticula, 146
Africa, The Birds of, 231
Agapornis pullaria, 252
,, *roseicollis*, 252
Alauda arborea, 68
,, *arvensis*, 68
,, *crassirostris*, 247
,, *cristata*, 194
,, *gulgula*, 194
Alaudidæ, 68
Alca torda, 165
Alcedinæ, 83
Alcedo ispida, 83
Alcidæ, 165
Amadina bicolor, 232
,, *castanotis*, 292
,, *erythrocephala*, 232
,, *fasciata*, 232
,, *gouldiæ*, 292
,, *lathami*, 292
,, *mirabilis*, 292
,, *modesta*, 292
Amazon, Levaillant's, 280
America, The Birds of, 273
Ampelidæ, 28
Ampelis garrulus, 28
Anas gibberifrons, 327
,, *pœcilorhynchus*, 212
,, *superciliosa*, 327
Anatidæ, 107
Anous stolidus, 284
Anseranus melanoleuca, 327
Anser brachyrhynchus, 107
,, *cinereus*, 107
,, *indicus*, 212
,, *segetum*, 107
Anthornis melanura, 293
Anthracoceros coronatus, 197
,, *malabaricus*, 197
Anthus arboreus, 22
,, *pratensis*, 22
Aprosmictus erythropterus, 306
,, *scapulatus*, 306
Apterygidæ, 340
Apteryx australis, 340
,, *mantelli*, 340
Aquila audax, 323
,, *chrysaetus*, 90
,, *verreauxi*, 256
Arboricola torqueola, 221
Archibuteo lagopus, 90
Ardea cinerea, 104
Ardeidæ, 104
Artamidæ, 287
Artamus superciliosus, 287
Asio brachyotus, 86
,, *capensis*, 256
,, *grammicus*, 277
,, *otus*, 86
Asionidæ, 205
Astur approximans, 323
,, *novæ hollandiæ*, 323
,, *palumbarius*, 90
Athene brama, 205
Australia, The Birds of, 287
Avadavat, Common, 182
Avadavat, Green, 182
Avocet, 153

B

Balæniceps, 261
Balearica chrysopelagus, 270
,, *pavonina*, 270
Barbet, Blue-cheeked, 199
,, Great, 199
,, Hodgson's, 199
Barita destructor, 298
Baza lophotes, 207
Bearded Tit, The, 13
Bernicla antarctica, 278

Bernicla brenta, 107
,, *canadensis*, 278
,, *hutchinsi*, 278
,, *jubata*, 327
,, *leucopsis*, 107
,, *magellanica*, 278
,, *rubidiceps*, 278
Birds of Africa, The, 231
,, America, The, 273
,, Australia, The, 287
,, India, The, 168
Bittern, 104
Biziura lobata, 327
Blackbird, 4
,, Grey-winged, 169
Blue-Bird, Common, 273
Blue, or Tom Tit, 18
Boathead, Hook-billed, 261
Bohemian Chatterer, 28
Bolborhynchus monachus, 280
Botaurus stellaris, 104
Bower-Bird, Silky, 294
,, Spotted, 294
Brambling, 43
British Empire, What it is, 1
Broadtails, The, 317
Brush-Turkey, 335
Bubo bengalensis, 205
,, *capensis*, 256
,, *cinerescens*, 256
,, *coromandus*, 205
,, *lacteus*, 256
,, *maculosus*, 256
,, *poensis*, 256
Bucerotidæ, 197
Bucorvus abyssinicus, 248
,, *rhinoceros*, 197
Budgerigar, 316
Bulbul, Black, 174
,, Brown-eared, 176
,, Green Blue-winged, 177
,, Green Malabar, 177
,, Red-eared, 176
,, Rufous-bellied, 177
,, White-cheeked, 176
,, White-eared, 175
Bullfinch, 48
Bunting, Cirl, 54
,, Corn, 53
,, Crested Black, 186
,, Lapland, 52
,, Red-headed, 186
,, Reed, 54
Bustard, 142
,, Australian, 337
,, Burchell's, 270
,, Denham's, 270
,, Red-necked, 270
Bustard, Senegal, 270
Butcher-Bird, 25
,, Long-billed Crow, 298
Buteo auguralis, 256
,, *borealis*, 277
,, *jacal*, 256
,, *vulgaris*, 90
Buzzard, Common, 94
,, Crested Honey, 207
,, Honey, 95
,, Red-tailed, 277
,, Rough-legged, 94

C

Cacatua galerita, 305
,, *gymnopis*, 305
,, *leadbeateri*, 305
,, *roseicapilla*, 305
,, *sanguinea*, 305
Cacatuinæ, 305
Caccabis chukar, 221
,, *rufa*, 131
Calænas nicobarica, 216
Calcarius lapponicus, 35
Calidris arenaria, 152
Callocephalon galeatum, 306
Calyptorhynchus banksii, 306
,, *funereus*, 306
,, *naso*, 306
Cape Pigeon, 271
Capercaillie, 129
Capitonidæ, 199
Caprimulgidæ, 75
Caprimulgus europæus, 75
Carduelis elegans, 35
Carpophaga luctuosa, 330
,, *ænea*, 215
Carpophagidæ, 215
Carrion Crow, 59
Cassowary, 342
,, Australian, 344
,, Beccari's, 344
,, One-wattled, 344
,, Painted-necked, 344
,, Westermann's, 344
Casuariidæ, 344
Casuarius australis, 344
,, *beccari*, 344
,, *picticollis*, 344
,, *uniappendiculatus*, 344
,, *westermanni*, 344
Cat-Bird, 294
Centropus phasianus, 304
,, *rufipennis*, 200
,, *senegalensis*, 249

Cereopsis novæ hollandiæ, 327
Ceriornis melanocephala, 221
,, *satyra*, 221
Chaffinch, 41
Chalamydodera maculata, 294
Chalcophaps indica, 216
,, *afra*, 263
,, *chalcospilos*, 263
,, *puella*, 263
Charadrius pluvialis, 146
Chaulelasmus streperus, 107
Chera progne, 232
Chibia hottentotta, 180
Chiffchaff, 6
Chionis minor, 271
Chough, Cornish, 67
,, White-legged, 298
Chrysomitris spinoides, 186
,, *spinus*, 35
Chrysotis levaillanti, 280
Ciconia episcopus, 261
Ciconidæ, 211
Ciconiidæ, 261
Cinclidæ, 13
Cinclus aquaticus, 13
Circus æruginosus, 90
,, *cineraceus*, 90
,, *cyaneus*, 90
,, *gouldi*, 323
Cissa venatoria, 191
Clangula glaucion, 107
Coccothraustes vulgaris, 34
Cockatiel, 318
Cockatoo, Bare-eyed, 309
,, Black, 311,
,, Blood-stained, 305
,, Ganga, 311
,, Goliath Aratoo, 311
,, Great Lemon-crested, 308
,, Leadbeater's, 305
,, Pastinator, 310
,, Roseate, 309
,, Slender-billed, 310
,, Triton, 308
Coliopasser macrurus, 232
Columba arquatrix, 263
,, *carribbæa*, 278
,, *guinea*, 263
,, *leucocephala*, 278
,, *livia*, 122
,, *œnas*, 122
,, *palumbus*, 122
Columbidæ, 122
Colymbidæ, 162
Colymbus arcticus, 163
,, *glacialis*, 163
Conure, White-headed, 282
Coot, Australian, 336
Coot, Common, 141
Copsychus saularis, 168
,, *seychellarum*, 168
Coracopsis barklyi, 252
Corcorax melanorhamphus, 298
Cordon-bleu, 234
Cormorant, Common, 103
Corn Crake, 138
Corvidæ, 57
Corvus australis, 297
,, *corax*, 57
,, *cornix*, 57
,, *corone*, 57
,, *culminatus*, 191
,, *frugilegus*, 59
,, *monedula*, 57
,, *splendens*, 191
Corythaix albocristata, 250
,, *buffoni*, 250
,, *erythrolophus*, 250
,, *machrorhyncha*, 250
,, *persa*, 250
,, *porphyreolophus*, 250
Coturnix communis, 131
,, *coromandelica*, 221
,, *pectoralis*, 335
Coucal, Common, or Indian, 200
,, Pheasant, 305
,, Senegal, 249
Cracidæ, 283
Crake, Corn, 138
Crane, Balearic, 270
,, Cape Crowned, 270
,, Sarus, 228
,, Stanley, 270
,, White, 229
Crateropodidæ, 303
Crax alector, 283
Crested Tit, 19
Crex pratensis, 137
Crithagra albogularis, 243
,, *butyracea*, 243
,, *chrysophyga*, 243
,, *musica*, 243
,, *sulphurata*, 243
Crow, Australian, 297
,, Carrion, 59
,, Hooded, 60
,, Hunting, 192
,, Large-billed, 192
,, Piping, 298
,, Senegal, 247
,, Tasmanian, 299
Crows, The, 57
Cuckoo, Black, or Koel, 200
,, Common, 81
,, Long-tailed, 304
Cuculidæ, 81

Cuculus canorus, 81
Curassow, Crested, 283
,, Lesser Razor-billed, 283
,, Razor-billed, 283
Curlew, 156
Cushat, 124
Cut-throat, 238
Cygnus atratus, 327
,, *olor*, 107
Cypselidæ, 73
Cypselus apus, 73

D

Dacelo cervina, 301
,, *gigantea*, 301
Dafila acuta, 107
Daption capensis, 271
Darter, Indian, 209
,, Levaillant's, 260
Dartford Warbler, 6
Daulias luscinia, 2
Dendrocitta vagabunda, 191
Dendrocolaptidæ, 303
Dendrocopus major, 77
,, *minor*, 77
Dendrocygna javanica, 212
,, *major*, 212
Dichoceros bicornis, 197
Dicruridæ, 180
Dipper, 13
Diver, Black-throated, 164
,, Great Northern, 164
Donacola castaneothorax, 292
Dotterel, Common, 149
,, Ringed, 148
Dove, Barred, 216
,, ,, Shouldered, 331
,, Cape, 263
,, Crested, 332
,, Diamond, 331
,, Graceful, 331
,, Green-winged Australian, 332
,, ,, Indian, 217
,, Martinican, 278
,, Mountain Witch, 278
,, Peaceful, 331
,, Placid, 331
,, Red Under-winged, 278
,, Ring, 124
,, Stock, 122
,, Tambourine, 168
,, Turtle, 125
,, White-winged, 278
,, Zebra, 216
,, Zenaida, 278
Dromæus novæ hollandiæ, 344
Drongo, Indian, 181
Dunlin, 154
Dunnock, 8
Duck, Australian Wild, 327
,, Blue, 329
,, Chestnut-breasted, 327
,, Eider, 120
,, Hymenolæmus, 329
,, Indian Tree, 213
,, Larger Tree, 213
,, Musk, 327
,, Pink-headed, 214
,, Slender, 327
,, Spotted-billed, 214
,, Striped, 327
,, Tufted, 118
,, Wild, 116
Dyal Bird, Indian, 170
,, Seychellean, 170

E

Eagle, Golden, 96
,, Wedge-tailed, 323
,, Mace's Sea, 208
,, White, 324
,, White-headed Sea, 277
,, White-tailed, 95
Eagle-Hawk, Ceylon, 208
Eclectus pectoralis, 306
Eeratogymna elata, 248
Ectopistes migratorius, 278
Eider-Duck, 120
Elanus melanopterus, 323
,, *scriptus*, 323
Emberiza cirlus, 35
,, *citrinella*, 35
,, *luteola*, 186
,, *miliaria*, 35
,, *schœniclus*, 35
Emu, or Emeu, 344
Entomyza cyanotis, 293
Erithacus rubecula, 3
Erne, 95
Erythrœnas pulcherrima, 215
Estrelda amandava, 181
,, *bichenovi*, 292
,, *cinerea*, 232
,, *cœrulescens*, 232
,, *dufresni*, 232
,, *formosa*, 181
,, *melpoda*, 232
,, *phaeton*, 292
,, *phœnicotis*, 232
,, *rubriventris*, 232

Estrelda ruficauda, 292
,, *subflava*, 232
,, *temporalis*, 292
Estreldæ, 181
Eudromias morinellus, 146
Eudynamis orientialis, 300
,, *taitensis*, 304
Euphema bourkii, 307
,, *chrysogaster*, 307
,, *chrysostoma*, 306
,, *elegans*, 306
,, *pulchella*, 306
,, *splendida*, 306
Euplectes afer, 233
,, *capensis*, 233
,, *flammiceps*, 233
,, *nigriventris*, 233
,, *oryx*, 233
Euplocamus albo-cristatus, 221
,, *horsfieldi*, 221
Eupodotis australis, 337
,, *denhami*, 270
,, *kori*, 270
,, *ruficollis*, 270
,, *senegalensis*, 270

F

Falco æsalon, 90
,, *biarmicus*, 257
,, *jugger*, 206
,, *peregrinus*, 90
,, *subbuteo*, 90
Falcon, Ash-coloured, 257
,, Greenland, 277
,, Peregrine, 97
Falconidæ, 90
Falconry, 102
Fieldfare, The, 3
Finch, Alario, 243
,, Beautiful, 292
,, Bicheno's, 292
,, Cape Palmas, 238
,, Chestnut-bellied, 184
,, Chestnut-breasted, 292
,, Crimson, 292
,, Dusky, 275
,, Gouldian, or Gould's, 289
,, Hooded, 236
,, Malacca, 184
,, Modest Grass, 292
,, Parson, 291
,, Pied Grass, 236
,, Red-tailed, 292
,, Ribbon, 238
,, Singing, 244
Finch, Striated, 184
,, White-eyebrowed, 276
,, Zebra, 289
Finches, The, 34
Floriken, Bengal, 227
Flower-Bird, Black-tailed, 293
Flycatcher, Pied, 29
,, Red-breasted, 30
,, Spotted, 30
Flycatchers, The, 29
Food of Hawks, 99
,, Soft-billed Birds, 9
Foudia erythrops, 233
Fowl, Guinea, 136, 269
,, Jungle Bankiva, 222
Francolinus afer, 268
,, *bicalcaratus*, 268
,, *capensis*, 268
,, *gularis*, 221
,, *pictus*, 221
,, *ponticerianus*, 221
,, *rubricollis*, 268
,, *vulgaris*, 221
Fratercula arctica, 165
Fringilla cælebs, 34
,, *montifringilla*, 34
Fringillaria capensis, 243
Fringillidæ, 34, 186
Fulica atra, 137
,, *australis*, 336
,, *cristata*, 107, 269
Fuligula ferina, 107
,, *marila*, 107
,, *novæ zelandiæ*, 327
,, *rufina*, 212
Furnarius rufus, 303

G

Gadwall, 113
Gallinago cœlestis, 152
Gallinula chloropus, 137
,, *nesiotis*, 269
,, *phœnicura*, 226
,, *tenebrosa*, 336
Gallinule, Island Hen, 269
,, Sombre, 336
,, White-breasted, 226
Galloperdix ceylonensis, 220
,, *lunulata*, 220
,, *spadicea*, 220
Gallus bankivus, 221
,, *sonneratus*, 221
,, *stanleyi*, 221
Gannet, 102
Garganey, 115

Garrulus glandarius, 57
Gecinus auratus, 77
Geochichla citrina, 168
Geopelia cuneata, 331
,, *humeralis*, 331
,, *placida*, 330
,, *striata*, 216
,, *tranquilla*, 330
Geotrygon sylvatica, 278
Geronticus alba, 262
Goatsuckers, 75
Godwit, Bar-tailed, 156
,, Black-tailed, 156
Golden-eye, 120
Goldfinch, 44
Goosander, 121
Goose, Bar-headed, 215
,, Bean, 108
,, Bernicle, 108
,, Black-backed, 214
,, Brent, 108
,, Canada, 278
,, Cape Barron, 328
,, Grey Lag, or Wild, 108
,, Hutchin's, 278
,, Kelp, 278
,, Loggerhead, 278
,, Maned, 327
,, Pink-footed, 128
,, Ruddy-headed, 278
,, Upland, 278
Goshawk, 97
Goura coronata, 331
Goura Pigeon, 334
Gracula intermedia, 187
,, *religiosa*, 187
Great Tit, 17
Grebe, Great Crested, 164
,, Little, 163
,, Red-necked, 163
Greenfinch, 39
Grossbeak, Blue, 275
,, Rose-breasted, 275
Grouse, Banded Sand, 220
,, Black, 127
,, Prairie, 282
,, Red, 130
,, Sharp-tailed, 282
Gruidæ, 228
Grus antigone, 228
,, *leucogeranos*, 228
Guan, Little, 283
,, Marail, 283
,, Piping, 283
,, Red-tailed, 283
Guillemot, 166
Guinea Fowl, 136, 269
Guiraca cærulea, 275
Gull, Black-headed, 160
,, Buller's, 339
,, Common, 159
,, Dominican, 340
,, Falkland Island, 284
,, Glaucous, 159
,, Greater Black-backed, 159
,, Jameson's, 339
,, Lesser Black-backed, 159
Gymnorhina leuconota, 298
,, *organica*, 298
,, *tibicen*, 298
Gypohierax angolensis, 257
Gyps bengalensis, 207

H

Hæmatopus niger, 271
,, *ostralegus*, 146
Haliaetus albicilla, 90
,, *leucoryphus*, 206
,, *leucocephalus*, 277
Haliastur indus, 206
Harrier, Hen, 92
,, Marsh, 92
,, Montagu's, 94
Hawfinch, 38
Hawk, Berigora, 324
,, Sparrow, 96
Hawks, Their Food, 99
Hedge Sparrow, 8
Hedymeles ludovicianus, 275
Helotarsus ecaudatus, 256
Hemipode, Australian, 335
,, Lepurana, 269
Hemixos flavala, 174
Hen, Black Wood, 336
,, Island,
Heron, Common, 104
,, Nankeen Night, 325
Heteralocha gouldi, 298
Hieracidea berigora, 323
,, *novæ zelandiæ*, 323
Hierofalco candicans, 277
Hirundinidæ, 31
Hirundo riparia, 31
,, *rustica*, 31
,, *urbica*, 31
Hobby, 98
Honey-Eater, Blue-faced, 293
,, Warty-faced, 293
Hooded Crow, 60
Hoopoe, 249
Hornbill, Abyssinian Ground, 248
,, Concave-casqued, 198
,, Crowned, or Pied, 198

Hornbill, Great, or Rhinoceros, 197
Huia Bird, 298
Hydrochelidon nigra, 158
Hydrornia halleni, 269
Hymenolæmus malachorhynchus, 327
Hyphantornis capensis, 233
,, *castaneofusca*, 233
,, *textor*, 233
Hypochera nitens, 232
,, *splendens*, 232
Hypsipetes maclellandi, 174

I

IBIS, BALDHEADED, 262
,, Straw-necked, 326
Introduction, 1
Iyngidæ, 80
Iynx torquilla, 80

J

JACKDAW, 62
Jay, 65
,, American Blue, 274
Jay-Thrush, Striated, 179
,, White-throated, 178
,, White-crested, 178
Jay-Thrushes, 178
Jungle-Fowl, Bankiva, 223
,, Sonnerat's, 223

K

KEA PARROT, 319
Keewee, 340
Kestrel, 98
Ketupa ceylonensis, 205
Kingfisher, 83
,, Laughing, 301
Knot, 154
Kite, Black, 257
,, Brahminy, 207
,, Common, 99
,, Egyptian, 257
,, Forster's, 277
Kittacincla macrura, 168
Kittiwake, 158
Koel, 200

L

Lagopus scoticus, 127
Lamprocolius auratus, 245
,, *rufiventris*, 245
Lamprotornis æneus, 245
Laniidæ, 25
Lanius collurio, 25
,, *excubitor*, 25
,, *rufus*, 25
Lapwing, or Peewit, 150
Laridæ, 157
Lark, Crested, 195
,, Madras Bush, 195
,, Sea, 148
,, Shore, 285
,, Thick-billed, 247
,, White-headed Bullfinch, 247
Larus argentatus, 157
,, *bulleri*, 339
,, *canus*, 158
,, *dominicanus*, 284
,, *fuscus*, 157
,, *glaucus*, 157
,, *marinus*, 158
,, *novæ hollandiæ*, 339
,, *ridibundus*, 158
Laughing Jackass, 301
Laughing-Thrush, Red-headed, 178
Leipoa ocellata, 335
Leptoptila jamaicensis, 278
,, *rufaxilla*, 278
Leptoptilus argala, 211
Leucosarcia picata, 331
Licmetis pastinator, 306
,, *tenuirostris*, 306
Ligurinus chloris, 34
Limosa ægocephala, 152
,, *lapponica*, 152
Linnet, 45
Linota cannabina, 35
,, *flavirostris*, 35
,, *linaria*, 35
,, *rufescens*, 35
Liothrix luteus, 172
Liothrix, Yellow-bellied, 172
Lobivanellus lobatus, 338
Lomvia troile, 165
Long-tailed Tit, 19
Lophoaetus occipitalis, 256
Lopholæmus antarcticus, 330
Lophophorus impeyanus, 221
Loriculus asiaticus, 201
,, *galgulus*, 201
Lorikeet, Swainson's, 313
Lorius domicella, 201
Lory, Blue Mountain, 313
,, Purple-capped, 203

Lovebird, Peach-faced, 254
,, Red-faced, 252
Loxia curvirostra, 35
Lyre-Bird, 299

M

Machetes pugnax, 152
Macropygia phasianellus, 331
Magpie, 63
,, Australian, 298
Mallee Hen, 335
Manucodia chalybeia, 295
Mareca penelope, 107
Marsh Tit, 18
Martin, House, 32
,, Sand, 32
Megalæma asiatica, 199
,, *hodgsoni*, 199
,, *virens*, 199
Meleagris gallo-pavo, 131, 282
Melierax monogrammicus, 257
,, *musicus*, 257
Meliphagidæ, 293
Melopus melanicterus, 186
Menura, 299
Merganser, Red-breasted, 121
Mergus merganser, 107
,, *serrator*, 107
Microglossa aterrima, 306
Milvago australis, 277
Milvus ægyptius, 257
,, *govinda*, 206
,, *ictinus*, 90
,, *isurus*, 323
,, *migrans*, 257
Mirafra affinis, 194
Missel Thrush, The, 3
Mitua tomentosa, 283
,, *tuberosa*, 283
Miyophonus horsfieldi, 168
Monaul, Himalayan, 222
Moorhen, 140
Mooruk, 342
Morepork, 300
Motacilla alba, 22
,, *lugubris*, 22
,, *melanope*, 22
,, *raii*, 22
Motacillidæ, 22
Mother Carey's Chicken, 162
Munia acuticauda, 182
,, *cantans*, 232
,, *cucullata*, 181
,, *malabarica*, 182
,, *malacca*, 181
Munia punctularia, 181
,, *rubro-nigra*, 182
,, *striata*, 182
,, *topela*, 181
Muniæ, 181
Muscicapa atricapilla, 29
,, *grisola*, 29
,, *parva*, 29
Muscicapidæ, 29
Musophaga violacea, 250
Musophagidæ, 250
Mynah, Common, 188
,, Indian, or Bank, 188
,, Larger Hill, 91
,, Malabar, 199
,, Pied, 187
,, Smaller Hill, 191

N

Neophron percnopterus, 257
,, *pileatus*, 257
Nestors, 319
Nightingale, 4
Ninox boobook, 322
,, *novæ zelandiæ*, 322
Noddy, 284
Numenius arquata, 152
,, *minutus*, 339
,, *phæopus*, 152
Numidia cornuta, 268
,, *cristata*, 268
,, *meleagris*, 268
,, *pucherani*, 268
,, *vandelli*, 268
,, *vulturina*, 268
Nuthatch, 21
Nutmeg-Bird, 183
Nycticorax caledonicus, 326

O

Ocydromus australis, 336
,, *earli*, 336
,, *fuscus*, 336
Ocyphaps lophota, 331
Odontophorus guianensis, 282
Œdemia nigra, 107
Œdicnemidæ, 144
Œdicnemus grallarius, 338
,, *scolopax*, 144
Œna capensis, 263
Oriole, Black-naped, 180
Oriolidæ, 180

Oriolus indicus, 180
,, *kundoo*, 180
Ortalis motmot, 283
,, *ruficauda*, 283
Osprey, 90
Ostrich, Common, 272
,, Pacific, 342
Otidæ, 142
Otis tarda, 142
Otocorys alpestris, 285
Ouzel, Ring, 4
Owl, American Hawk, 277
,, Barn, or White, 86
,, Barred, 277
,, Ceylon Fish, 206
,, Gosse's Eared, 277
,, Indranee, 209
,, Long-eared, 87
,, Short-eared, 87
,, Tawny, or Wood, 86
,, White-fronted, 322
Owls, Food of, 89
Oxeye, 17
Oyster-catcher, Black, 271
,, Common, 271

P

Palæornis alexandri, 201
,, *columboides*, 201
,, *cyanocephalus*, 201
,, *docilis*, 252
,, *fasciatus*, 201
,, *rosa*, 201
,, *torquatus*, 201
Palæornithidæ, 201
Pandion haliaëtus, 90
Panuridæ, 16
Panurus biarmicus, 16
Paradisea minor, 295
,, *rubra*, 295
Paradise, Birds of, 294
,, Emerald Bird of, 295
,, Golden Bird of, 295
,, Lesser Bird of, 295
,, Red Bird of, 295
,, Twelve-wired Bird of, 295
Paradiseidæ, 295
Parrakeet, Adelaide, 307
,, Alexandrine, 201
,, Auriceps, 318
,, Banded, 204
,, Beautiful, or Paradise, 318
,, Blossom-headed, 203
Parrakeet, Blue-bonnet, 318
,, Blue-crowned Hanging, 205
,, Bourke's, 316
,, Ceylonese Hanging, 204
,, Malabar, 204
,, Many-coloured, 318
,, Masked, 319
,, Monk, 280
,, New Zealand, 318
,, Pennant's, 307
,, Pileated Broad-tail, 318
,, Quaker, 281
,, Ring-necked, 202
,, Rose-ringed, 252
,, Rosy, 204
,, Shining, 319
,, Stanley, 318
,, Yellow-rumped, 307
Parrot, Brown-headed, 255
,, Brown-necked, 254
,, Grey, 254
,, Hawk-headed, 281
,, Jardine's, 255
,, Levaillant's, 255
,, Meyer's, 255
,, Philip Island, 321
,, Praslin, 254
,, Ruppell's, 255
,, Senegal, 255
,, Timneh, 254
Parrots, Pigmy, or Dwarf, 321
Partridge, Grey, 131
,, Guiana, 282
,, Red-legged, 133
Parus ater, 17
,, *caudatus*, 17
,, *cæruleus*, 17
,, *cristatus*, 17
,, *major*, 17
,, *palustris*, 17
Passer alario, 242
,, *diffusus*, 242
,, *domesticus*, 34
,, *luteus*, 242
,, *montanus*, 34
,, *simplex*, 242
Pastor, *blythi*, 187
Pastor, Rose-coloured, 190
,, White-headed, 190
Pavo cristatus, 221
Peacock, 136
,, Pheasant, 224
Peafowl, Common, 224
Peewit, Black-breasted, 338
,, Wattled, 338
,, Yellow-wattled, 229
Pelecanus conspicillatus, 325

Pelecanus mitratus, 209
,, *rufescens*, 260
Pelican, Australian, 325
,, Mitred, 209
,, Red-backed, 260
Penelope marail, 283
Penguin, Falkland Island, 284
,, Gentoo, 284
,, Jackass, 284
,, Rock Hopper, 284
Perdicula asiatica, 221
,, *cambaiensis*, 221
Perdix cinerea, 131
,, *hodgsoniæ*, 221
Pernis apivorus, 90
,, *ptilorhyncha*, 206
Petrel, 162
Petronia petronella, 243
Pezoporus, Australian Ground, 311
Phalacrocoracidæ, 102
Phalacrocorax carbo, 102
,, *graculus*, 102
Phaps chalcoptera, 331
,, *elegans*, 331
,, *histrionica*, 331
Phasianidæ, 131
Phasianus colchicus, 131
,, *wallichii*, 221
Pheasant, Common, 134
,, Reeve's, 135
Phonipara bicolor, 275
,, *olivacea*, 275
Phyllornis aurifrons, 174
,, *hardwicki*, 174
Phylloscopus loquax, 3
,, *rufa*, 3
,, *sibilatrix*, 3
,, *trochilus*, 3
Phyrrhulauda verticalis, 247
Piapec, 247
Pica bootanensis, 191
,, *rustica*, 57
Picidæ, 77
Pie, Occipital Blue, 192
,, Wandering, 192
,, Yellow-billed Blue, 192
Pigeon, Bronze-winged, 332
,, Crowned, or Goura, 334
,, Double-crested, 330
,, Harlequin Bronze-winged, 331
,, Nicobar, 218
,, Passenger, 279
,, Pheasant-tailed, 331
,, Ring-tailed, 278
,, Rock, 123
,, Superb Fruit, 330
,, Triangular-spotted, 263
Pigeon, White-crowned, 278
,, White Fruit, 330
,, Wonga-Wonga, 332
Pinicola enucleator, 35
Pintail, 117
Pipile cumanensis, 283
Pipit, Meadow, 25
,, Tree, 24
Pitta, Bengal, 196
Pittidæ, 196
Plant-cutters, 250
Plantain-eater, Violet, 250
Platalea leucorodia, 106
Plataleidæ, 106
Platycercus adelaidæ, 307
,, *barnardi*, 307
,, *eximius*, 307
,, *flaveolus*, 307
,, *flaviventris*, 307
,, *icterotis*, 307
,, *pallidiceps*, 307
,, *pennanti*, 307
,, *pileatus*, 307
,, *semitorquatus*, 307
Plectrophanes nivalis, 35
Ploceidæ, 181
Ploceus bengalensis, 182
,, *manyar*, 182
Plover, Green, 150
,, Grey, 147
,, Golden, 146
,, Ringed, 148
Plotidæ, 209
Plotus levaillanti, 260
,, *melanogaster*, 209
Pochard, Common, 119
,, Red-crested, 215
Podargus cuvieri, 301
Podiceps auritus, 163
,, *griseigena*, 163
Poe, 293
Poëphila cincta, 292
Pœocephalus fuscicapillus, 252
,, *gulielmi*, 252
,, *meyeri*, 252
,, *robustus*, 252
,, *ruppelli*, 252
,, *senegalus*, 252
Polyplectron chinquis, 221
Polytelis barrabandi, 306
,, *melanura*, 306
Porphyrio, Black-backed, 336
,, Grey-headed, 226
Porphyrio melanotus, 336
,, *poliocephalus*, 226
Porzana maruetta, 137
Pratincola rubetra, 3
Procellaria pelagica, 161

Procellariidæ, 161
Prosthemadura novæ zelandiæ, 293
Psittacidæ, 252
Psittacus erithacus, 252
,, *timneh*, 252
Pseudotantalus leucocephalus, 211
Psycanistes subcylindricus, 248
Pterocles fasciatus, 219
Pteroclidæ, 219
Ptilonorhynchus smithi, 294
,, *violaceus*, 294
Ptilopus jamboo, 215
,, *superbus*, 330
Ptilorhis paradisea, 295
Ptilostomus senegalensis, 247
Pucrasia microlopha, 221
Puffin, 166
Puffinus anglorum, 161
Pycnonotidæ, 174
Pycnonotus hæmorrhous, 174
,, *jocosus*, 174
,, *leucogenys*, 174
,, *leucotis*, 174
,, *pygæus*, 174
Pyrenestes albifrons, 233
Pyrrhocorax graculus, 57
Pyrrhula europæa, 35
Pytelia citerior, 232
,, *melba*, 232
,, *phœnicoptera*, 232
,, *wieneri*, 232

Q

QUAIL, AUSTRALIAN, 335
,, Common, 132
,, Tasmanian, 335
Queest, 124
Quelea russi, 233
,, *sanguinirostris*, 233
Querquedula circia, 107
Quiscalus lugubris, 276

R

RAIL, AUSTRALIAN, 336
,, Bar-winged, 336
,, Earl's, 336
,, Water, 137
,, Weka, 336
Rallidæ, 137
Rallilus cristatus, 221
Rallina pœciloptera, 336
Rallus aquaticus, 137
Rallus pectoralis, 336
Ramphastus dicolorus, 276
,, *erythrorhynchus*, 276
,, *toco*, 276
Raven, 57
Razorbill, 166
Recurvirostra avocetta, 152
Redbreast, 9
Redpoll, Lesser, 46
,, Mealy, 48
Redshank, 155
Redstart, 8
Redwing, 3
Reed Warbler, 8
Reeve, 155
Regent Bird, 287
Rhizothera longirostris, 221
Rhodonessa caryophyllacea, 212
Rifle-Bird, 295
Ring-dove, 124
Ring Ouzel, 4
Rissa tridactyla, 157
Robin, Blue, 273
Rock-Pigeon, 123
Rook, 60
Rosella, 317
Ruff, 155
Rufous Chiffchaff, 6
Ruticilla phœnicurus, 3

S

SANDERLING, 155
Sandpiper, 155
Sarcidiornis melanonota, 212
Sarciophorus bilobus, 229
,, *pectoralis*, 338
Saxicola œnanthe, 3
Scaup, 119
Sceloglaux albifrons, 322
Schizorhis africana, 250
Scolopacidæ, 152
Scolopax rusticola, 152
Scops leucotis, 256
Scoter, Common, 120
Seed-eater, Hartlaub's, 244
,, St. Helena, 244
,, Sulphury, 244
,, White-throated, 245
,, Yellow-rumped, 244
Seleucides nigricans, 295
Sericulus melinus, 287
Serinus canicollis, 243
Serpentarius reptilivorus, 258
Shag, 103
Shamah, 172

Shearwater, Manx, 161
Sheath-bill, Black-billed, 271
Sheldrake, Common, 110
,, Ruddy, 110
Shoebill, 261
Shorelark, 72
Shoveller, 118
Shrike, Great, 25
,, Grey, 25
,, Pied Crow, 25
,, Red-backed, 26
Shrikes, The British, 25
Sialia wilsoni, 273
Sibia, Black-headed, 179
Silverbill, African, 238
Siskin, Indian, 186
Sitta cæsia, 21
Sittidæ, 21
Skua, 158
Skylark, British, 68
,, Indian, 194
Snipe, Australian, 339
,, Common, 154
,, Tasmanian, 339
Somateria mollissima, 107
Song Thrush, 3
Sparrow, Black-breasted, 243
,, Diamond, 289
,, Grey-headed, 243
,, Hedge, 8
,, House, 35
,, Tree, 37
Sparrow-hawk, 96
Spatula clypeata, 107
Spectacle Birds, 288
Spermestes cucullata, 232
,, *fringilloides*, 232
Spermospiza hæmatina, 233
Sphagolobus atratus, 248
Sphenicidæ, 284
Spiloglaux novæ zelandiæ, 322
Spilornis cheela, 206
Spizaetus caeliatus, 206
,, *ceylonensis*, 206
Spoonbill, 106
Spur-Fowl, Hardwick's, 221
Squatarola helvetica, 146
Starling, Purple-headed Glossy, 246
,, Rufous-vented Glossy, 246
Starlings, The, 55
Stercorarius catarrhactes, 157
Sterna hirundo, 158
,, *macrura*, 158
Stock-dove, 122
Stone Curlew, 144
Strepera arguta, 298
,, *fuliginosa*, 293
Strigidæ, 86
Stringops habroptilus, 306
Strix capensis, 256
,, *delicatula*, 321
,, *flammea*, 86
,, *novæ hollandiæ*, 321
Struthidea, Grey, 303
Struthio camelus, 272
Struthionidæ, 272
Sturnia malabarica, 187
Sturnidæ, 55
Sturnopastor contra, 187
Sturnus vulgaris, 55
Sula bassana, 102
Surnia funerea, 277
Swallow, 31
,, White-eyebrowed, 287
Swallows, The, 31
Swan, Black, 329
,, Food of, 109
,, Mute, 109
Swift, Alpine, 75
,, Common, 73
Sylvia atricapilla, 2
,, *cinerea*, 2
,, *curruca*, 2
Syphcotides bengalensis, 227
Syrnium aluco, 86
,, *indranee*, 205
,, *nebulosum*, 277
,, *woodfordi*, 256

T

Tachybaptes fluviatilis, 162
Tachyeres cinereus, 278
Tadorna casarca, 107
,, *tadornoides*, 327
,, *variegata*, 327
,, *vulpanser*, 107
Talegallus lathami, 335
Tanager, Sayaca, 285
Tanagridæ, 285
Tantalus, Indian, 212
Teal, 114
Tern, Arctic, 161
,, Black, 161
,, Common, 160
Tetrao cupido, 282
,, *phasianellus*, 282
,, *tetrix*, 127
,, *urogallus*, 127
Tetraogallus himalayensis, 221
Tetraonidæ, 127
Tetrapteryx paradisea, 270
Thick-knee, Australian, 338
,, British, 144

Thrush, Falkland Island, 273
,, Horsfield's, 169
,, Missel, 3
,, Song, 3
Thrushes, The, 2
Tinnunculus alaudarius, 90
,, *conchroides*, 323
Tit, Blue, or Tom, 18
,, Coal, 17
,, Crested, 19
,, Great, 17
,, Long-tailed, 19
,, Marsh, 18
Tits, The, 17
Tocus melanoleucus, 248
Totanus calidris, 152
Toucan, Green-billed, 276
,, Red-billed, 276
,, Toco, 276
Touracou, Variegated, 250
,, White-crested, 251
Tragopan, Horned, 223
Treron bicincta 215
,, *phœnicoptera*, 215
,, *viridis*, 215
Tribonyx mortieri, 336
,, *ventralis*, 336
Trichoglossus chlorolepidotus, 306
,, *novæ hollandiæ*, 306
Tringa alpina, 152
,, *canutus*, 152
Tringoides hypoleucus, 152
Troupial, Black, 276
Turdidæ, 2
Turdus falklandicus, 273
,, *iliacus*, 2
,, *merula*, 2
,, *musicus*, 2
,, *pilaris*, 2
,, *pœcilopterus*, 168
,, *torquatus*, 2
,, *viscivorus*, 2
Turkey, 136
Turnix lepurana, 269
Turnstone, 151
Turtle-dove, Cambayan, 254
,, Common, 125
,, Vinaceous, 266
Turtur aldabranus, 216
,, *chinensis*, 216
,, *communis*, 122
,, *humilis*, 216
,, *meena*, 216
,, *picturatus*, 216
,, *semitorquatus*, 263
,, *senegalensis*, 263
,, *suratensis*, 216
,, *vinaceus*, 263
Twite, 46
Tympanistria bicolor, 263

U

UNDULATED GRASS PARRAKEET, 316
Upupa epops, 249
Upupidæ, 249
Urobrachya albonotata, 232
,, *axillaris*, 233
Urocissa occipitalis, 191
,, *flavirostris*, 191

V

Vanellus vulgaris, 146
Vidua ardens, 232
,, *paradisea*, 232
,, *principalis*, 232
Vultur calvus, 207
Vulture, Egyptian, 258
,, Pondicherry, 208
,, Secretary, 258

W

WAGTAIL, GREY, 24
,, Pied, 23
,, Ray's, 24
,, White, 24
,, Yellow, 24
Waterhen, Black-tailed, 336
,, Mortier's, 336
Waxbill, Australian, 292
,, Cinereous, 235
,, Common, 233
,, Crimson eared, 234
,, Crimson-faced, 236
,, Crimson-winged, 236
,, Dufresne's, 234
,, Green, 182
,, Orange-cheeked, 234
,, Red-bellied, 233
,, St. Helena, 235
,, Wiener's, 238
,, Zebra, 236
Waxwing, 27
Weaver, Bengal, 184
,, Black-bellied, 242
,, Birds, 181
,, Crimson-crowned, 242
,, Grenadier, 241

Weaver, Long-tailed, 241
,, Manyar, 184
,, Shining, 241
Whalehead, 261
Wheatear, 8
Whimbrel, 157
Whinchat, 8
Whitethroat, 5
,, Lesser, 6
Whydah, Paradise, 240
,, Pin-tailed, 240
,, Red-chested, 241
,, Yellow-backed, 241
Wigeon, 117
Willow Warbler, 6
Wonga-Wonga Pigeon, 332
Woodchat, 26
Woodcock, Australian, 339
,, Common, 153
Woodlark, 71
Woodpecker, Greater Spotted, 78
,, Green, 78
,, Lesser Spotted, 78
Wood Quest, 124
Wood Swallows, The, 287
Wryneck, 80

X

Xanthomyza phrygia, 293

Y

Yellowhammer, 53

Z

Zonotrichia leucophrys, 275
Zenaida amabilis, 278
,, *leucoptera*, 278
,, *martinica*, 278
Zosterops dorsalis, 288
,, *lateralis*, 288

Printed by Cowan & Co., Limited, Perth.

www.ingramcontent.com/pod-product-compliance
Lightning Source LLC
Chambersburg PA
CBHW030912270326
41929CB00008B/674
* 9 7 8 3 7 4 3 3 0 9 2 6 5 *